The Colonel and I

The Colonel and I

My Life with Gaddafi

Daad Sharab

Pen & Sword
MILITARY

First published in Great Britain in 2021 by
Pen & Sword Military
An imprint of
Pen & Sword Books Ltd
Yorkshire – Philadelphia

ISBN 978 1 52679 598 4

Typeset by Mac Style
Printed and bound in Great Britain by
CPI Group (UK) Ltd, Croydon, CR0 4YY

Pen & Sword Books Limited incorporates the imprints of Atlas,
Archaeology, Aviation, Discovery, Family History, Fiction, History,
Maritime, Military, Military Classics, Politics, Select, Transport,
True Crime, Air World, Frontline Publishing, Leo Cooper, Remember
When, Seaforth Publishing, The Praetorian Press, Wharncliffe
Local History, Wharncliffe Transport, Wharncliffe True Crime
and White Owl.

For a complete list of Pen & Sword titles please contact

PEN & SWORD BOOKS LIMITED
47 Church Street, Barnsley, South Yorkshire, S70 2AS, England
E-mail: enquiries@pen-and-sword.co.uk
Website: www.pen-and-sword.co.uk

Or

PEN AND SWORD BOOKS
1950 Lawrence Rd, Havertown, PA 19083, USA
E-mail: Uspen-and-sword@casematepublishers.com
Website: www.penandswordbooks.com

Contents

Introduction

For more than two decades, Daad Sharab was Muammar Gaddafi's troubleshooter and fixer. Despite being an outsider she won the trust of a man who is still regarded in the West – almost ten years after his death – as a tyrant and a terrorist.

In her autobiography, *The Colonel and I: My life with Gaddafi*, she gives a unique insight into the character of the former Libyan leader and lifts the lid on many of the secrets of his crazy regime. Daad inhabited a world of suitcases stuffed full of cash, espionage and dirty tricks. She became a confidante of the Lockerbie bomber, visiting him in prison in Scotland where she became convinced of his innocence, and played a key role in bringing Libya in from the cold following years of sanctions.

During her time globetrotting for 'the Colonel' she rubbed shoulders with the likes of Hillary Clinton, George Bush and billionaire arms dealer Adnan Khashoggi. Daad is scathing about self-serving politicians who cosied-up to the dictator, and reveals how he was covertly wooed by Israel to try to broker a peace deal in the Middle East.

She also befriended many ordinary Libyans, including members of Gaddafi's famous Amazonian Guard of female minders, and through them experienced everyday life under the regime. Daad's close relationship with Gaddafi made her enemies in Libya's notorious intelligence services who, deeply suspicious of her influence, accused her of being the dictator's mistress and a spy. Ultimately her time in Libya ended in betrayal. For twenty-one months she was held in Tripoli, under house arrest, and became embroiled in the 2011 Arab uprisings when Gaddafi was overthrown and killed by his own countrymen. As his empire crumbled Daad narrowly survived a NATO bombing raid, witnessing the horrific aftermath. Saved only by the kindness and bravery of strangers, she came under fire as she fled across the Libyan Desert to neighbouring Tunisia. Daad's timely book is written in collaboration with British journalist Adrian

Lee, who worked on staff for several national newspapers including *The Times* and is now a freelance journalist and writer. *The Colonel and I: My life with Gaddafi* is published ahead of the tenth anniversary of The Arab Spring and Gaddafi's death, in 2021. Daad does not set out to defend the former Libyan ruler, but in this remarkable account offers herself as a witness and asks readers to be his judge. Was Muammar Gaddafi really a monster, or a revolutionary who was widely misunderstood by the West? The book also deals with the struggles the author faced as an Arab woman and single mother, who has strived to break the glass ceiling in a male-dominated world. She made legal history by taking on the Saudi royal family in a British court. Daad bravely delayed brain surgery to deal a humiliating defeat to Prince Al-Waleed bin Talal, a nephew of the kingdom's ruler and one of the world's richest men, in a case fought over her key role in a $120 million private jet deal.

Chapter 1

Endings and Beginnings

I know the planes will come soon, just as they have done every night for the last six months. By now I have learned that these aircraft fly so high that you don't hear their approach. So there is no drone of engines, or any other warning.

All I can do is wait. Wait and pray that somewhere else is hit. When the bombs begin falling, as I know they will, only fate will determine whether I live or die. Never have I felt so frightened and alone.

Sleep is impossible during the raids, so I try to snatch some rest during the day when it is quieter. I look at my watch now and it is only 5.30 on this balmy September evening. It is also Ramadan, the holy month, and I am fasting. Outside it is still light.

Time drags relentlessly here and I wonder how I will fill the next hour and a half before my guard brings food. At least then I will also enjoy a few minutes' human contact. I curse myself for waking early, but it is hardly surprising my body clock is playing tricks.

When the bomb lands I am sitting on the bed, reading.

There is a deafening blast and the building begins to rock violently. I curl up like a baby in the womb, screaming over and over again: 'I'm dying, I'm dying'. But my shouting is futile, because no one can hear me.

The roof collapses, showering me with chunks of concrete. One big piece strikes my head a glancing blow but I'm so shocked, or more likely so terrified, that I feel no pain.

Although it can only be a matter of seconds, the shaking seems to last hours. Being caught in an earthquake must feel exactly like this. Clouds of dense, black, choking smoke and dust engulf the room and I think to myself: 'My body will never be found.'

And yet I am still alive. It is not just luck but a miracle that two huge slabs of fallen masonry have formed a sort of protective tent above my bed.

I'm scared to move in case my struggles bring the whole lot crashing down, crushing me to death, but after about ten minutes lying helpless in the dark I realise I have no other choice. Survival is in my hands alone.

Somehow I wriggle free from my tomb without disturbing the slabs and begin to crawl, sharp debris on the floor tearing skin from the palms of my hands and knees.

I am in Tripoli, the capital of Libya. It is the Arab Spring of 2011 and swathes of the Middle East are being turned upside down. Governments in Tunisia and Egypt have been overthrown and now what I once considered unthinkable is happening around me.

The forty-two-year regime of Muammar Gaddafi, the president who took me under his wing before his mind was poisoned against me by my enemies, is in its death throes. Abandoned by my country, I am at the mercy of a man who is regarded as a monster by millions of people. For over two decades he treated me like a favourite daughter, but then he turned against me. For nineteen months I have been his prisoner.

All around me NATO bombs are pounding government targets in the city I have come to love, and regard as my second home. Throughout Libya, rebels are taking control of the streets, but right now I care nothing about revolution.

I slowly feel my way through the murk and discover that the main door frame is badly damaged, and I can feel faint breaths of air. But my heart sinks as I realise that the locked outer gate with its impenetrable iron bars is still intact.

In any case, it dawns on me that even if I can escape, I don't know where I can go to.

On the one hand I am Gaddafi's prisoner, but on the other he was once my protector. I have no idea if the rebels who are now roaming lawlessly, intent on revenge against the Colonel and his despised regime, will regard me as friend or foe. Someone to be liberated, or an accomplice of the dictator to be killed amid the chaos?

'Think Daad, think,' I repeat to myself, as my reserves of courage ebb away.

As I stand gazing through the bars, pondering what to do next, the smoke gradually clears. I can see the outline of a man walking purposefully towards me. He is carrying an automatic rifle.

The words of my father, from all those years ago, are ringing in my ears: 'Daad, I am begging you, don't go to Libya. It is not safe. If anything happens we cannot help you there.'

I didn't listen. I've always had a stubborn streak and a steely determination never to be downtrodden because I happen to be a woman. Those qualities served me well as, fighting against centuries of tradition, I first carved a successful niche in the deeply sexist Arab business world and then prospered for so long amidst all the madness surrounding Gaddafi.

Now I wonder: is this where my story ends?

The beginning was more than 2,000 miles away, in Saudi Arabia.

My father, Mohammad, a Jordanian, trained as an agricultural engineer but he became an economic migrant who was tempted to Saudi Arabia in 1955 by the offer of a reliable and well-paid teaching job.

As is still the Arab custom, he took a young bride. My mother, Amal, also Jordanian, was just 17 years old and seven years his junior when they were married in 1958.

Her main duty was to run the household and produce a male heir but, to their disappointment, when I was born in 1961 I was the second of four girls. Linda, Rana and Reem are my sisters.

In Arabic my name Daad means 'giver of life', deriving from part of the root of the palm tree. Many years later my father let slip that Daad was also the name of his first love, which I did not find very amusing at the time.

Although I am proud to be Jordanian, I suppose you could also describe me as a child of the Middle East.

My family's roots are in Palestine and when I was a little girl we would spend summer holidays there. My first hazy memories are of playing on the sunny terrace of my grandfather Ahmad's house, in the town of Tulkarm, while he kept watch over me from his wooden chair and contentedly smoked a shisha pipe.

Those carefree days didn't last. After the Six Day War of June 1967, when Israel went into battle against its Arab neighbours and occupied what was then Jordanian land, I could not visit again. The house was eventually lost, along with treasured family photographs and other possessions, following my grandfather's death as Israel seized empty properties.

My parents kept trying for a boy. Finally a cherished son, Wael, was born in 1971 followed by two more boys – Firas, in 1973, and finally Ezalden, in 1978, bringing the brood to seven.

In the 1960s and early 1970s, when I did my growing-up, Saudi Arabia under King Faisal was a repressive country despite his reputation as a moderniser.

One of his reforms was to abolish slavery but, under a law that would persist until 2018, it was forbidden for women to drive. We could watch strictly controlled state television, but cinemas were banned.

Yet in many ways we were fortunate because the atmosphere in Jeddah, where we lived, was a lot more relaxed than in the capital Riyadh some 600 miles distant. In those days all the embassies were in Jeddah, so all the visiting diplomats and their families were based there.

Home was a modern villa on a compound with a mix of other foreigners, thrown together by their work, which meant I had to switch constantly between two very different lives.

Going to and from my private all-girls' school I had to be covered from head to toe in black. At the malls in Saudi Arabia I remember seeing the Islamic Religious Police, who enforce Sharia law, shouting at foreign women to cover up.

Later, I came to loathe the custom of people having to conceal their faces. It strips away identity and individuality, almost reducing women to animals. There is nothing in the Muslim religion, which I follow, that says you must be covered in black.

Another rule required women to have a male 'wali', or guardian. His consent was required for anything major, such as travelling, obtaining a passport, getting married and signing contracts. In the Arab world, the final word is always with the man.

However, during my childhood I didn't question anything like this. My father always told me: 'Daad, we are strangers here, so we must follow and respect their rules.'

It's a lesson I have carried with me through the rest of my life. I like to think I am tolerant of different cultures, even though there may be aspects I don't like.

Growing up in Saudi Arabia, my other life revolved around our modest rented chalet on a private beach on the Red Sea, about ninety minutes' drive away from our home, where we'd go every weekend to swim with other foreign children. It was liberating to be able to wear shorts and play in the sun with my face uncovered. I loved splashing in the warm sea and riding my bicycle.

That period, when we also travelled to Jordan and Lebanon for family holidays, also sowed a seed of desire to discover more about other countries and how they tick. In future, I would always be ready to embrace an adventure.

In the region at the time, just as now, turmoil was never far away.

When I was 8 years old, a disenchanted soldier called Muammar Gaddafi seized power in Saudi Arabia's next-door-but-one neighbour. He was born in June 1942 in a Bedouin tent near the coastal town of Sirte, in the rocky desert midway between Tripoli and Benghazi. His father was a camel herder and his mother an illiterate nomad, both members of one of Libya's poorer tribes, the Qadhadhfa.

I was an excellent scholar, so focused on my lessons and pleasing my father that I was only vaguely interested in the wide world around me. So I cannot pretend I was anything other than blissfully unaware of Gaddafi's bloodless revolution that toppled King Idris of Libya in 1969, or how he came to be loathed in the West. He styled himself as a man of the people, standing up against those he regarded as oppressors and imperialists. At home and abroad he stamped down strongly against dissent. As I was growing up he became a thorn in the side of the United States and Britain, helping to arm so-called liberation groups such as the Irish Republican Army and dispatching hit men across Europe to murder his own countrymen for having the temerity to criticise his methods.

When I was 14 years old, King Faisal of Saudi Arabia was assassinated by his nephew, Prince Faisal bin Musaid. I do remember the next day we didn't have to go to classes, and all the Saudis mourning, but for us foreign schoolgirls life seemed to go on much the same.

After a few years in Saudi Arabia, my father decided to quit teaching and founded a business in the agriculture sector. It went well, meaning we wanted for nothing. I had plenty of new clothes and my father, who loved cars, drove a Cadillac.

At home we had a housekeeper so I didn't have to do any cleaning, cooking or make my bed. As the family grew in size I shared a bedroom with my three sisters. My parents could afford to move to a bigger house, but were settled on the compound where they had some close friends. So we all made do. I didn't mind sharing a room and we all seemed to get by without too many squabbles. I've always been closest to my older sister, Linda, and we'd play Mummy to the younger girls.

It was a privileged beginning but there's no doubt life would have been much easier in Arab society for me if I'd been born male. Yet I have never regretted my gender.

As an Arab girl you have two choices: either you get married very young and have children, or you learn to fight hard against the system. At quite a young age I decided to take the second path.

I didn't want to be like my mother or elder sister, Linda, who got married to one of our cousins when she was 17 years old. She wasn't forced to marry this relative, but it was a match manufactured by the family.

I didn't feel like a rebel and there were no big rows, but I just knew instinctively that kind of life wasn't for me. Anyway, much as I liked them, none of the remaining cousins were to my taste. There was never going to be a romance.

Fortunately, my father saw a spark in me. At school I was an A-star pupil in all my subjects and showed a maturity beyond my years. He would joke: 'Daad, I never have to phone to see if you've passed your exams.'

I was closer to him than my mother, who got married after finishing High School and had a much more traditional Arab approach. She came from a large family herself and would have liked me to get married and have lots of children, but my father knew better than to try to arrange another wedding.

Then, in my early teens, my serene upbringing was shattered by terrible news.

Wael, the first son, initially seemed to be progressing normally but then our mother noticed that he could not stand up or start taking his first toddler steps. He was diagnosed with an incurable developmental condition, which meant he would never walk.

My brother, who still needs constant care, was taken to England to get the best treatment and remained there for ten years. We used to go and visit him at his specialised care home, staying in the best hotels and also making side trips to places such as Paris.

In Arab families, the first-born boy is the most important child so for my parents, who had waited so long for a son, Wael's condition was a tragedy.

With my older sister Linda married, and by then living in the United States, my father seemed to turn even more of his attention on me. I'm not sure if it was deliberate on his part but maybe, in his eyes, I took Wael's place. Being the apple of his eye had its advantages, of course, but I felt under even more pressure to do well at school. I spent the rest of his life trying to live up to his expectations.

At first I dreamed of being a doctor but I didn't want to spend another eight years studying. Although we were well off, I also wanted my own money. To me money meant independence and power. I always hated asking for hand-outs.

In 1978, when I was 17 years old, my father decided to move the family to Jordan, where he knew we would get a more rounded education and there was more freedom for his children to make choices.

I was glad to move but for him it was a huge sacrifice because by then he had four or five businesses in Jeddah, almost 1,000 miles away, which he could not just abandon.

While a smart new family villa was being built in the Jordanian capital, Amman, he rented a nearby property for us all and commuted backwards and forwards for the next six years. There were long separations, which I found difficult to bear.

Saudi Arabia was a closed society, so the upheaval also meant saying goodbye to all the friends I had made at school in Jeddah. I never saw or even spoke to them again, because telephone links between the two countries were poor in those days.

In stark contrast to Saudi Arabia, where I'd spent the first seventeen years of my life, the outlook in Jordan under King Hussein was very European and liberal. The country was in the middle of an oil boom, foreign investors were welcomed with open arms and the economy was growing wildly.

I enrolled at the University of Jordan to study Business Administration and Economics. As soon as possible I passed my driving test. These days the streets in Amman are a nightmare of traffic jams and frantic car horns, but back in the late 1970s the place was a lot less hectic. My father presented me with a gleaming new sports car, in bright red, so I could make the daily thirty-minute journey to lectures.

In Jordan I could not only drive, but wear a skirt outdoors and even date boys. What an eye-opener for a teenage girl.

It felt like starting my life all over again.

Chapter 2

London

It was only when I went to university that it really began to dawn on me that I needed to broaden my horizons. Until then I was, like most teenagers, utterly self-absorbed. I inhabited my own little bubble in which I worked hard at school, but otherwise barely had to lift a finger.

At the University of Jordan my studies still came first, but politics can hardly be avoided when you are surrounded by students. The Middle East was, as always, a cauldron of unrest. Although Jordan was a stable country, the overthrow of the Shah of Iran in my first year at university, 1979, was a reminder that nothing could be taken for granted.

About this time in my life, in my late teens, among all the powerful figures in the region one began to stand out from the crowd: Colonel Muammar Gaddafi.

Let me make it clear that I was never a revolutionary, I'm not anti-American and I wasn't drawn to Gaddafi by his politics. Yet I was at an impressionable age and there was something about him that began to fascinate me.

I didn't dare confide in my father, who would have been horrified, but I started admiring Gaddafi from afar. It's hard to put my finger on the exact reasons, but I have always been captivated by power and how it is used.

At the time Gaddafi, who was 28 years old when he took control of Libya, was still only in his mid-thirties and much younger than most other world leaders. He struck me as a proud, idealistic and deeply religious man who took a very different approach to many other Arab leaders who were rushing to align themselves with the United States. Even the way he dressed was different.

You have to remember that it was the late 1970s and there was no Internet, no Google. I had to rely entirely on Jordanian TV news and couldn't just flick on the set and tune into one of hundreds of satellite channels, such as Al Jazeera, the BBC World Service or CNN, to get a different view. It's not like now, when if something happens on the other side of the world you know all about it in ten minutes.

However, I was hungry for information about Libya and its leader and even in the brief glimpses I got of him on Jordanian TV it was obvious that Gaddafi had great charisma.

But enough of him, for now, because I had my own problem to worry about.

As my first year unfolded at university I realised there was a hole in my education. In Saudi Arabia, compared with Jordan, there wasn't a heavy emphasis on learning English, and as a consequence of my early upbringing I was now lagging behind my fellow students. Looming ahead were exams in English, which were part of my degree, and I was anxious that for the first time in my life I would be branded a failure.

A drastic step was called for. At the end of that first year it was decided that I should go to London, for three months in the summer of 1979, to learn the Queen's English.

I'd been many times to Britain, to visit my disabled brother and on family holidays, but this was a very different experience.

Previously we'd always stayed in upmarket hotels and eaten at the best restaurants. I had happy memories of walking through Hyde Park, visiting Buckingham Palace and London Zoo. I had only fond memories of London, but now I found myself living in a large, sprawling house with other foreign students, in Forest Hill, in the south of the city.

It was not the best area of London but the host family, who made money by renting out five rooms and providing an evening meal, were kind. They were also strict. For the first time I had to make my own bed, clean my own room, wash and iron my own clothes, and be at the meal table on time. The food wasn't very good, and I suspect the hosts were siphoning off some of my father's funds which were meant to pay for my dinners. We ate a lot of spaghetti Bolognese but very few vegetables, so sometimes I would skip meals and use my pocket money to buy better food.

For even the tiniest deed I had to say 'thank you', which I was not used to. The English say 'thank you' all the time, and I remember being told off constantly for forgetting this politeness. My landlady would tell me: 'Daad, thank you is the magic word.'

Every day I had to catch a train, then the London underground to my language school in Oxford Street. I was shocked by the number of homeless people, and the British habit of going to the pub after work to drink away money that had just been earned. My upbringing had been rather sheltered and, in my eyes, it was also a much more aggressive country than Jordan where I never had to worry about walking at night.

Later my perceptions changed and I came to appreciate London, not just as a good financial base for my companies but because of the justice and political systems which are the best in the world. In Britain you are free to think and talk about anything.

I still detest the weather and high taxes but there is more equality; men and women can share raising the family and being the breadwinner. You can have a career and be a mother.

I was also impressed that Britain had a female prime minister, Margaret Thatcher, but in those first few weeks of the summer of 1979 I hated London with all my heart.

Although I got on fine with the other students, and we'd sometimes go to the theatre or on shopping trips, I missed my family back home. I didn't make any close friends, as English lessons were intensive and everyone was working hard during the day before disappearing off to their digs. In the house in Forest Hill, where everyone was coming and going, we'd only really meet to eat evening meals. I often felt very lonely.

The only time there was any respite were the rare occasions my father came to visit, when it was like the old days. I stayed in a hotel, ate out and went shopping at Selfridges.

Twice I called him long distance, in tears, begging to be allowed to come home to Jordan. Twice my father replied: 'Daad, you must stick with it, things will get easier.'

As usual, he was right. I ended up going to London every summer for the next three years, even staying with the same family despite their stinginess when it came to providing meals.

Looking back, I realise now that my father was testing me and trying to toughen me up. At that time it was almost unheard of for an Arab girl to be packed off alone to a western country. I felt like a child being abandoned in the jungle and left to try to survive. That might sound harsh but my father had lofty ambitions for me.

Another part of this process was the new responsibility I was given at home, in Amman, during term time.

While studying at university I continued to live with my mother and remaining brothers and sisters.

During my father's long absences for work in Saudi Arabia he put me in charge of running the household, including being responsible for shopping for food for the family and paying all the bills.

Like my summers in England, it was another reversal of the pampered existence I'd enjoyed throughout my childhood. As a result, I grew up quickly.

The youngest child, Ezalden, was only 9 months old when I started at college and both he and Firas, who was then aged 5, seemed more like sons than brothers.

My mother, who didn't then drive and tended to spoil the children, was more than happy for me to take on this parental role. In fact, we became much closer and the dynamic between us also changed. It felt more like we were two sisters than mother and daughter. That was partly due to us spending more time together socially, in coffee shops and going to concerts, but also down to the small age gap between us. She was only nineteen years older than me. I even managed to persuade her to take driving lessons, so she wasn't so reliant on me.

There was still one source of tension, however.

My mother did not value education for girls and we rarely spoke about my studies. She just wanted me to get married. We didn't have screaming matches but she just kept quietly chipping away.

We would be drinking coffee and sure enough her favourite conversation would begin: 'Daad, you will become too old and no man will want you. If you don't get married soon then people will begin talking and asking what is wrong with you?'

Or it might go something like this: 'Daad I'm worried I will die before you are married and I will never see you have children.'

All I could do was fix my smile and remain silent, because there was no point attempting to change her point of view. Her outlook never altered, whatever I achieved, but that was simply the traditional Arab mother's way of wanting the best for her daughters and I don't blame her. The pressure from Arab society was exactly the same, so I was very fortunate that my father's aspirations for me were so untypical.

What with running the house and my studies there was little time for romance while I was at university. With one exception.

A Palestinian engineer invited me out and we had a few very innocent dates. When I was in Forest Hill he used to send me long letters, which I'm sorry to say I haven't kept. It was clear he was interested in me.

Still it came as a surprise when, out of the blue, he proposed. At the age of 19 a wedding wasn't part of my plans and, anyway, I didn't love him. For the first, but not the last, time in my life I very politely turned down an offer of marriage.

On my twenty-first birthday, 14 February 1982, I graduated from university.

My father would have supported me in any career I chose but I decided to go to work for The Jordan Investment Bank. I opted for banking because I remembered one of my father's friends telling him, in front of me: 'If you want to be a successful businessman you need to know what's going on inside banks. Then you learn how to make money.' His words made a big impression on me.

My boss in the bank's marketing department was an imposing man called Basil Jardaneh. He could be very demanding and tough, so everyone was scared of him. They were terrified to knock on his office door but I stood up to him, even arguing sometimes. I think he liked my headstrong personality and youthful self-confidence.

It was the start of a habit of speaking my mind to powerful men, which was not always wise and would eventually lead me into grave danger.

My job at the bank involved seeking investors and Basil Jardaneh introduced me to the maxim 'follow the money'. He taught me to seek out companies which had just won government tenders.

In my time working at the Jordan Investment Bank I also encountered the rampant sexism which is still rife today within the Arab business world. If you think there is a glass ceiling in US and European board rooms then multiply that by twenty times in the Arab business community.

Lots of women worked in my bank but mainly in secretarial jobs, not the senior posts which would allow them to meet clients and government officials. So, in my executive role, I mixed and worked almost exclusively with men.

Most of the businessmen I met didn't take me seriously. Many Arab men don't value a woman's opinion – they trust other men more so they are constantly trying to prove you wrong, or undermine you.

It sometimes seems to me that all Arab men want to date you, especially if you are young. It's hard to get them to talk to your brain, not your body. It seems that every man has to try it on with a woman, almost as if it is his male duty.

I learned to be diplomatic and say 'no' politely, without causing them to lose face or become offended by the rejection. In the end they gave up and we could concentrate on doing business. The truth is they didn't really care if they succeeded in seducing me or not, but they had to be seen to try.

If I'd been working in a European or American bank I would have been taken more seriously. I encountered sexism every day, but it made me tougher and I also learned how to hide my feelings. I didn't have a rule not to date colleagues and contacts, but I was able to put emotions to one side.

Some Arab women are driven to breakdowns because of the constant harassment. Others lose direction and end up going out with these men, or even marrying them. Many Arab women live with men they don't love, or are forced to marry someone they don't really know, and then have to stay with them solely for economic reasons. Half the married women in the Arab world would be divorced if they had their own money!

I didn't want to be end up like this. I wanted to be financially independent. When I got married I wanted it to be for love, not for financial support. I didn't regard myself as some sort of pioneer for Arab women – I was just trying to make my own way in a man's world. Sadly, I do not believe much has changed since I began working more than thirty years ago.

One thing I did realise was that, despite the misogyny I witnessed and suffered, I much preferred the company of men socially. Even now almost all my best friends are male. I don't enjoy being around groups of women who just talk about fashion, make-up, their children and the problems they have with their husbands. I don't like sitting in the hairdresser's all day, or going to a spa to gossip. It's just not for me.

When my sisters went to London they'd spend days in Bond Street and Knightsbridge shopping but I didn't enjoy that. It doesn't mean I don't follow fashion, or buy brand names and like to look good, but I just find what I need as quickly as possible.

Even now I would rather be surrounded by men, talking about business. As a result I still often find that women don't like my company. Early on it became a joke: 'Go Daad, go, sit with the men.'

There is no doubt that working at the bank made me a stronger person, but after five years in the post I felt I had little more to learn there and sought a change of scene.

I am not interested in money for money's sake but I still had a thirst for education, so I decided to quit my job and finish my Master's degree.

I opted for university in Cairo, which at the time also happened to be the most liberal of all the Middle East countries. I lived alone, in a small flat paid for by my father. He had contacts in Egypt, which opened doors for me socially and I attended lots of parties. Always, I had one eye on building up my book of business contacts. Without good contacts you are nothing in business.

One of them was a wealthy man in his mid-seventies called Sayed Marei. His son was married to a daughter of Anwar Sadat, the Egyptian president who had been assassinated by his own army officers six years earlier, in 1981.

Marei, an old friend of my father, was a former Minister in the Egyptian government then Chairman of the People's Assembly, mentored me when I moved to Cairo. At weekends he often invited me to his farm, where he bred horses, and I'd mingle with the other guests. Marei and his wife, Soad, treated me like a daughter, and after my father and Basil Jardaneh he was the third important man in my life.

Through Marei, who was still involved in Egyptian politics and regarded as a wise elder statesman, I got to meet Yasser Arafat.

By a stroke of good fortune Arafat, the leader of the Palestine Liberation Organisation, just happened to be visiting Marei at his farm when I was also there. Knowing about my Palestinian heritage, Marei invited me to meet him.

It was hugely exciting because the name of Arafat, who was then at the start of peace talks with Israel, resonated all over the world. Seven years later he would win the Nobel Peace Prize and he eventually became president of Palestine.

Arafat had no idea who I was but, to my surprise, after we were formally introduced he agreed that I could sit in on talks between him and Marei about the peace process.

I was impressed by Arafat's negotiating skills, but it's an amusing interlude that sticks most in my mind. During the hour-long meeting, one of Marei's horses gave birth and he was called away for a few minutes.

When he returned, Arafat smiled at me and said to Marei: 'You must name this foal Daad.' It was quite an honour, because these pure-bred Arab horses were worth a small fortune.

A little later the jet black foal was sold to King Hussein of Jordan, for one of his daughters. However, when it came to load the horse on to the cargo plane for the short flight to Jordan, it became terrified and refused to be led into the hold. No amount of encouragement worked and the sale had to be abandoned.

Marei used to poke fun at me: 'The horse is just like the girl it is named after. Too headstrong for its own good.'

During my short time in Egypt I also learned how to enjoy life more, and relax. I liked the Egyptian outlook on life, which was much more laid back than in Jordan where people are more serious. In Egypt they had a talent for laughing at setbacks and dramas, which I tried to carry away from the country with me. Like me, they believe in fate. Their attitude is that God will decide what happens.

For a while I worked back in Amman for my father's new company, The Three Group, which traded in foreign currencies and commodities. He made me managing director, earning commission on deals of up to $10 million, and I became well known in the Jordanian business world. I dealt with some extremely rich individuals, in Jordan and abroad.

One business trip took me to the United Arab Emirates where I met a Lebanese journalist who lived in Sharjah. We got chatting about a forthcoming conference she was attending in a few months' time, in Libya. It was organised by the Libyan Women's Union and she told me they were looking for strong, high-achieving women to invite. The journalist asked if I would like my name to be put forward for the event in Tripoli, which was scheduled to last a week.

I agreed without a moment's hesitation, never thinking I would be accepted. Then, a few weeks later, an invitation arrived in the post.

I was determined to discover more about this mysterious country, led by the enigmatic Gaddafi who was still one of my idols, but there were two stumbling blocks.

Although there were direct flights between Amman and Tripoli, relations between King Hussein and Gaddafi had not been good for several decades. The background was alleged Libyan support for Palestinian guerrilla groups which were opposed to the monarchy in Jordan.

At the time of my invitation, in 1988, relations had deteriorated to the point where there was no Jordanian ambassador in Tripoli. Neither was there an embassy, nor even an old embassy building, for the simple reason that it had been destroyed in riots said to have been organised by Gaddafi four years earlier. Of all the countries in the Middle East, Libya was the place Jordanians didn't visit without looking nervously over their shoulders. All this I was willing to take in my stride, but first I had to overcome the second and potentially more serious obstacle. My father.

I'd always been a dutiful daughter who'd caused him very few problems and, in turn, he'd always indulged me. But now we were on a collision course. He pleaded with me not to go to Libya, pointing out quite correctly that if anything happened I would be isolated without any diplomatic assistance. Communications between the two countries were so bad that there was no guarantee I would even be able to make a telephone call to Jordan for help.

This very strained conversation took place a few months before Pan-Am Flight 103 was blown up over the Scottish town of Lockerbie, killing 270 people, in December 1988. A few years later I would come face to face with the Libyan man who was convicted of planting the bomb, and reach my own conclusion about his guilt.

However, already the perception in Jordan was that Libya was a dangerous, lawless country full of terrorists. The general view in my homeland was that if any atrocity happened in the world Gaddafi was bound to be to blame.

My father told me straight: 'You are not going.'

Here I was, 27 years old and a grown woman who was trusted with millions of dollars, yet I felt my father was still treating me like a child. For perhaps the first time in my life I was prepared to defy him on a matter of any consequence. I was going to Gaddafi's Libya, whether my father liked it or not. I nagged and nagged day and night. Eventually he gave me his blessing – very reluctantly.

Chapter 3

First Impressions

He enters the hall, almost theatrically, flanked by eight female bodyguards who are clad in khaki. Without any prompting the entire room stands and there is a long, thunderous burst of applause. Even though I am far away I can see he is wearing traditional, brown, Arab robes. He is tall and I sense an aura about him, which is almost religious. This is beyond my wildest dreams. So why do I feel little bit scared?

In idle moments, when I have reflected on that first glimpse of Gaddafi, I have wondered countless times how my life would have turned out if I'd listened to my father and stayed at home in Jordan. For sure it would have been a lot less interesting – and I'd never have met the Colonel.

When I boarded that Royal Jordanian Airlines flight from Amman to Tripoli in March 1988 I was 27 years old but was still brimming with youthful impetuousness. Taking my seat in the economy section for the two-and-a-half hour journey, it felt like I was setting out on a big adventure.

I was curious to discover more about Libya, beyond the meagre scraps I'd managed to obtain from Jordanian television news. Was the country really as terrible as I'd been led to believe, or was everything wildly exaggerated propaganda?

On a practical level I was well aware that the Women's Union conference would be attended by hundreds of influencers from all over the Middle East and Africa. Naturally, my contacts book was tucked inside my handbag and I was determined to fill it. Mixed with excitement was also a feeling of trepidation.

This is not intended to be a history book, but I believe the following is important to provide some context.

When I first visited in early 1988 Libya was a pariah country. Gaddafi's vision of setting up a federation of Muslim and Arab states had alarmed the US, which feared the emergence of a new super power. He was accused in the West of sponsoring numerous terrorist organisations, including sending explosives to the Irish Republican Army. Libyan Semtex was alleged to have been used by the IRA, which was fighting for a united Ireland, in atrocities on the British mainland and in Northern Ireland. In the same position today I would search the Internet for all the background, but I didn't have that luxury in the 1980s.

At home, Gaddafi was suspected of starting a secret nuclear weapons' programme. The final straw was the alleged involvement of his agents in the bombing of La Belle nightclub in West Berlin on 5 April 1986, which killed three people including two American servicemen. Another 229 were injured in the blast, including 79 Americans.

Ten days later, Ronald Reagan authorised the bombing of strategic targets in Libya, describing Gaddafi as 'the mad dog of the Middle East'.

The Colonel and his immediate family escaped, by the skin of their teeth, after being tipped off by the Italian prime minister, Bettino Craxi, who opposed the raid. Italy was Libya's former colonial power and there were still close links between the two countries.

Later Gaddafi would recount to me with great glee how he had outsmarted the mighty Americans, but there was collateral damage that night. It was claimed by Libya that Gaddafi's 15-month-old adopted daughter, Hana, was among the innocents killed when bombs hit his Bab al-Azizia compound in Tripoli.

More of her later but, in short, two years after the US attacks Libya was still not a place on anyone's holiday wish list. Even in the Middle East Gaddafi didn't have too many friends, so it was only natural that my father was very anxious.

Unsure of what to expect, I was keen not to be totally unprepared. So my suitcase was bulging with an array of medicines, which I feared would be impossible to come by in Tripoli due to embargoes. I also made sure to pack soap and my favourite brand of shampoo.

Yet, while Libya's historical links with terrorism did not sit easily with me, I did not share my father's grave concerns about my personal security.

Although I was travelling independently, also on the flight were the official delegation of women from Jordan and the Lebanese journalist who'd been my original contact. It was a case of safety in numbers. The conference was happening in full view of the world and was an opportunity for Libya to enhance its reputation. I told myself that there was nothing to be gained from harming me, or any of the other delegates.

As far as I was concerned I would be in Tripoli for a week, attend a few presentations and fly home richer for the experience. I couldn't help noticing that I was the youngest woman attending, so it felt even more of an honour to be there. I reckoned that by networking hard in my spare time I might even be able to attract some investment for our company, The Three Group.

Hopefully a few of my questions about what this mysterious country was actually like would also be answered. Perhaps I would be able to watch Gaddafi speaking on Libyan television and get a different slant, or catch a few ordinary Libyans off guard and ask them about everyday life under the man I secretly idolised.

What could possibly go wrong?

As it transpired, nothing went along the lines I envisaged as I twisted in my seat to get my first glimpse of Tripoli out of the window as we began our descent.

For a start my preconceptions about the country were far wide of the mark. I had anticipated vast inhospitable desert, an uncivilised nation, grim state-run shops with empty shelves and unfriendly people. Instead, we were greeted warmly at the airport with garlands of flowers, and my first impressions of Tripoli were of a developed city with lots of new buildings and, to my surprise, street lights. I noticed that many of the cars were being driven by women who made no effort to cover their faces.

On the thirty-minute transfer to our resort hotel on the Bay of Tripoli, where the conference was taking place, there were none of the signs of poverty I'd envisaged. All that set Libya apart from other countries that I'd visited in the region were the myriads of huge posters of Colonel Gaddafi, whose image stared out from everywhere.

The food at the hotel was excellent and, a little to my embarrassment, there were plentiful supplies of shampoo and soap in my bathroom. Part of me wondered, rather cynically, if this was all a show for our benefit, but I came to realise over the next few days that Libya was intent on using its oil riches, first unearthed in the late 1950s, to become a modern country. The discovery of 'black gold' transformed Libya from one of the world's poorest to one of the richest nations.

Also, to my surprise, there were no soldiers on the streets. Despite its reputation for fostering terrorism, Tripoli felt peaceful and safe.

The only glitch came when I tried to telephone home to reassure my family and discovered it was impossible to get a line out of the country. My father was correct on that score, at least. It preyed on my mind because I knew he would be worried sick by my silence, but it seemed there was nothing to be done.

The following morning I was introduced to the woman who would, over the next few years, become my unlikely best friend.

Naima al-Sagir was the head of the Libyan Women's Union and one of the most powerful women in the country. At the time she was also the head of Colonel Gaddafi's group of all-female bodyguards, known as the Revolutionary Nuns. I discovered that she was the very first recruit. Gaddafi valued her very highly.

It has always puzzled me that Western journalists were so fixated on these women, nicknaming them the Amazonian Guard. Later I got to know many of them, as well as most of the other women in Gaddafi's life, and I can assure you that most of the stories are false.

At the time Naima was 35 years old. Like all the other bodyguards she regarded Gaddafi as a god and was prepared to die for him. Despite the age gap we eventually became like twins and every time I visited Libya she would leave her home and stay at my hotel.

I admired her immediately and we quickly realised we had so much in common, despite our very different backgrounds. Like many of the other Libyan women involved in organising the conference, Naima wanted to know all about my life and the world beyond Libya's borders. It was refreshing to see so many women holding responsible posts, in stark contrast to the Arab business world with which I was familiar. Naima told me she reported directly to President Gaddafi.

She was very beautiful with long, dark hair, but what struck me first about Naima, who was wearing a skirt suit, was her hairy legs and lack of make-up. I would never dream of leaving the house without looking my best.

One day much later, when I got to know her a lot better, I plucked up the courage to ask her about this. Naima explained: 'The Nuns of the Revolution should not alter their appearance just to please men.'

At the start of the conference Naima gave a short welcome address, then dropped a bombshell. Instead of the entire event taking place in Tripoli, as scheduled, all 700 delegates would be flying to Benghazi, more than 400 miles away in the east of the country.

As the reason was given a murmur went round the room. We were going to hear a speech by Gaddafi, in person.

This had never been part of the arrangements, so I cannot begin to describe my own feverish excitement as we were all driven back to the airport in a convoy of official cars and loaded on to two large private jets. The prospect of seeing Gaddafi in the flesh was thrilling.

That night I barely slept a wink at our hotel in Benghazi, and was still buzzing with anticipation the following morning when we were ushered into the large conference hall. To my dismay, however, I was directed to a seat right at the back of the room and far from the main stage where Gaddafi would be speaking.

Due to his presence, Libyan TV was beaming the conference live all over the country and the cameras added to the sense of excitement. It felt like the United Nations with all the delegations having little cardboard signs showing their nationalities, and microphones. Syria, Palestine, Lebanon, Jordan etcetera….and me.

After the applause had died down Gaddafi began speaking. And went on, and on. For over two hours. I didn't fidget or let my attention waver for a second, and not just because I had to concentrate intently on his lips to understand his dialect of Arabic. I was captivated.

Much to my surprise, Gaddafi did not exploit the occasion to speak out against America, or the West. In fact, he filled the entire time talking about the important role of women in his country and how other nations should give us more opportunities in government and other key posts, such as defence and foreign affairs.

'In your countries why do women only get jobs in education or social services?' he demanded to know, and urged us all to go home and fight for our rights. He added: 'Men lie to you but they are no better than you.'

It was inspiring, because I'd never heard an Arab man argue like that in favour of women. As well as Indira Gandhi of India, Gaddafi even mentioned Margaret Thatcher, who was still prime minister of Britain at the time, as a good example.

When he finished speaking, Gaddafi invited questions from the floor and a hundred arms shot up simultaneously. He pointed to the lucky ones in turn and I listened with growing incredulity as each woman gave the same short monologue, stating how honoured she was to be there, what a great leader he was and sending sincere greetings from her country.

I was shocked. It was political bullshit.

Everyone knew Gaddafi had oil money and they wanted a piece. Some of the countries attending were very poor and thought that by winning his favour they could secure investment from Libya.

Gaddafi listened politely, scribbled a few notes but gave the impression he'd heard it all a thousand times before. I felt sorry for him, having to listen to this drivel.

Up until that point I had no intention of speaking, mindful of my unofficial status at the Women's Union conference and my relative youth. Then, without really thinking matters through properly, I was raising my hand.

Suddenly, Gaddafi was pointing at me. 'Where are you from? Please raise your sign so I can see.'

The camera was still rolling and panned from Gaddafi to each questioner. As it focused on me I placed my sign, face down, and explained that I was not part of the official delegation but if he wants to know I am from Jordan.

'Are you Jordanian-Jordanian, or Palestinian-Jordanian?' he demanded.

It was the most loaded of questions, because relations between King Hussein of Jordan and Libya were so bad. Gaddafi was anti-Jordan, but pro-Palestine because of the Israel situation. At the time almost half of Jordan's 3 million population had, like me, Palestinian heritage.

'I am Palestinian-Jordan,' I replied.

Even from so far away I could see a smile spread across Gaddafi's face. It was a naughty smile, as if to say he got the response he wanted.

'What is your name?'

I told him: 'It's Daad.'

'OK, what is your question?'

After all that I'd heard in the past few minutes I was determined to ask a proper and relevant question, but I had nothing prepared. Then, words were coming out of my mouth instinctively and it was almost as if they were being uttered by some other, crazy, woman.

I grabbed a microphone and told him: 'For the last two hours you have been talking about women's rights and you are pushing us to fight. I agree 100 per cent with what you say, every word of it, but if this is truly what you believe then where is the most important person? Where is your own wife in this movement? Why don't we see her here today?'

I didn't mean to be provocative but everyone knew that his wife, who had once been a nurse, was always in the background. In that respect she was much like my own mother and, in another similarity, she had given Gaddafi seven children.

When I put the question I didn't appreciate that she preferred it that way, and had no political aspirations.

I could tell by Gaddafi's reaction that he was taken aback by my rather brazen manner, but he was fully aware that the whole of Libya was watching on live television. He couldn't just cut the broadcast.

Years ago, when I was learning English, I was taught the phrase 'you could hear a pin drop'. At that moment that was true in the packed hall, where there was a hush as 699 other women waited to see how the Colonel would react.

When I look back it was a question that changed my life. As you know, I believe in fate and only God knows what would have happened if I had stayed silent that day. You can call it bravery, but maybe it was also a bit foolish. It wasn't my aim to cause upset, or offence, or try to make a name for myself. Unwittingly I was playing a dangerous game with Gaddafi, who had a reputation for stamping down hard on dissent.

Playing for time to think, he again asked for my name and country and I repeated both. Gaddafi took a few more moments, before answering: 'Look, I don't want to have in my country Jehan al-Sadat number two.'

He was referring, pointedly, to the wife of the former Egyptian president, Anwar Sadat. It was always said by Gaddafi, insultingly, that the First Lady ruled Egypt in all but name.

When Sadat was alive the two men despised one another. Their mutual loathing dated back to the 1970s, when Gaddafi was taking a stand against Western interference and influence in the Middle East. He constantly attacked Sadat for allowing bars, night clubs and gambling in Egypt. Sadat's response was to dismiss the upstart Gaddafi as 'a boy' and the two countries briefly went to war in 1977.

So Gaddafi's reply to my question was a clever riposte which got him off the hook as far as the audience in the hall, and no doubt those watching on live Libyan television, were concerned.

He continued: 'I don't want to put my wife in a position to start using power and gain a bad reputation outside the country. My wife, she is a normal wife who looks after my children and that's it. This is my answer. Are you convinced?'

Even then I didn't bite my tongue and simply accept his response. By conservative Muslim standards Gaddafi was a feminist, who did not espouse the traditional Arab view that females should be subservient. I knew women were allowed to serve in the Libyan armed forces, for example. But I still believed that Gaddafi's wife should have been there making those remarks about women's rights and leading the movement in Libya. It would have sent a good message to the leaders of all the countries represented at the conference, so I felt justified in challenging him.

'No,' I replied firmly, although my heart was racing.

When I met his wife some time later she struck me as a generous, good woman but very naive. Safia Farkash was a typical, pure Bedouin wife, not very well educated. Not for one minute did she strike you as the wife of a president. I would also learn much more about how she met Gaddafi, and why he married a woman who did not appear to me to be a very good intellectual match.

I waited to hear his next response, but Gaddafi made it clear that our little exchange was over and the camera zoomed away. Soon he was gone and the day's other business drew to a close without further drama. On the way out of the hall I got the impression that the other delegates were keeping me, the trouble-maker, at arm's length. No one said a word about the episode, although Naima gave me a quick smile as we filed out.

We all checked out of the hotel in Benghazi and flew back to Tripoli, where there was another surprise.

After numerous failed attempts to contact my family I discovered that I could now make priority long distance calls to Jordan as often as I liked and that was an order from Mr Mubarak Al Shamekh, the Minister of telecommunication whom I met in Benghazi.

I couldn't help reliving the day's events in my head and wondering whether angering the Colonel, in full view of his people, would have more serious repercussions for me before I left Libya. However, as the conference continued normally the next day I began to relax. I reassured myself: 'Daad, he has other matters on his plate without worrying about a girl like you.'

That evening I was in my hotel room at about 11 p.m. when a loud knock startled me. Composing myself, I answered the door to find two men in military uniform on the threshold. They were perfectly polite but their few words, with no other explanation given, sent a chill through my entire body.

'President Gaddafi wants to see you.'

Chapter 4

Face-to-Face

When the soldiers left I was in a blind panic. Was I going to be sent home in disgrace, causing a diplomatic incident between Libya and Jordan? Or could I be in such deep trouble for provoking Gaddafi that I was I going to be arrested and slung in jail? My imagination was running riot – maybe all those awful stories I'd seen and heard about the Colonel were true?

My first instinct was to flee, but even in my state of absolute terror I quickly came to the conclusion that running away in the middle of the night was futile. So I threw on some clothes and dashed downstairs to an office which was being used by my new friend Naima. In fact, it was dawning on me – as I almost tripped down the stairs – that in Libya she was my only friend and I had no plan B. If Naima wasn't there at this late hour, or turned me away, what could I do next?

Bursting into the room I found her working late and explained what had just happened. Close to tears, I told her: 'I don't want to go anywhere.'

To my astonishment, she burst out laughing.

'Don't worry, there is nothing to be scared of,' said Naima. 'All that is happening is that President Gaddafi will be having private audiences with a few hand-picked delegates. You are lucky Daad – he has chosen you. You will be safe. Just calm down.'

Part of me refused to believe her, but I realised that this could be a once-in-a-lifetime chance to meet a president face-to-face. How many people can say they have achieved that? When I was a student at university, admiring Gaddafi from afar, I would have given anything for such a unique opportunity.

Either way, I decided that I didn't really have any choice. I had only been in Libya for a couple of days but already knew that Gaddafi invariably got what he wanted.

I had also learned that in this country nothing could be taken for granted and so it proved again. Having just flown from Benghazi to

Tripoli we were going all the way back again, that evening. There was barely time to pack a few clothes before we were off to the airport in official limousines and boarding another private jet.

This time it was a much smaller aircraft, of the type you associate with rich business people and celebrities, with just twelve seats. It was my first introduction to that kind of exclusive travel, where there are no tickets, no passports needed or laborious check-in procedures. I could easily get a taste for it, despite the circumstances, I reflected.

I was glad that Naima was among the women on board, because I'd placed my entire trust in her. The others were from South Lebanon, Palestine and The Polisario Front, an organisation seeking independence from Morocco in the Western Sahara.

We'd hardly settled in to our seats for the ninety-minute flight and been served a drink before we were landing in Benghazi, where it was now after midnight. I expected to be transferred to the hotel and be taken the next day to meet Gaddafi but instead we were driven away from the city centre.

It became clear that we were on our way to see the Colonel that very night, or, to be more accurate, in the small hours of the following morning.

'What kind of president meets people at 2 a.m.?' I asked Naima, as our small convoy of three black cars arrived at some sort of military base about thirty minutes' drive from the airport. 'In Jordan our king has meetings during the day.'

Peering into the darkness, I could just make out guard towers and soldiers carrying machine guns. I began feeling nervous, wondering if this might be some sort of trap.

Naima explained that Gaddafi often kept strange hours and worked late at night dealing with mail and reading books until 3 a.m. Meetings like this were nothing out of the ordinary, even for his government ministers.

When I got to know Gaddafi better I realised that the clock didn't matter for him and everyone around him had to get used to his unusual timekeeping. One of the perks of being leader is that you can see people when you choose.

Inside the base there was a warren of small rooms and, after eating a hasty meal, we were moved around frequently over the next hour or so.

I was last in line to meet Gaddafi but, worryingly, as the other invited delegates emerged from their meetings many were in tears.

'What happens inside there?' I asked Naima. 'Is he beating them?'

She explained: 'They are talking to him about how they suffer and they cry to try to gain sympathy, so he will give money to their countries.'

It was approaching 3 a.m. when it was my turn to see Gaddafi and by then I was feeling exhausted.

I remember an overpowering aroma of bakhoor, a type of Arabic incense made from wood chips soaked in essential oils, which I came to associate with Gaddafi, as I was guided by Naima into his private office.

It was sparsely furnished, with just a desk in the corner and a single chair. In the traditional Arab style, there were mats and a scattering of red cushions on the floor. Gaddafi, dressed in brown robes, was sitting on the chair behind his desk but got to his feet as we entered.

Momentarily I lost my composure. A few feet away was the man that everyone back home told me was a terrorist and a monster.

There followed an awkward few minutes as Gaddafi spoke to Naima, completely ignoring me. It was just small talk but felt very staged, as if he had never met her before when I was fully aware that they knew one another well.

Maybe he'd seen my unease and this charade with Naima was intended to give me an opportunity to relax. At one point he signed a document. I just felt even more intimidated, but finally he turned to me and we shook hands.

Then, after the initial formalities were over, there was another even more awkward and embarrassing moment.

Gaddafi invited me to sit on the floor, which is the traditional Bedouin way of conducting meetings, and pointed to one of the ornately decorated mats.

Now I had a new dilemma. After our exchange in the conference hall the last thing I wanted was to cause further offence, but I was not dressed for sitting cross-legged on the floor.

This was the late 1980s, the era of power-dressing. I was wearing a black jacket, with big shoulder pads, a matching black skirt and teetering on high heels. My skirt was already above the knee, according to the fashion of the day, and much too tight to allow me to sit on the floor without hitching up. For reasons of comfort and modesty I did not want to sit like this. How I wished I'd opted for a smart trouser suit.

I could see it was his intention to sit on the chair, so he could take notes.

Apologising, I explained my difficulty to Gaddafi who smiled and rearranged the cushions to provide a low barrier between us. He gestured to the mats.

Somehow I managed to sit on the floor while retaining my dignity and he joined me, using the row of cushions as a sort of table so he could take notes. I accepted his offer of coffee.

He spoke in a low voice and, as before, I had to focus hard to understand his accent. To my surprise, knowing his fierce reputation, there was nothing threatening or aggressive about him. Close up I noticed that his face was already lined by sun exposure and from being blasted by the wind in the desert.

Gaddafi began firing questions, about every aspect of my background and work. I told him all about my family's roots in Palestine, my upbringing in Saudi Arabia, my studies in economics and my diverse business dealings in the Middle East, London, and other corners of the world.

Occasionally he would nod, or glance at Naima. Sometimes he would make a joke with her and laugh. Thankfully, there was no further mention of my impertinent question to him at the conference – for which I was extremely grateful.

This continued for twenty minutes, then the meeting was finished. Gaddafi turned to Naima. In my hearing and with an enigmatic smile, he said: 'This is a very nice gift you have given me.'

I asked myself: 'What just happened in there?' Was I the 'gift' and if so, how?

There didn't seem to be any purpose to the encounter and I was left wondering why Gaddafi had gone to the trouble of flying me all the way back to Benghazi from Tripoli.

He was very difficult to read and I didn't know what first impression I'd made on the Colonel.

I should have left the meeting feeling elated but actually I was rather deflated and disappointed. I was even a tiny bit hurt that he didn't give me some sort of parting gift or keepsake. Still, at least I wasn't destined for prison.

By now it was 4 a.m. and I was shattered. I just wanted to get back to Tripoli as soon as possible, but it was another three hours before the same private jet delivered us all back to the capital and I finally snatched a few hours' sleep.

A mere four hours' rest, as it happened, before there was another hammering on my hotel room door and I was greeted by a representative from the president's office. What now? I asked myself.

I was politely informed that I was to attend a meeting but, as usual, there was the bare minimum of information.

Again, I sought advice from Naima who was very positive. 'Go,' she urged me. 'This message will have come directly from President Gaddafi himself.' I had the feeling that she knew exactly what was going on.

Less than an hour later I was sitting in the office of Ahmad Ramadan, whose very grand official title was Director of Information of the Office of Muammar Gaddafi. In reality, I came to discover, he was the Colonel's right-hand man. Although he looked unremarkable, wearing a cheap-looking suit, he was one of the most powerful and feared figures in the Libyan regime. For reasons I never quite fathomed, he was nicknamed Black Box. I can only assume it's after the flight recorder in an aircraft, which holds all the information.

Now Ramadan informed me that President Gaddafi wanted to make me a business proposal. It was his intention that I should become a special advisor for the government-run Libya Arab Foreign Investment Office (LAFICO), which handled all the country's foreign deals.

All Gaddafi's questions and probing about my business background suddenly made sense. My late-night trip to Benghazi must go down as one of the most unconventional job interviews in history. There was no social media, so this was his way of finding out everything about me. He could have just asked for my CV!

The proposal was flattering, of course, but I remained cautious. Yes, I'd come to Libya with half an eye on making contacts for my company and LAFICO was a big fish which handled many millions of dollars. But I wanted LAFICO as a client, not my employer.

Upsetting Gaddafi again was not on my agenda at that moment, however, so I agreed to see Mohamed El Huwej, the organisation's chairman. Ramadan scribbled a brief letter, which he asked me to hand to the boss.

The following morning I was driven in one of the now familiar official cars, a black Mercedes, to LAFICO's odd-looking headquarters which resembled an inverted bottle.

El Huwej didn't pay me much attention when I was eventually shown into his office. With a slightly bored manner he opened and unfolded the note I had delivered, read the contents – and almost jumped out of his seat.

Like flicking a light switch, his mood was transformed and suddenly he could not have been more polite and welcoming. Hilariously, he seemed to forget we had already shaken hands and we went through the entire greeting process for a second time.

He could not have been more enthusiastic and his manner became almost deferential as he set about telling me about LAFICO's structure.

'We are an organisation worth $85 billion,' El Huwej boasted, handing me a pile of glossy brochures, which explained how Gaddafi had set up LAFICO in 1981.

The chairman became even more rapt when the telephone rang a few minutes later, interrupting him mid-flow.

'She's here,' he told the caller, glancing at me. By the manner in which El Huwej was visibly shaking, I deduced that it was Ahmad Ramadan on the other end of the line. He was obviously checking that I had not had any last-minute second thoughts, and briefing the LAFICO chairman on my future. Judging by El Huwej's reaction, you did not want to make an enemy of Ahmad Ramadan.

El Huwej ran through the fine detail of the job offer. My role would involve identifying businesses, including foreign hotel chains, factories, oil refineries and banks, which the state could buy. The Libyan government, or Gaddafi to be precise, wanted someone with good contacts in the Middle East and abroad.

Crucially because I carried a Jordanian passport it was anticipated, quite correctly as it turned out, that I could gain much better access and open doors which would otherwise remain firmly shut in Libya's face. At the time it was a country that was intent on trying to restore its reputation and build bridges after decades of looking inwards.

One aftermath of the US bombing raids on Libya in 1986 was sanctions, which prevented American organisations doing business with the regime.

Gaddafi didn't want to remain isolated from the rest of the world, so he looked elsewhere. One of his priorities was Europe, where he owned stakes in banks and was also building up a property portfolio in London worth millions of pounds.

The UK had broken off diplomatic relations with Libya in 1984, after a shot fired from inside the Libyan embassy in London killed a policewoman, Yvonne Fletcher. The bullet was intended for anti-Gaddafi demonstrators.

Despite the strain between the two countries, Libyan money continued to pour legally into Britain because there were no sanctions.

At one stage Libya had a stake in Fiat, until Ronald Reagan forced the Italian car manufacturing company to put the brakes on the partnership. It was often a game of cat and mouse with the US which, as the Fiat case showed, could exert huge pressure on countries which did business with Libya.

As a Jordanian it would be easier for me to operate under the radar, while Libya discreetly spent its cash.

This side of Gaddafi is overlooked, but he was a shrewd man who realised that by buying foreign businesses he could generate even more wealth for Libya. At the time of my first meeting with El Huwej, in 1988, the country was the biggest oil producer in North Africa.

Money is power and Gaddafi also knew that every dollar would also help him retain his own grip on his country.

On the table for me was a £50,000 per annum consulting fee, which was trifling compared to the money I earned at The Three Group. It would barely cover all my overheads, but what I heard next almost caused my jaw to hit the table.

In addition to the fee, I would receive 5 per cent commission on every deal I completed successfully. Mentally, I quickly did the maths.

I would be at the very heart of Libyan foreign investment policy and if only a fraction of the deals El Huwej talked about came to fruition I could earn a fortune. Even better, under the terms of the proposed offer I could continue working for The Three Company or any other firm I launched. It was an offer I couldn't refuse.

Putting aside any misgivings about throwing in my lot with Libya, I shook hands with the chairman. A contract was drawn up and signed there and then. I left the LAFICO building congratulating myself, hardly able to take in my good fortune.

I'd set out a week earlier for what could have been a fairly mundane conference. Now, here I was going home having met Gaddafi and clutching a piece of paper that could set me up for life financially.

On a personal level it would mean spending more time in Libya, a country that still intrigued me, meeting more of its people and forging new business links there. The possibilities seemed endless.

When I flew home to Jordan and back to my relieved family I was still on a high, determined to grasp this wonderful opportunity with both hands. I was sure my father would be proud.

Had I known then exactly what Gaddafi had in mind for me, perhaps I would not have put pen to paper so hastily.

Chapter 5

Khashoggi

The words of Gaddafi when I next met him at his base in Tripoli sent a chill through my body.

After a few polite formalities, he said: 'Forget everything you have been told by LAFICO, you will be working for me and reporting directly to me.'

It was three months after I'd signed the agreement which I hoped would allow me to broker deals between Libya and companies throughout the rest of the world.

Arriving back in Tripoli from Abu Dhabi, where I'd been working, I was given word that the Colonel wanted to meet me and was taken by private limousine to his vast Bab al-Azizia compound in the southern suburbs of Tripoli. I've seen the place described as a palace, but this could not be further from the truth. Bab al-Azizia, which means Splendid Gate, was a glorified military barracks which operated as Gaddafi's headquarters in the capital. Behind two thick concrete perimeter walls were his offices and an ordinary-looking two-storey villa where he lived on the first floor. Downstairs was a sitting room where he sometimes held night-time meetings. There was also a simple, brightly coloured Bedouin tent where he liked to greet foreign visitors. I'd heard there had once been a zoo and fairground at Bab al-Azizia, but when I first visited in 1988 the compound still bore the scars from the US bombing raid of 1986 and some of the buildings were derelict. Any comparisons with Michael Jackson's theme-park style Neverland ranch, which the singer bought in 1988, were well wide of the mark. The Colonel shuttled round the compound in a golf buggy and the complex was actually more like small village, with palm trees dotted around the wide green spaces, and a scattering of other villas. I was told Bab al-Azizia, which was heavily defended, covered more than two square miles.

Over the next few years I became a regular there, jumping on a plane from wherever I happened to be in the world the moment Gaddafi summoned me. My routine involved telephoning Ahmad Ramadan, the information director, and he would arrange security clearance.

That first trip, I just tried to take it all in. The Colonel received me in his modern office block, next door to his private quarters. I was surprised by how modest the compound was, but later realised that this was typical of Gaddafi's approach. He shunned most of life's luxuries, not even wearing a watch.

I'd taken the precaution of wearing a sensible trouser suit but was relieved that this time he chose to use conventional chairs for our talk.

'You signed the contract, that's good,' he began, offering me dates and coffee with camel milk before outlining precisely what he wanted.

'You will be working for me under the umbrella of LAFICO. It's your job to give me second opinions on Libya's foreign investments, because I'm not an expert on business or economics, but I do not want this information to be shared with LAFICO. Don't worry about LAFICO.'

He scribbled down the telephone number of his private office, while I tried to make sense of his intentions.

In all my years working in Libya I was never given an official title, which was unusual in the regime. I was often described as Gaddafi's 'special advisor', so let's settle on that. My exact role caused all sorts of speculation, both in Libya and abroad. I couldn't help smiling when, years later in an American newspaper article which sought to discover what had become of 'Gaddafi's women', I was described as 'the Jewel of Jordan'.

It did occur to me that I was going to be some sort of spy for the Colonel, who wanted me to be his eyes and ears. Certainly, that is how many people in his inner circle came to regard me and it would soon begin to cause many problems. I would be caught in the middle. Ultimately, being regarded by my enemies as Gaddafi's personal spy would put my life in danger.

Straight away on that first visit it was clear that the leader did not trust most of the senior people around him and wanted me, an outsider, to give him an independent view on how the millions of dollars of Libya's oil revenue were being invested. Gaddafi told me that every deal worth more than $10 million required his personal approval, but he wanted more control.

I still felt nervous around him, unable to push the stereotypical media descriptions of the dictator out of my head. It was at least a year before I got to understand his personality and finally began to relax in his company. Initially we'd shake hands when greeting but after a few meetings he started giving me a kiss on both cheeks, in the Arab way.

At that early stage I didn't feel able to refuse anything he suggested, despite my reservations. I wasn't confident I had the experience or skills to live up to his expectations. Inside I was thinking: 'How can I do all this?' but I simply replied: 'I will do my best.' At that first meeting he did not explain that my duties would soon go far beyond mere economics and that, in reality, I would be caught up in the highly complex and volatile politics of Libya. That was a wise move on his part, as I was already wondering if I was out of my depth. He must have sensed my lack of confidence and was economical with the truth so as not to scare me off.

Over the next few years not only would I rub shoulders with some of the most powerful businessmen in the world, but I'd have a private audience with the president of the United States. I would also expose corruption at the heart of Gaddafi's government, and encounter Libya's so-called 'dogs of war' who roamed the globe in the 1980s assassinating opponents of the regime.

My first mission took me to London to the office of Tiny Rowland, the chief executive of the Lonrho conglomerate.

Rowland was a larger-than-life tycoon who had his fingers in many pies in the Middle East. In Britain, he owned *The Observer* newspaper but failed in a later bid to take control of the Harrods department store.

He was once described by former British Prime Minister Edward Heath as 'the unacceptable face of capitalism'. Rowland considered himself a personal friend of Gaddafi, who was considering buying a stake in his Metropole Hotels Group. Despite the antipathy towards Libya in his own country, Rowland had no qualms about doing business with Gaddafi.

The Colonel wanted to know from me if Rowland could be trusted and how a deal would be greeted in Britain. Margaret Thatcher was prime minister at the time and she had not been forgiven by Gaddafi for allowing British bases to be used by US bombers in the 1986 attack on Libya. In turn, the killing of policewoman Yvonne Fletcher was still raw in Britain.

Adnan Khashoggi was one of the middle men in the proposed Metropole deal and it was the fabulously wealthy Saudi businessman who paved the way for my visit to Rowland.

The two of us sat down in a huge boardroom and talked mainly about the price, then had dinner.

Initially the valuations by Rowland and LAFICO were wide apart, but I was also there when hands were eventually shaken by Rowland and the LAFICO chairman El Huwej. The final price paid by Libya was £177 million ($309m at the time), which proved to be a bargain.

Rowland had a reputation for being utterly ruthless, but I found him to be a straightforward negotiator. Unlike so many of the Arab men I'd done business with, I felt he treated me as an equal. He had little time for Margaret Thatcher or the British establishment, and I always wondered if there was a touch of spite in his enthusiasm for doing business with Gaddafi. The hotel deal was concluded soon after Libya was indicted for the bombing of Pan Am 103 over Lockerbie but that did not prevent Rowland describing Gaddafi as 'my friend' and announcing his intentions to do future business with Libya. When I reported back a few weeks later, Gaddafi deemed the trip a success – which was a relief. I felt I'd proved myself on this important first mission, although I didn't receive a penny in commission because I had not initiated the deal.

I had several more meetings with Rowland, also meeting his wife Josie, and we stayed in touch until his death ten years later, aged 80.

On each visit to Libya during this period my friend Naima would stay with me at the Grand Hotel, in Tripoli. On Gaddafi's instructions I was placed in a twin room and she would sleep in the second bed. When I asked Naima about this she explained that it was to safeguard me against uninvited amorous advances from local men.

'You are a young woman, on your own in a strange country and you wear nice clothes,' she said. 'You have to take care.'

This struck me as odd, because I never felt threatened in that way in Libya. Looking back, I'm sure now that Gaddafi was more concerned about the danger posed to me by members of his own inner circle, who did not welcome my arrival on the scene. However, by then I was learning not to ask too many questions so I accepted my new roommate. Anyway, by that stage Naima already felt more like a lifelong friend. Although there was an eight-year age gap we really clicked and it was good to have her companionship. There wasn't much else to do in Libya, where there were no cinemas or theatres in the late 1980s.

My arrangement with LAFICO allowed me to continue working on my own business deals and in 1989 I moved my base to London, where I rented a flat in Mayfair. I built a good working relationship with the chairman, Mohamed El Huwej, who was diligent and honest.

I divided my time between London, Amman and Tripoli and it sometimes felt that my feet barely touched the ground.

Next I was dispatched by Gaddafi to New York. The purpose was to meet his ally Khashoggi, who was then under investigation by the US authorities. He was alleged to have helped President Ferdinand Marcos of the Philippines and his wife Imelda plunder millions of dollars when they fled the country in 1986. It was claimed the looted money was invested in Manhattan real estate.

At the time of my visit in 1989, Khashoggi, often described as the richest man in the world and known for his weapons deals, had been extradited from Switzerland and was banned from leaving the US. Although I never saw it, I believe he was wearing some sort of ankle bracelet or tag which allowed his movements to be tracked while he awaited trial. Khashoggi would be acquitted of all charges the following year, but when I visited New York in 1989 Gaddafi was worried about the fate of one of his chief fixers. The Colonel wanted me to find out what was going on and offer his assistance.

In my business career I'd mingled with plenty of wealthy men but meeting Khashoggi was, to borrow a baseball analogy, the equivalent of graduating from the minor to major leagues. At the height of his success he was said to be worth $4 billion, mainly made from commission on his deals. He never created anything, he was always the middle man as in the Metropole Hotels deal.

I had been to the States three times previously, first when I was 17 years old to see my sister Linda in Miami following her marriage, then twice on holiday.

This time I arrived in style, flying by Concorde from London to save time. I was surprised by how small and cramped the supersonic aircraft felt, despite the $5,000 ticket price. It was also very noisy.

On all these trips on behalf of Gaddafi I'd take two big suitcases, even though I might only be staying for a short time, so I had appropriate clothes for every possible situation. They were mainly by Italian designers, always in dark colours, always conservative. Cleavage was never on display. I saw that tactic used by some businesswomen, to try to gain an advantage, but my view is that using your body in this way is very cheap.

Being collected from an airport by limousine was nothing new, but riding in a car fitted with a bubbling Jacuzzi was something I'd never experienced until that moment. En route from JFK airport to Manhattan, I received a call from Khashoggi inviting me to make use of this ostentatious customisation. There were blacked out windows and a screen separating me from the driver, but I declined the kind offer to take a dip!

Khashoggi lived in a palatial penthouse in a block near Central Park, reputedly created by buying sixteen apartments and knocking them together. He'd built a swimming pool and the views of the city from the floor to ceiling windows were breathtaking.

We spoke in Arabic about his difficulties with the US authorities and in front of me Khashoggi recorded a short message for Gaddafi, explaining the detail of the pending court case and stating that he would come to Libya as soon as he was able. The following morning we went for a stroll and could hardly move for Americans wanting to have their pictures taken with the billionaire.

I also met his Italian wife, Laura, and their young son but didn't take much notice when he also introduced me to a very attractive young Iranian woman who was doing some interior design work. A couple of years later I recognised her photograph in the newspapers when she was unveiled as Khashoggi's third wife, Shahpari.

I stayed in a beautiful serviced apartment on a lower floor, which he also owned. On the morning I was due to leave New York I found a small jewellery box on my bed. Inside was a farewell gift of a gold necklace with a ruby pendant, and a note signed by him and his wife. The present was probably worth about $20,000 but to him it was a mere trinket. Khashoggi's gift for Gaddafi was a traditional Kashmiri camelskin robe, which was embroidered with his name. It was chosen from Bijan, on Fifth Avenue, which has always been a favourite with US presidents. It has been described as 'the most expensive store in the world'. The price tag for the robe was $33,000.

I got on well with Khashoggi, meeting him many times subsequently. He would later be a guest at both my engagement party and my wedding in Jordan. However, I always felt that all he really cared about was making money.

The Colonel seemed very happy with both the robe and the tape recording. Mission number two accomplished, even if acting as a glorified go-between was not what I expected when I signed on the dotted line for LAFICO. Another development was the launch of my new company, which I called Prime Oil, in 1990 to handle the sale of Libyan crude oil to Mediterranean countries. It was all done with the blessing of Gaddafi, who was happy for me to profit as long as I did his bidding on the other tasks. I was handling about four shipments of oil every month, amounting to approximately 10 per cent of Libya's total exports.

It was an exciting time. Life felt good but that was about to change.

Chapter 6

The Dogs of War

My third mission for the Colonel was the most challenging of them all. Nothing I had learned at university, or in the tough and sexist Arab business world, prepared me for my visits to maximum security prisons to meet murderers.

Long before I set foot in Libya, its reputation as a rogue state was sealed by its methods of dealing ruthlessly with anyone who opposed the regime.

Its reach extended far, seeking out and assassinating dissidents throughout Europe. It is claimed in the West that this was official policy, sanctioned by Gaddafi.

In April 1980, Libya's Revolutionary Committee decreed that all opponents of the government who were living abroad should be executed. It described these irritating and often outspoken exiles as 'stray dogs', calling on them to return home or face 'revolutionary justice'.

A wave of thirty-five murders followed across Europe, mainly in Italy, Britain and Greece. Within the space of two weeks in 1980, a journalist and a lawyer, both Libyan dissidents, were killed in London. The former had been openly critical of the regime; the latter had the temerity to defend members of the overthrown King Idris's government.

As a result there was a series of high-profile trials, in which the killers were brought to justice and handed life sentences. Others who failed in attacks, caused injury or were on the fringes, were also imprisoned. In one incident, the two young children of a Libyan businessman who was undergoing medical treatment in England were fed poisoned peanuts, which left them temporarily paralysed. It was a terrifying warning that their father had overstayed. Newsagents stocking dissident magazines, a restaurant and a nightclub were bombed indiscriminately. By good fortune no one was killed.

By the end of the 1980s, the men who were responsible for all these crimes were still languishing in British jails, having shown no remorse.

This, much to my shock, was the point where I entered the scene.

At one of my now regular briefings with Gaddafi he instructed me to go to the office of Ahmad Ramadan, where the official was waiting with a bulky file.

'This is a list of Libyan prisoners in Britain,' he said, handing over the paperwork. 'President Gaddafi would like you to try to visit them.'

Glancing quickly at the file, I could see there were eight or nine names. Ramadan explained that Libyan intelligence officials claimed the authorities in Britain were refusing visiting rights. Somehow, I was meant to sidestep this barrier, speak to them all and report back on their condition and state of mind.

This was not a business task, but an intelligence one. I had no diplomatic status, so how on Earth could I gain access to the prisoners when Gaddafi's intelligence officers had failed? After such a promising start in my role as special advisor, had I been handed mission impossible?

As usual in times of crisis I sought out my friend and confidante Naima who suggested a solution.

'You must go there as a representative of the Libyan Women's Union,' she told me. 'The prisoners' mothers have come crying to us that they are forgotten, begging for our help. They are desperate for information.'

Before setting off for London, I arranged a meeting with the mothers, who were distraught because they had not seen their sons for up to ten years. I was their only hope, which was a heavy burden to carry on my inexperienced shoulders. At the time I was not yet 30 years old and was still a relative novice when it came to international politics and diplomacy. I must admit I was especially uneasy about taking on this job, involving murderers. It was a reminder of Libya's shady side. However, after meeting the mothers I could at least justify it in my mind as a humanitarian mission.

I contacted a lawyer in London, who made a request on my behalf to the British Home Office. We took the approach that it was a human right of the mothers to know that their sons were being well treated.

Out of the blue I received a call from the lawyer, informing me that permission had been granted to visit all the men. It was a surprise, given the impenetrable wall into which Libyan intelligence officers claimed to have run. I was sent a programme of dates for my visits, at different prisons.

'No one has approached the Home Office about this until now,' I was told by my British lawyer. It seemed that Gaddafi had good reason not to trust his own people. I could only conclude that he was being lied to by his intelligence officers.

London was, by now, a familiar and cosy place where I felt at home but I was stepping out of my comfort zone. I'd never been inside a prison in my life.

Most of the men were delighted to see me, pressing photographs and letters into my hand to take home to Libya to their families, along with messages and tape recordings for Gaddafi. Many of them complained that they felt abandoned by Libya and the only legal representation they had received was provided routinely by the British justice system. Between them these prisoners were responsible for killing four men in London. They told me everything, claiming they had been assured by Libya that in return for acting as hit men they had been promised that they, and their families back home, would be properly looked after.

They felt betrayed because they vehemently believed that they had only been doing their duty for Libya. They thought they were soldiers on foreign soil and had no shame.

I asked each of them: 'Did Gaddafi order you to kill?'

This question was personal, not part of my mission, because I was curious to understand all I could about the character of my new master. After my arrival in Libya in 1988 he seemed to be intent on a path of rapprochement but I wanted to know if the Colonel, my childhood hero, had once pulled the strings of these hit squads.

Every prisoner replied: 'I never met Gaddafi.' Make of that what you will. They would only tell me that their orders came from the revolutionary office – which covered the whole government.

One visit sticks most in my memory. I travelled from London to the south coast and boarded a car ferry for the short crossing to the Isle of Wight to meet a convicted murderer. At the prison office I was told he did not wish to see me, so I returned to London leaving my telephone number. Two days later my phone rang and it was the prisoner calling.

'What proof do I have that you come from Gaddafi?' he demanded. Of all the prisoners he was the only one who queried my credentials, which indicates how desperate these men were to have any contact from Libya.

'It's up to you, if you see me or not,' I replied, providing a few more details. He seemed satisfied and a meeting was arranged.

The prisoner, Khalid, who was in his late twenties and wore his hair in a ponytail, spoke good English. He had studied while he was in prison and was likeable. I had to remind myself that I was sitting across the table from a killer who, according to my sources, was the most dangerous of all the Libyans held in Britain. He too gave me a letter and photo for his family, but nothing for Gaddafi.

I discovered that most of these prisoners would be eligible for early release after serving two-thirds of their sentence. My final meeting was with the British lawyer, instructing him to begin the parole process as soon as I had Gaddafi's say so.

Carrying the tape recordings and the information I'd gathered I flew back to Tripoli to relay all this to the Colonel.

'What, you were able to meet these men?' he said, clearly taken aback.

I'd taken the precaution of having my photograph taken with each prisoner, as irrefutable proof that visits had taken place.

'Yes, here are their photos,' I said, pushing them across the desk, along with letters written by the men.

The next minute he was screaming down the phone at some hapless person, demanding to know why he'd been lied to. It was the first time I'd seen Gaddafi lose his temper.

It emerged that millions of dollars of government money intended for the prisoners' legal costs and care had gone missing from under the leader's nose. This had happened not only in Britain, but in other countries where Libyans were being held. The only conclusion was that corrupt officials had stolen the money intended for the men and their families. No wonder the prisoners felt abandoned by the state. When they eventually arrived home, some of them came to visit me at my hotel to pass on their gratitude. Among them was Khalid, who had originally been so suspicious. I later learned that Gaddafi set up a committee to investigate who was to blame for the missing cash, and that several officials were jailed. Whether the money was ever recovered I have no idea.

Corruption like this was rife in Libya, but I also discovered that people around Gaddafi were rendered helpless by fear of failure. They would simply bury their heads in the sand rather than admit the job was beyond them, or lie that everything was fine. Sometimes it was impossible to determine whether it was a case of corruption or incompetence. The prisoners' case struck me as a mixture of the two. Other officials in quite senior posts were just plain lazy and told the leader only what they thought he wanted to hear. All in all, it was a very strange and paranoid environment. There were some good people, but it often seemed the rotten apples had more influence.

It put me in a difficult position because I didn't set out to prove that his people were lying to him, or cheating him.

Despite Gaddafi's fury he was once again pleased with my work and, coming on top of my successes with Tiny Rowland and Adnan Khashoggi, I believed I had his complete trust.

However, I had unwittingly stirred up a hornets' nest. My visits to the prisoners were supposedly secret but it seemed everyone knew about this mission. I didn't appreciate it immediately, but behind my back people in the intelligence service were beginning to scheme against me.

They were jealous of the growing influence of a foreigner and, one way or another, didn't want me in Libya.

One of the obvious examples of this growing menace was being followed at almost every step. There was nothing subtle about their methods. Sometimes I'd be walking down the street when I'd notice a black car in my shadow, driving slowly. This was meant to intimidate – and succeeded.

Naima told me to ignore these 'silly games', but I realised that I was now totally reliant on Gaddafi for my safety in Libya.

I discovered through a contact in Gaddafi's office that the intelligence service had opened a file on me. Although I reasoned that my enemies daren't touch me without incurring his wrath, I wasn't so naive to take it for granted that some sort of 'accident' might not happen in Libya. I tried to be alone as infrequently as possible.

With hindsight, I was in much more danger than I realised at the time. This was a bad misjudgement because I now realise they would not have hesitated to kill me. It would have been so easy to poison my food, or have me run down in the street.

There were two particular thorns in my side. The names of Abdullah Senussi and Moussa Koussa were feared in Libya and almost from the outset these two men, who are said to have been responsible for carrying out much of the regime's dirty work, tried to make my life a misery.

Senussi, the brother-in-law of Gaddafi, was head of internal security when I arrived in Libya in 1988. From the start I had a bad feeling about him; he seemed to be a loose cannon. He operated much as he pleased, and I suspect many of his acts were carried out without Gaddafi's knowledge or permission. In my opinion, Senussi was an evil character, capable of anything. He was my first enemy in Libya. He could be charming but I soon worked out that he was two-faced and a very dangerous man to cross. By all accounts he was natural with his wife and children, but I soon learned that he could not be trusted. He was close to Gaddafi and guarded his position jealously, ensuring the leader was fed his version of events. He was ruthless towards anyone he regarded as a threat and I have no doubt that he schemed against me. Because of his family connections with Gaddafi, this man also had a strong influence over the Colonel's children when they were growing up. He was effectively responsible for supervising their upbringing and I'm convinced his malign guardianship is one of the main reasons why so many of Gaddafi's offspring turned out badly. One of Senussi's roles was to cover up the children's misdeeds, so that even their father did not know the extent of what was happening.

Koussa was a former Libyan ambassador in London and based there in 1980 at the height of the assassinations of the Libyan dissidents. He gave an extraordinary newspaper interview with *The Times* newspaper, in London, in which he celebrated the two recent murders – of the lawyer and the journalist – in the capital.

'The revolutionary committees decided last night to kill two more people in the United Kingdom,' he said. 'I approve of this. They are resident in Britain. I do not know how it will be done or if it will be soon. We don't like breaking the law here but we are fighting these people because they worked against our revolution.'

Koussa, who was promptly nicknamed 'the envoy of death', was expelled from London in disgrace. He was welcomed back into the intelligence service fold in Tripoli, where he became close to Gaddafi.

When I first arrived in Libya in 1988, I was only vaguely aware of Koussa, who was deputy head of the intelligence service, but as time passed I learned that he was also one of the key figures in the campaign against me. From 1992 he was Minister of Foreign Affairs, until 1994 when he replaced Senussi and became head of the intelligence services.

Koussa was a well-educated man who had completed his Master's degree at Michigan State University and understood the ways of the West.

It was he who orchestrated much of the intimidation against me, including surveillance and eavesdropping on my telephone calls. He was quite open and unapologetic about this when I met him, telling me with a smile: 'Don't be angry, I am only doing my job to protect the president. You are not a Libyan and we can't control your movements outside the country. If you were in my place you would do exactly the same.'

I remember the exact words he then used to describe me. 'You are like a time bomb,' he added. 'We don't know when you might explode.'

The dirty tricks against me were endless. To give just one more example, a guy called Abdulsalam Al Zadmah, who held a senior rank in the intelligence office, promised to make my life easier if I became his girlfriend. The implication was that it would be made more difficult if I refused and he wasn't happy when I shrugged off this clumsy advance. I didn't have to wait long before Al Zadmah, who was renowned for doing the regime's dirty work, took his revenge for my snub.

One day my passport was snatched away from me at Tripoli airport as I tried to fly home to Jordan. I had no choice but to return to my hotel.

I reported the incident to the intelligence office, according to protocol, but time passed and there was no sign of the passport. It wasn't a huge hardship as I simply worked from my room, but eventually I sought Gaddafi's intervention. An investigation was ordered and I was informed that the culprit had been found to be Al Zadmah. Next I was told that he was to be prosecuted in court for theft.

It seemed completely out of proportion for an incident I'd dismissed as an act of petty spite, and at the lower end of the scale in terms of some of the many attempts to undermine me in Libya. The case was widely reported in Libya as a raft of VIPs, including Abdel-Salam Jalloud, a former prime minister of the country, were wheeled out to give evidence. Jalloud, who became an ally of mine, was an interesting character. He was one of Gaddafi's classmates at school and part of the 1969 revolution against King Idris. For twenty years he was the president's most trusted lieutenant. Although there was a fall-out over the direction of relations with Egypt and his influence waned, he remained an important figure in Libya. Jalloud spoke against Al Zadmah in court and the outcome was that he was convicted and his military rank downgraded. It was one of those times when I felt sure I only knew half of what was really going on behind the scenes in the regime. Al Zadmah was not being punished for merely stealing my passport. He was a powerful figure but ended up being humiliated in public. Maybe the Colonel, tiring of all the back-stabbing against me, also wanted to send a message that I should be left alone to get on with my work.

However, the man who finally returned my passport was Abdullah Senussi and with it came a warning.

'You are not welcome here,' he told me.

Mustering courage I replied: 'If that really is the case I need to hear it from Gaddafi, not you.'

Yet I don't want to give the impression that I spent my entire time living in fear, because there was much to like and enjoy about Libya.

Now I was spending so much time in the country, with a remit from the Colonel that went well beyond business deals, I was determined to immerse myself in its culture and politics.

When I first set foot in Libya for the Women's Union conference in 1988, all the delegates were given a copy of the famous Green Book. It was written in three parts by Gaddafi from the 1970s – social, political and economic – and was said to have been inspired by Chairman Mao's Little Red Book. It was compulsory for schoolchildren to study its contents and slogans from the booklet were splashed on billboards all over the country. It is 82 pages long and runs to about 21,000 words, which is about three times the length of the American Constitution – if that counts for anything.

In my excitement at meeting the Colonel I'd barely had time to glance at the Green Book after a copy was first pressed into my hands, but now I set about studying the Colonel's political philosophy. Thirty years after he first came to power Libya was still, supposedly, run according to those principles. I took the view that you can't work in a country without understanding the system. Gaddafi rejected both capitalism and communism, which perhaps explains Libya's isolation. The Green Book sets out a direct democracy, where there are no political parties. Instead there was a network of people's committees at local level. Gaddafi called the Libyan system his 'Jamahiriyah', which roughly translated means 'state of the masses'. Gaddafi described this approach as the 'Third Way' after capitalism and communism. In 1977 he'd changed the country's name from the Libyan Arab Republic to the Great Socialist People's Libyan Arab Jamahiriyah.

From 1980, he held no official position in the hierarchy but remained in absolute control. He portrayed Libya as a state governed by the people, with himself as a sort of guiding father. He was advised by a small inner circle, including some of his relatives from the Sirte area. Around him there was a constant jockeying for power and favour, like a medieval court. At the centre of all this, as I increasingly found to my cost, was Abdullah Senussi's intelligence service.

The Green Book has been widely ridiculed but much of it struck me as sensible, in theory at least. It has also been called simplistic and stating the obvious but this was a book intended to be read by everyone, not just intellectuals. I liked his basic assertion that men and women were equal, and that education was a right for everyone. Gaddafi's position at the top of the Libyan political pyramid was set in stone but citizens could vote for local representatives in health, education and so on.

I was keen to discover if the theories in the Green Book were actually put into practice, so in 1990 I followed local elections in Libya with great interest.

I was initially impressed but then I happened to see a television broadcast by Gaddafi, who was attacking certain candidates but praising others. He made it perfectly obvious which he favoured, even calling one existing representative a thief.

'I am helping my people to vote,' said Gaddafi, without a trace of irony. 'I know the best people.'

He would also pay unannounced visits to the polling stations in Tripoli, while votes were being cast. This was democracy, Libyan style.

During the election there was an incident when Gaddafi was confronted by an old man, walking with the help of a stick. The man showed Gaddafi the curve of the top of the stick, telling him that it mirrored Libyan politics. In other words, it was bent at the top.

I was sure he would be hauled away to prison for daring to say this, but Gaddafi just smiled and walked away, saying: 'You are right.'

A slightly dog-eared copy of the Green Book still sits, gathering dust I am afraid, on the shelf of my office in Amman.

Whenever possible I also seized the opportunity to savour everyday life in Libya, which was a welcome escape from living out of suitcases in a hotel.

Usually that was limited to a few hours spent at a coffee shop or a restaurant but one day I was lucky enough to be invited to a wedding.

Through Naima I got to know several of Gaddafi's female bodyguards, the Revolutionary Nuns, and one of them happened to be getting married.

As I've mentioned, so much I have read about the bodyguards is false, including the myth that they must all be virgins. In truth the young women were permitted to marry, but if the husband came from outside the security service the bodyguard had to leave her job.

The wedding party was in a large tent, pitched in a middle-class neighbourhood of Tripoli. At the height of the celebrations, a modest white Peugeot 505 saloon car pulled up. Out stepped the Colonel with only his driver, not a security guard in sight, to join the 200 guests. He'd given his guards the slip, to keep a promise to the girl to attend her wedding and enjoy a few minutes of normality. About fifteen minutes later they eventually caught up with the president, and soon the entire area was surrounded by soldiers.

Gaddafi stayed for about half an hour and it was quite a sight to witness everyone chanting his name, clapping and dancing. He was taken into a house to pose for photographs with the thrilled bride and groom, who did not mind being upstaged at all.

By the time Gaddafi left he was besieged by ordinary people and his guards formed a cordon so he could reach his car. He suddenly grabbed my arm and pushed me to his side.

'Protect me from the left,' he laughed. 'It is not properly guarded.' As Gaddafi reached his car he looked at me and asked: 'Do you have a gun?'

I'd never even held one, so I replied: 'No.'

He laughed again: 'So I was not properly protected then?'

The Colonel often complained that he could not behave like a normal person and that day I couldn't help feeling a little sorry for him. He was in his element, surrounded by his people, but he could only stay for half an hour. As Gaddafi was driven away, I noticed an old woman of about 90, crying. I asked her what was the matter and she told me: 'I love him. I am crying with happiness. My dear, people your age cannot understand what he has done for us. I lived during the kingdom, under Idris, and he freed us. Before, we were living in shacks with tin roofs. Now we have concrete homes and free education. We know his value. Gaddafi is more than a son to me. I was praying to God to meet him before I die.'

This reaction was typical in my early days in Libya. At that time there is no doubt that the Colonel was still adored.

Some people, especially from older generations, thought Gaddafi was a god.

Chapter 7

A Very Strange Proposal

After my time spent behind bars visiting the prisoners, and the resulting fall out with the Libyan intelligence service, it was with some wariness that I wondered: 'What next?'

It was becoming obvious that Gaddafi was using me in a scattergun sort of way, to tackle any problem that was occupying his mind. By 1990, only two years after my arrival, I was regarded as his number one troubleshooter and I still feared disappointing him.

So it was something of a relief after being embroiled in Libya's complex politics to be given a task for which, with my business background, I appeared perfectly suited.

One day I was summoned to the Colonel's now familiar office, inside the Bab al-Azizia compound.

'You know about oil don't you?' asked Gaddafi rhetorically, handing me another file. It related to a Swiss company which was trading Libyan oil, in much the same way as I now handled the country's most precious natural resource through my own business, Prime Oil. At this time about 40 per cent of Libya's production was sold through brokers like myself, while the rest went directly to refineries. In 1990, Libya was producing 1.4 million barrels of oil a day and the income from sales was bankrolling the country. Oil revenue was worth about $20 billion a year to Libya and its reserves were the largest on the continent. Without the natural resource Libya would still have been a poor desert nation.

Despite his lack of interest in day-to-day economics, Gaddafi was no fool. He'd nationalised the Libyan petroleum industry in 1974 and booted out all Western companies. So, in theory, he had complete control over the oil. However, when it came to the overseas sales, he appeared to have taken his eye off the ball.

This Swiss company, owned by an Algerian, was responsible for oil deals worth many millions of dollars but Gaddafi was suspicious.

'I want you to investigate the company and find out whether the money is coming back to Libya, or staying in Switzerland,' he said. He'd been told that some of the proceeds which should have flowed back to Libya, to a branch of the military called Al Sadi, were going missing.

It appeared to be a reasonably simple case of following the money trail and establishing if fraud was indeed happening on this grand scale, as the Colonel seemed convinced was the case.

I should have known better than leaping to the conclusion that anything in Gaddafi's Libya was straightforward. My investigations would open a can of worms and further deepen my rift with the intelligence service. They would also result in a proposal of marriage from a man I'd never met. It was to prove one of the most bizarre episodes of my life.

Initially, I arranged to meet the Algerian owner and his Libyan business partner at the head office of the Swiss company in Geneva. I discovered that Al Sadi was run by a man called Sayed Gaddaf Al-Dam, who happened to be a cousin of Gaddafi. Alarm bells started ringing in my head as soon as I learned of the family connection, but all I could do was press ahead with my enquiries. It emerged that Gaddaf Al-Dam was given a quota of oil, in lieu of a budget from the government, and was meant to use the sales proceeds to fund this section of the Libyan military.

The story that Gaddafi had been fed was that his cousin was planning a revolution and siphoning off large amounts of the oil money to fund his plot. It might sound a little far-fetched but I can assure you that in Gaddafi's long reign he faced numerous attempts to overthrow him from within, so he had a keen nose for the first whiff of trouble. Family loyalty counted for nothing as far as Gaddafi was concerned, including his own children.

It was alleged that Gaddaf Al-Dam was keeping the money for his own use in a Swiss bank account, so it was a matter of going through all the paperwork meticulously.

My analysis of the accounts eventually showed that every cent of oil revenue, amounting to $200 million a month, was going back to Libya as intended. It didn't take long to establish that, when it came to oil at least, Gaddaf Al-Dam was an honest man.

I took this discovery back to Gaddafi informing him that everything was above board and that Al Sadi was not being short-changed.

The Colonel asked: 'Are you sure? Because I can tell you now that five men, including my cousin, are currently in prison for fraud. You are telling me they are innocent?'

I wasn't entirely surprised to discover that it had been a case of guilty until proved innocent. I guessed that you don't hold power in a country like Libya for decades by sitting on your hands.

I had the paperwork to support my findings and as I assured him they could be trusted he picked up the telephone. After a short conversation Gaddafi gave the order: 'Release these men.'

I could not remember ever having seen the Colonel so elated. He leapt from his chair, clasped my face in his hands and kissed me on the top of the head.

'You have made me very happy,' he said. 'You have saved a man who is dear to my heart. Thank you.'

Pleased as I was to have cleared the name of an innocent man, there was a sting in the tail. The so-called case against Gaddaf Al-Dam and his alleged co-conspirators had, almost inevitably, been built by the intelligence service. There never had been a plot against Gaddafi but, no doubt as some sort of power struggle, the five men had been framed. I'd exposed yet more lies by the shady secret service and I feared there would be a price to pay.

Still, another mission was ticked off and seismic events in the Middle East soon pushed the Al Sadi case from my mind.

On 2 August 1990, Saddam Hussein invaded neighbouring Kuwait, triggering the first Gulf War. No one knew how it would pan out, or how the hostilities would affect other countries in the region including Libya. Despite Gaddafi's apparent enthusiasm to rejoin the world fold Libya was the only Arab country to support Iraq over the invasion, which did nothing for his international standing.

I took the precaution of flying to London, seeking sanctuary in my flat from where I followed the growing global crisis on CNN. It was a novelty after my early years, when I grew up in a media void, to be able to keep up to speed on satellite television with every development.

One evening, my viewing was interrupted by the ring of the telephone. On the line was an operator with a strong Libyan accent, and I assumed it was Gaddafi trying to drag me back. I sat on the line waiting for fifteen minutes until a connection was made. It was not the Colonel, however, but a voice I'd never heard previously.

'Hello, how are you?' he began, before launching into a speech that was obviously carefully prepared. 'This is Sayed Gaddaf Al-Dam. I read the Al Sadi file you prepared for the president and I want to thank you. I have nothing to give you apart from my name. I don't know if you are young or old, ugly or beautiful, but I am in your debt and I would like to offer you marriage. You saved my life and this is what I can do for you.'

In the Middle East, marriage is still often regarded as a type of business arrangement. Although it is becoming less common, many parents insist it is their right to marry off sons and daughters to cousins. In my homeland, Jordan, about one in five weddings happen in this traditional way. Marriage comes first and, if you are lucky, love follows.

Even rarer, but still not entirely consigned to history, is marriage as a way of paying off a perceived debt, or out of a sense of honour. This is more a Bedouin tradition. They have complicated customs of loyalty, revenge and hospitality which can be difficult for westerners to comprehend.

It is often said that this is why Gaddafi married his second wife, Safia, the former nurse. As I've said they did not seem to me to be a good match, but legend has it that when he was being treated for appendicitis in hospital in 1970 she thwarted an attempt to poison him. To show his eternal gratitude he gave his greatest gift, marriage. Whether this is true or not I don't know, but it would explain a lot.

I've also said that I was set on the modern Arab way of marrying for love.

It's not often that I am lost for words, but what could I possibly say to Gaddaf Al-Dam? I knew next to nothing about him, including his age, and had never before set eyes on the man. Even now, in the era of online match-making, you can at least see a photograph before getting romantically involved!

I managed to stammer a few hasty words down the line: 'Thank you. It's an honour for me but I was just doing my job. I didn't know who you were when I started out on my investigation.'

I ended the call as quickly and as politely as possible, promising to speak to him again when I had gathered my thoughts. Privately, I hoped this would be the end of the matter.

The famous Indian member of Parliament Amar Singh and I, when I first met Hillary Clinton in New York.

Mr Sant Singh Chatwal, who invited Mrs Hillary Clinton and I to dinner at his house.

Photographs taken at the court when I won against Prince Al-Waleed Bin Talal.

Muammar Al Gaddafi and my daughter Noor Abdul Hakim Al-Tamimi when she was 9 years old, in his tent in Tripoli during Prince Al-Waleed Bin Talal's last visit to Libya.

Muammar.

My youngest brother Izeldine and Head of Military Security of President Gaddafi Salmeh during Muammar Al Gaddafi's last visit to Paris.

Naima Al Saghyr, the Head of Security for Al-Gaddafi.

Muammar Gaddafi, my father and I at Gaddafi's office in Libya.

Muammar Gaddafi and my father during my father's first visit to Libya.

The Lockerbie prisoner Abdelbaset al-Megrahi and I when I visited his prison in Scotland.

Al-Waleed Bin Talal and I inside the plane which Gaddafi bought.

Muammar Al Gaddafi, my late brother Firas and my brother Izeldine when Gaddafi visited Jordan.

Suha Arafat, wife of the late Yasser Arafat, President of the Palestinian Authority, in a hotel lobby in Libya.

Leaving the plane from Sirt to Tripoli, for my last meeting with Gaddafi before being put under immediate detention.

A childhood photograph of me with my father and eldest sister Linda, along with his late Majesty King Hussain of Jordan.

Two photographs of me in my wedding dress (this page and next).

Former US Secretary of State James Baker, during his visit to Jordan.

My ex-husband on my right during our wedding. My dress was designed by Tina Green, a successful English businesswoman and billionaire.

My ex-husband Abdul Hakim Al-Tamimi with Adnan Khashoggi and his famous Iranian wife Shahbari. Adnan Khashoggi was the richest man at that time.

Fred Trammell Crow, General Scowcroft (the United States National Security Advisor under George Bush Snr.), the President of the election campaign for George Bush, Mrs Scowcroft and I at Mr Trammell Crow's house in Dallas.

James Baker, Ambassador Mr Edward Djerejian and I in Mr Baker's office in Austen.

Very deliberately I hadn't said 'no', but I hoped my reticence spoke volumes. It was a tactic I'd used in the past, in my banking days, to fend off unwanted advances from men. All I could hope was that my new suitor would consider any debt to me was now repaid and we could both get on with our lives, with no hard feelings.

Straight away I called Naima in Libya and asked her to intervene on my behalf. I had no intention of accepting Gaddaf Al-Dam's proposal but, because of the family connection to Gaddafi, I was still wary of having caused offence. I feared that the Colonel would wrongly jump to the conclusion that I had somehow engineered a relationship with his cousin, to improve my own position in Libya.

So I pleaded with Naima: 'Please tell the president that his cousin is offering to marry me, yet I've never met the guy. I don't want the president to think I am going behind his back.'

I was caught in the middle yet again.

Maybe my skills of diplomacy had become a little rusty, because Sayed Gaddaf Al-Dam hadn't got the message. That, or he was used to getting his own way and chose to completely ignore it.

Over the next few weeks I was besieged by the man, starting with daily telephone calls in which he implored me to marry him. He was constantly pushing, pushing for commitment. Next he managed to get hold of a photograph of me, which I later discovered came from Naima who thought this relentless pursuit by Gaddaf Al-Dam was all a huge joke. I felt a tiny bit flattered, but the bigger picture was that I had a growing feeling that his smothering attention could end badly for me. I didn't need any more enemies in Gaddafi's inner circle, but my admirer was not giving up.

He decided the way to my heart was through grand gestures. In February 1991, Gaddaf Al-Dam organised a surprise thirtieth birthday celebration for me at Villa dei Cesari, an Italian restaurant on the River Thames in London. It was all arranged behind my back, with the assistance of my business partner at Prime Oil who had good intentions but misjudged my mood. By the time I found out what was going on more than fifty guests had been invited, including Adnan Khashoggi's son Mohammed. I could hardly refuse to attend.

Gaddaf Al-Dam booked out the entire place, filling the room with balloons and sending two Italian friends to choose the menu.

It seemed there was to be no avoiding him now. I was still set against accepting his proposal but I was curious about what sort of man goes to all this trouble to woo a stranger.

However, I would have to wait a little longer to meet him. It was the height of the Gulf War and travel from Libya was still difficult. On my birthday, I arrived at Villa dei Cesari to find a place set next to mine at the table. Unable to fly to London, he had arranged for it to remain empty.

Much as I enjoyed the evening it was all rather surreal. I was slightly on edge, half expecting him to show up after all. I wouldn't have put it past Gaddaf Al-Dam to suddenly jump out of the cake shouting 'surprise!'

My birthday present from him was a stunning diamond necklace. Whatever else I thought of Gaddafi's cousin, he had good taste in gifts.

I noticed that the entire party was being recorded on video camera and a few days later the reason became apparent, as I received a call from Gaddaf Al-Dam describing in detail everything that had happened on my birthday. I certainly couldn't fault his effort.

Then matters took an even stranger turn. He called from Libya and asked me to listen to a recording that he was about to play. It was a telephone conversation between him and my father in Jordan. I listened, speechless, as I heard Gaddaf Al-Dam formally request my hand in marriage. In the West this tradition is symbolic, but in the Arab world it is much more significant. The approval of the bride-to-be's father is very important. Legally a woman can get married without her father's consent but there is a social stigma if she weds against his wishes.

Although I knew my father would never try to force my hand, it was a worrying development. I feared I'd never shake off Gaddaf Al-Dam now, although my father had the good sense to give him a non-committal reply. It was along the lines that he needed to know more about Gaddaf Al-Dam's background.

From Libya, news reached me that Gaddafi's cousin was also telling everyone that we were already engaged. He began writing poems and love songs for me. This was spiralling out of control. He was obsessed.

I made it my business to find out more about my very persistent suitor. He came from Sirte in the north-west of the country, the same birthplace as his relative Gaddafi, and at the time he was 43 years old. Both were from the Qadhadhfa tribe, which was one of the most influential in Libya.

In Roman times, Libya was three separate states which were only shoe-horned together under Italian occupation in the early twentieth century. One of Gaddafi's pledges after he came to power in 1969 was to properly unite Libya. In his Green Book he wrote: 'Tribalism undermines national identity because tribal loyalty weakens national loyalty.'

However, with up to 140 different tribes of varying influence spread throughout the country he hadn't really succeeded in persuading Libyans to embrace their Arab rather than tribal heritage. I remember one American writer stating: 'Libya is not a real country; only a bunch of tribes with flags.'

It was a crass description but at the end of the twentieth century clan loyalties still ran deep. The Colonel understood this and chose to surround himself with his own people, like a security blanket, even if he didn't fully trust them.

The more I learned about Gaddaf Al-Dam, the more my conviction was reinforced that I must tread carefully. Gaddafi's cousin had held various senior positions in the government, including Libyan ambassador in London and roles within the intelligence service. He was a man of influence and in Libya that could spell danger. His ties to the intelligence service didn't provide any comfort, so I resolved to act.

Two weeks after my birthday, coalition forces engaged in Operation Desert Storm drove Saddam Hussein out of Kuwait, bringing the Gulf War to a conclusion. In the Middle East, Saudi Arabia and Egypt were the two main financial contributors to the war against Iraq. I was thankful that Gaddafi did not get sucked into the war, despite his contempt for both the US and Britain, which were also at the forefront of this conflict on Arab soil. He'd learned in 1986, when he narrowly escaped the American bombs with his life, that head-on conflict against the US was futile. Gaddafi had met Saddam many times and loathed the Iraqi leader, regarding him as a thug. The West tended to lump them together, under the terrorist banner, but they were two very different characters. At the time of the first Gulf War, Gaddafi was very much moving towards compliance with international law and mending fences. He was even embracing capitalism, in his own way, by allowing Libyans to run their own businesses. Coffee shops, restaurants and hotels could now be privately run under the watchful eye of the state.

In many ways it suited Gaddafi for America and the rest of the West to have someone to hate more than him. In that regard, Saddam filled the Colonel's shoes perfectly.

The ceasefire also meant I was now free to return safely to Libya and I quickly sought a meeting with the Colonel, intending to enlist his help in extricating myself from Gaddaf Al-Dam's clutches.

I could think of no other solution, but my direct approach did not go according to plan. Right from the start I could see that Gaddafi was wrestling with a dilemma.

'Look,' he said. 'My cousin has an addiction to painkillers.' A type of drug was mentioned but it didn't mean anything to me.

Gaddafi then went on to reveal the history of Gaddaf Al-Dam's dependency. The reason for the Colonel's delight when I helped clear his cousin's name became crystal clear. Gaddafi told me that some years earlier a gift of a sports car had been received from Italy but, as I knew, he was not motivated by luxuries so he did not try it out. The car, either a Ferrari or a Lamborghini, I forget which, sat in his compound until Gaddaf Al-Dam was the first to take the wheel. When he started the engine the vehicle burst into flames, causing serious injuries. According to Gaddafi it was an assassination attempt.

'So, as you see, I feel responsible for my cousin,' said the Colonel. 'He was treated for two years for his injuries and during this time he became addicted to painkillers.'

Numerous attempts had been made to wean Gaddaf Al-Dam off the drugs, including sending him to rehab in Hong Kong, but he'd never gone through with any of the various programmes.

'Do me a favour,' added Gaddafi. 'Don't refuse his offer of marriage straight away but make it a condition that he starts the treatment first.'

Sensing nothing but more trouble ahead I asked: 'So you want me to lie to him?'

Gaddafi shrugged: 'Don't consider it a lie. Think of it as saving him. You will be doing a good deed. Just get him into a hospital. Later, after he recovers, you can tell my cousin you don't want to marry him.'

Gaddafi had spoken. Refusal would potentially undermine everything I had worked so hard to achieve in Libya. I did not feel at all comfortable that my personal life was being manipulated, but I decided to treat it as just another mission for the Colonel.

Over the course of the next six months I spoke regularly to Gaddaf Al-Dam by telephone. I discovered that he'd been married and divorced twice, and had two sons and a daughter. He was quite open about his addiction and we spoke about him having treatment in Switzerland.

At last I was also going to meet him, at the Richmond Hotel in Geneva, where he was staying and we agreed to have dinner. I flew to Switzerland from London, making sure I booked a separate hotel in Geneva. I was afraid of how Gaddaf Al-Dam would behave, given his drug dependency and his obsessive behaviour towards me so far. So I took one other precaution: persuading Gaddafi to allow Naima to accompany me. Who better to act as a chaperone than one of Libya's famous bodyguards?

My overriding emotion was nervousness. I imagined that this was how Arab brides in arranged marriages must feel when they meet their future husband for the first time. The big difference here was that there was going to be no wedding, even if he did not yet know it.

When I arrived at the Richmond Hotel, where we were to dine in his private suite on an upper floor, Gaddaf Al-Dam was waiting to greet me in the corridor when I stepped out of the lift. My first glimpse revealed a tall, quite handsome man, who looked younger than his actual age. He'd served in the army and had that courteous military bearing about him. He embraced me, with no hint of embarrassment or awkwardness, as if we had known one another for years.

I was a lot less relaxed and the presence of a small army of security guards in dark suits, who would clearly be in the background for the duration of our first meal together, did nothing to put me at my ease. In all he had an entourage of about forty people, including his brother Ahmed who was also a powerful figure in Libya.

Despite all my reservations, as we dined in Gaddaf Al-Dam's suite and made small talk I couldn't help warming to this stranger. He was enthusiastic about his love of poetry, so I gathered that he had a sensitive side. I noticed that he introduced me as his wife to hotel staff, and during the meal he spoke of his plans for our marriage. I went along with this, telling myself that he would soon be in hospital having treatment and I would be free to leave. We parted that evening on good terms and I returned to my hotel.

Next morning we set out for a specialist clinic, in Montreux, about 70 miles away on the other side of Lake Geneva. Then, as we drove, Gaddaf

Al-Dam suddenly ordered the chauffeur to pull over. My first instinct, as he opened the door and climbed out, was that he had decided not to have treatment after all.

'Come with me down to the water,' he said, and we walked the few metres to the lakeside. Gaddaf Al-Dam next pulled out a box of injections and began throwing handfuls of them into the depths. 'This is my sign to you that I am serious,' he said. It was another grand gesture and it made a big impression on me. I was torn between my loyalty to Gaddafi and my conscience, which was telling me it was not fair to lead this man on and allow him to think I was going to become his next wife.

We'd barely arrived at the clinic and Gaddaf Al-Dam was admitted, before a doctor asked to speak to me.

'You are very important to my patient and he has made it clear that he is having treatment only to please you,' he explained. 'You must be here for him all the time because it will be difficult.'

It was not what I wanted to hear. I'd anticipated spending a couple of days in Switzerland, making sure that Gaddaf Al-Dam was safely in hospital, then flying back to my home in London.

My heart sank when the doctor told me it could take two or three months to complete the treatment, but I felt I had no choice. My one condition, that Naima stayed too, was agreed by Gaddafi.

There followed a gruelling period as we visited the clinic every day. I don't know what medication they gave Gaddaf Al-Dam, but he looked like a corpse. He suffered bad withdrawal symptoms, which left him dizzy and weak. I hated to see him suffering like this, but I told myself it was for the best. Gaddaf Al-Dam just made me feel even more guilty when he grabbed my wrist one day and said: 'Look at the pain I am in. It is all for you.' He was in such agony that he reached out for the bed frame and prised the metal rods apart.

The clinic, which was popular with VIPs and celebrities, was very expensive but not a pleasant environment for an outsider like me. There were other patients screaming and I found the place distressing.

After about a month the doctors were pleased with his recovery. He looked normal and we were able to spend sunny afternoons sitting in the clinic garden.

He was still convinced we would marry soon, telling me: 'If I don't marry you there will be no one else.'

Despite this I felt that my time in Switzerland was drawing to a close, particularly as there were growing tensions with Gaddaf Al-Dam's brother who was treating me like a member of his staff. Ahmed knew nothing of the deal I'd made with Gaddafi and assumed I was intent on marrying his brother Sayed. He made it clear by the manner in which he disrespected me that he didn't approve. I think there was also some political jealousy towards his brother. Maybe it suited Ahmed for Sayed, who was a favourite of the president, not to get better. Unlike Sayed, the other brother bore a close family resemblance to Gaddafi which I found unnerving. I knew Ahmed was involved in buying weapons for Libya.

My dark mood was not improved by the departure of Naima, who had been summoned back to Libya. 'Enough of all this,' I said to myself.

Secretly, I booked flight tickets to London and fled. It was out of character for me to behave like this, also taking the risk of upsetting Gaddafi, but I could no longer stand the atmosphere in Switzerland. If it came to a showdown with the Colonel I could argue that I'd gone the extra mile by staying longer than agreed, and that Gaddaf Al-Dam was almost fit to be discharged.

My final act in Switzerland was to write a letter to Gaddaf Al-Dam, explaining everything including my pact with Gaddafi and my problems with his brother. 'I am sorry but I did this to help you recover,' I wrote. 'Forgive me.' On my way to Geneva airport I made a detour and handed the letter to one of his doctors.

I believe Sayed Gaddaf Al-Dam genuinely loved me. Maybe too much. Although those strong feelings were not reciprocated I had grown very fond of him and had great sympathy for his plight.

I heard later that he offered to resign from his job with the military in order to marry me. For security reasons it was forbidden for members of the Libyan armed forces to marry foreigners. I think that showed he was a real man, with strong principles and I won't say a bad word about him. Perhaps if we'd met in different circumstances I would have married him but this way it was never going to happen. In any case, I don't think Gaddafi would have allowed it.

On my return to London I struggled to put events in Switzerland to one side. I prayed Gaddaf Al-Dam would not relapse because I had run away. I was worried sick he might harm himself and called all my contacts in Libya, seeking information.

Finally, a couple of weeks later, I heard that he was doing well and had returned to Libya from Switzerland looking ten years younger. Some of my guilt lifted.

At Gaddafi's command, and with good intentions, I was not entirely honest with Gaddaf Al-Dam. I hope he understands why.

Five years later I happened to bump into him in Libya. He was impeccably polite but we didn't discuss what had happened between us and the subject of marriage was not reopened. I am glad to say that he never became my enemy. He did not marry again.

Chapter 8

New York

Rewind to 1988 and I am sitting at home in Jordan one evening in late December when state television news carries a report about an aircraft crashing over the town of Lockerbie, near the border between Scotland and England.

These are the facts. Pan Am Flight 103 originated in Frankfurt, Germany, and landed at London Heathrow before its scheduled departure to New York JFK and Detroit. It was four days before Christmas and the Boeing 747 was carrying students, soldiers going home on leave, couples on shopping trips and families reuniting for the holidays. At ten seconds before 7.03 p.m. the voice recorder detected a loud sound as a bomb detonated on board, and radar images showed the plane breaking up into five sections in mid-air. Fatefully, three engines, still functioning as the aircraft disintegrated, carried large sections to the small Scottish town of Lockerbie.

Survivors on the ground reported hearing what they thought was a roll of thunder; others likened the trail of flaming wreckage to a meteor shower. Fully laden fuel tanks, intended to carry Pan Am 103 across the Atlantic, caused a fireball on the ground and debris was later recovered up to 80 miles away.

All 243 passengers and 16 crew, along with 11 people in the town, were killed. At 82, Jean Murray was the oldest on board, the youngest was 2-month-old Brittany Leigh Williams. More than sixty of the victims were American college students, who'd been studying abroad.

For many Britons and Americans I know this is one of those moments in history, like the shooting of JFK or the death of Elvis, when they instantly remember exactly where they were.

It was quickly apparent that the loss of the aircraft was no tragic accident. As fragments of debris were painstakingly collected and pieced together it was established that explosives were hidden in a brown suitcase, loaded into the forward cargo area. The aircraft was 300 miles from London, flying at 31,000 feet, when the bomb detonated. Had the flight departure not been delayed the bomb would have exploded somewhere over the Atlantic, as intended, and much of the evidence would never have been recovered.

The burning question was: 'Who was to blame?'

For the first two years of the investigation the finger pointed at Iran, which was said in the West to have hired a Palestinian terrorist organisation to carry out the atrocity. The bombing was supposedly in retaliation for the US's downing of an Iranian passenger jet over the Straits of Hormuz in July 1988. The aircraft, mistaken for an Iranian fighter jet, was struck by a missile fired from the US cruiser Vincennes. Most of the 290 passengers who died were pilgrims on their way to Mecca.

During my first two years visiting Libya, between 1988 and 1990, I never heard the word Lockerbie mentioned. I was not directly involved in policy making so I don't claim to have known about everything going on in Libya, but I was on the close fringes of government and I did not hear so much as a whisper.

When I returned to Libya in the summer of 1990 after an absence of six months – much of the time spent mulling over the marriage that never was to Sayed Gaddaf Al-Dam – that had all changed. Now, the Lockerbie issue was dominating the political agenda in Tripoli.

Libya was in the frame because it was alleged that a computer chip in the bomb's detonator matched parts found on two Libyans arrested in Senegal. The same type of detonator had, it was claimed, been used to destroy French UTA Flight 772 over the Sahara in 1989. The DC-10 aircraft was en route to Paris from The Republic of Congo, via Chad. The same green-coloured piece of circuit board was discovered in tiny bomb fragments. It was traced back to Libya, whose motive for bombing UTA Flight 772 was said to be revenge for France's support of Chad in a long-running border dispute with Libya. UTA 772 became known as 'the forgotten flight' because although 170 people on board were killed it never attracted the same international attention as Lockerbie. Now, though, it was a vital piece of the puzzle. Even the same type of Samsonite suitcase was used in both attacks.

This is just a short summary of the case against Libya. Investigators from Scotland and the US had followed up leads in fifty countries and interviewed 14,000 people. All the evidence appeared to stack up against Libya and there was a thirst for justice. Iran, Syria and Palestine, the other usual suspects at the time, were forgotten.

So I returned to a country where the people were worried about the prospect of food and other shortages, as Libya once again became a pariah state and the West thirsted to punish Gaddafi.

In November 1991, two suspects, Abdelbaset Al-Megrahi and Al-Amin Khalifa Fhimah, were named and charged in their absence by the authorities in the US and Britain. They were linked to the bomb by a shopkeeper in Malta, who remembered selling clothes that were found in the suitcase containing the Lockerbie bomb. It was claimed that the bomb began its journey in Malta, where Al-Megrahi was working as an agent for Libyan Airlines. Allegedly he was able to tag the suitcase containing the device and send it on a flight which connected with Pan Am 103.

Although I would subsequently meet the supposed Lockerbie bomber Al-Megrahi in his prison cell in Scotland, following his conviction, I had at that time never encountered either man. Their names had not cropped up in Tripoli and meant nothing to me when Lockerbie first became an issue in 1991.

The Colonel wasn't sure of his next move. He couldn't be seen to cave in to the US and Britain, but he didn't want to become an international outcast again. He refused to hand the pair over for trial in Scotland or a neutral venue, but his offers to try the men in Libya, Malta, or a neutral Arab country were rejected.

At one stage it might have suited Gaddafi, who hated America, to take the credit for Lockerbie but he was intent on a different path by now.

'The evidence against Libya is less than a laughable piece of a fingernail,' he insisted, but I knew he was worried. Lockerbie took up more and more of his time and committees were set up to deal with the crisis. As far as Gaddafi was concerned, the Americans and the British were like dogs with a bone over Lockerbie. He knew there would be no respite and, as far as he was concerned, Libya in general and he in particular made a convenient scapegoat. Someone had to pay, although international law appeared to be on his side when it came to surrendering Libyan citizens.

Sure enough the pressure on Libya to hand over the two suspects for trial was ratcheted up, and in the spring of 1992 the United Nations passed a resolution imposing sanctions. The US and Britain led the way among the fifteen voting nations of the UN Security Council. Wearing black for mourning, relatives of some of the victims of the Pan Am bombing watched from the visitors' gallery as the Council voted. The ruling also covered the bombing of the UTA airliner. A total of 440 people from some thirty countries died in the two disasters. Neither plane had fallen from the sky accidentally and it was not just the Americans and British who wanted answers from Gaddafi. In addition to surrendering Al-Megrahi and Fhimah for trial, Libya was required to renounce terrorism and accept responsibility for the actions of Libyan officials. I knew of at least two, Abdullah Senussi and Moussa Koussa, who might have good reason to be anxious as the net seemed to close on Libya. Both would come under suspicion for being the real masterminds behind the bombing of Flight 103.

The strong words from the UN also dealt with the thorny issue of paying compensation to relatives of victims on both flights. The Colonel tried to portray the pressure being put on Libya as an attack by the West on the Arab world as a whole, orchestrated by Israel. Morocco, the only Arab country on the Council, abstained in the vote, but once again Libya found itself short of friends.

Gaddafi did have one ally in Britain: his old pal Tiny Rowland wrote an article in *The Observer*, which he owned, condemning sanctions. The Metropole Hotels deal, which I'd been heavily involved in, was concluded and Libya bought a one-third stake in the chain.

Sanctions were exactly what Gaddafi dreaded. They prevented international flights to and from Libya, which made business difficult for everyone. Now to reach Libya from Amman or London I was forced to fly to Tunisia, cross the border into Libya by car then take a tortuous journey through the desert to Tripoli.

Sales of arms, commercial aircraft and spare parts to Libya were also banned. However, Libya was still permitted to trade its vital natural resource, oil, which also suited many countries in the West. So in many ways life carried on much as before.

Given my experience in dealing with the Colonel's overseas headaches, I knew it was only a matter of time before I got dragged into the fallout from Lockerbie. In fact, it was only a matter of days.

I was informed that I was to work in a small team including foreign affairs minister Omar Mustapha Al-Montasser and treasury minister Mohammed Al-Bukhari. My role was to become a sort of globetrotting spin-doctor, to try to put Libya's case to the West and ultimately have the sanctions lifted. The focus was to be on the US and Britain. Not much to ask!

The potentially insurmountable hurdle we faced was that Libya, long before any court case, had already been judged guilty by many in the West of planting the Lockerbie bomb. It seemed strange to me that they were already talking about compensation for the victims' families. Normally you establish guilt beyond reasonable doubt, then discuss compensation. I understood Libya's assertion that the suspects would not get a fair trial.

It was too early for me to reach my own conclusions but at no stage, then or later, did I ever hear Gaddafi admit that he had any involvement – either directly, or by sponsoring a non-Libyan terror group to carry out the act which was more likely. His position on that, in front of me at least, never wavered. Not then, and not when Libya eventually paid millions of dollars of compensation to the Lockerbie families. They were a vocal group and intent on blood money.

From the outset I was astounded by the naivety of Gaddafi and some of the so-called expert advisors around him. They wanted to change opinions in the US and Britain but they seemed to have no grasp that it was possible to hire lobbying firms to do this. It had echoes of my approaches to the Libyan prisoners – Gaddafi just assumed that everything had to be underhand, through subterfuge or by paying illegal bribes to corrupt officials and politicians.

Past experience had taught me that it was often the best strategy to aim high. I arranged a meeting in Geneva with an American lobbyist and business advisor called Gordon Wade and some of his influential associates including a British colleague, Geraldine I'Anson, and another American, William Bodine. Wade was a former chairman of the Republican Party in Kentucky, who I reckoned would be our best route to President George Bush, while Bodine was a top financial adviser. The American lobbyists were taking a calculated risk because they could be deemed to be busting their own country's restrictions on dealing with Libya, which went far beyond those imposed by the United Nations. My view was that they were grown men and knew what they were taking on. Also representing

Libya were Al-Montasser, Al-Bukhari and one of Gaddafi's most trusted advisors, Juma'a Al Marfi, who was head of a Libyan military organisation called Muammar Group (Legion). Al Marfi, who now lives in London where he's been granted political asylum, was as loyal as they come.

'We can help you,' Wade assured us, in exchange for a contract worth $8 million a year. The money, to be channelled through Switzerland, wasn't an issue for Libya. We shook hands on the deal which stated that the lobbyists would assist the Libyan government in the 'solution of the Lockerbie problem', and 'in enhancing relations with Western European nations'.

In 1992 we met Wade and Bodine again, against the backdrop of International Monetary Fund and World Bank meetings in New York and Washington which Libya was permitted to attend. Al-Bukhari was sweating on his US visa until the very last minute but was eventually granted entry and we travelled, with an entourage of other Libyans, via Tunisia and London.

It was much easier for me, a Jordanian, to enter the US and when we arrived at JFK airport I took a different immigration channel. The Libyan delegation was all carrying matching official flight bags, for personal effects and paperwork, and I had been given one for the trip by Al-Bukhari. I didn't give this a second thought until we were passing through security and customs on arrival. Then I realised the bag I was carrying felt much heavier than when I'd taken it on board. Moments later, as it was scanned and opened by US officials, the holdall was discovered to contain $2 million in crisp, new $100 bills. I felt foolish, realising it had been switched under my nose at some stage on the flight. I looked towards Al-Bukhari, who had just cleared immigration and was being enthusiastically greeted by a welcome party from the United Nations. The moment I caught his eye he gave me a knowing smile, and it didn't take a genius to work out what had happened.

Because Libyans were not permitted to use credit cards in the US, or make bank transfers, the stash of cash was for the treasury minister to pay all the bills during our trip. He just didn't want to risk a diplomatic row, or arouse suspicion, by being the one carrying it into the US and having to explain why it was needed. Libya's reputation as a terrorist state preceded him.

A Jordanian woman was less likely to be detained or refused entry but in any country a bag full of cash raises eyebrows.

'What's this?' asked the US security man.

'It's money,' I replied, not simply to annoy him but to buy a few moments to think on my feet.

'I can see that,' he said. 'Why are you carrying all this cash with you?'

'My boyfriend gave it to me, for shopping on 5th Avenue,' I said. 'If you don't like that I can get back on a plane and spend it in London.'

Without batting an eyelid, he replied: 'No Ma'am that won't be necessary. You just need to declare it. As soon as we stamp your papers you can enjoy your shopping.'

I wasn't finished with the treasury minister, who was by now convulsing with laughter. Striding towards him, I decided entering the spirit of the joke was the best approach. It had been an embarrassing episode, and I'd let my guard slip in allowing the switch to happen but no lasting harm had been done. If I had to play the stereotypical spoiled Arab girlfriend to ease the Libyans' path into the hostile US then so be it.

So I hugged the bag to my chest and declared, with a beaming smile of my own: 'This money is legally mine now.'

Al-Bukhari handed back my own identical bag, taking the one containing the money. 'If you keep it, how can we pay all our bills in America?'

I liked Al-Bukhari, who had a good sense of humour. He worked hard on the Lockerbie issue, unlike some of the other Libyans who just hoped it would go away, and he always seemed calm.

The following day, Al-Bukhari spoke against sanctions, reading a very good speech prepared with the help of the lobbyists. There was a mention of Lockerbie and the olive branch of allowing UN inspectors into Libya to check for nuclear weapons was offered.

The conciliatory speech, a far cry from the angry rhetoric usually associated with the Gaddafi regime, was covered by many of the US newspapers and included a little joke about George Bush who was in the audience.

It drew laughter and afterwards we were congratulated by some of the Americans. 'We didn't realise Libyans had a sense of humour,' they said.

Our trip to America had got off to a good start, and it was about to get a whole lot better.

Chapter 9

President Bush

I have always stressed the importance of contacts. Good connections can open many doors in the business world, and it's just the same in politics. Doors that would otherwise be firmly shut in your face can suddenly unlock if you know the right people.

I was about to receive a telephone call that would gain me access to the most powerful man in the world.

It came from Lucy Billingsley, the daughter of one of the US's leading real estate developers, Trammell Crow. He was a Texan who had reshaped the skylines of some of America's major cities in the 1980s and grown fabulously rich on the proceeds. He also happened to be a major donor to the Republican Party and in 1992, when I was with the Libyan delegation in New York, was organising a fundraising event at his ranch in Tyler county about 100 miles south-east of Dallas. It was the build-up to the US presidential election later that year and George Bush was fighting to stay in power.

'Would you like to join us?' enquired Lucy. I'd become acquainted with this diminutive redhead and her husband Henry after being introduced by the lobbyist Gordon Wade. She added: 'It will be a good opportunity to meet a few people who might be able to help you.'

Tickets for this type of function could not be bought and it was almost unprecedented for foreigners to be on the guest list. This was excellent news and as I seemed to be on such a roll I decided to chance my arm.

'Would it be possible for Mr Al-Bukhari, the Libyan treasury minister, to attend with me?'

Given America's poisonous relations with Libya I was anticipating a sharp intake of breath and a hasty refusal but, on the contrary, Lucy assured me that the minister would also be welcome at the ranch in a few days' time. Her husband Henry had kept the best bit back, adding: 'Oh, and President Bush will be there. I hope we can arrange for Mr Al-Bukhari to speak to him for a few minutes.'

This was the realm of dreams but, unfortunately, the terms of Al-Bukhari's hard-won US visa severely restricted his movements to New York and Washington.

As I recall he was allowed just far enough from his hotels to attend the scheduled meetings. At that time, Libyans were the last people the Americans wanted roaming around their country.

Texas was not on our itinerary, which had taken months to approve, and we were well aware that cutting through red tape to try to seek a travel extension would take weeks. We discussed this apparent impasse with our American contacts who assured us that the authorities would turn a blind eye, and urged us not to let this golden opportunity slip from our grasp. It was hard to believe but we felt there was nothing to lose.

So, dispensing with Al-Bukhari's usual posse of security guards, we set off for Dulles airport in Washington, more in hope than expectation. This was pre 9/11 when taking an internal flight in the States was much like hopping on a bus, but even so we were very surprised to be waved through departures. No one said a word to us, exactly as we'd been told.

I'd met Trammell Crow twice previously, on my own, and we'd got on well. He was one of those self-made billionaires that seem to pour off production lines in America and legend has it that he started out plucking chickens, while studying at night classes. After serving in the US Navy he turned his attention to real estate, beginning with warehouses in the late 1940s then making his fortune by building office and apartment blocks. His landmarks include the Peachtree Center in Atlanta, the Embarcadero Center in San Francisco and the 50-storey Trammell Crow Center in Dallas.

Crow, who personified the American rags to riches dream, was known as 'the largest landlord in the US' and was a generous donor to the Republicans.

All in all, a very useful man to know and likeable too. There was a humility about him, which included driving regular cars and buying his shirts from the budget chain Walmart. He seemed happiest messing around on his ranch.

Crow greeted us warmly there, the day before the fundraiser, and we were escorted to guest rooms in the main house. Our hosts were understandably nervous about a member of the Libyan government, with no security men in tow, staying in a local hotel. Equally, the notion of

Gaddafi's man rubbing shoulders with the great and the good of the Republican Party in election year would not go down well with many voters. You might even call it political suicide. A very low profile was in order and that suited me fine.

That afternoon I was enjoying a cosy lunch with Crow and Al-Bukhari when the phone began ringing off the hook. Two of the callers were Brent Scowcroft, the US National Security Advisor, and James Baker, the White House Chief of Staff, demanding to know why Al-Bukhari had been invited.

The general message from both was: 'Get this man out of the house before the president arrives.'

A series of almighty rows erupted, as Crow resolutely held his ground. He was a godfather of the Republicans and 78 years old at the time of our visit. I got the impression he didn't give a damn, and it did not sit easily with his Texan sense of hospitality to have to kick out an invited guest. There was also another motive to stand up to Scowcroft and Baker. Money. The Libyans had hinted that if strings were pulled they might be willing to sign commercial deals with Trammell Crow and his son-in-law Henry Billingsley after sanctions were lifted. One of their strategies was to buy cheap land in Dallas and sell it for development when prices rose, and they were keen on finding wealthy Arab partners. Like good connections, money opens doors and everyone knew the Libyans were rolling in oil dollars.

The upshot was that Al-Bukhari was not going anywhere, so a compromise was thrashed out. He would attend the fundraising event with me but remain in the background. Under no circumstances would he be introduced to, or come near, Bush. There would be no friendly handshakes, which could easily be misconstrued, or photo call.

However, a Jordanian being introduced to the president was not going to cause much of a stir so suddenly my position was elevated. I didn't have any diplomatic status in Libya, let alone in the US, but I'd be the face of the regime as far as the Americans were concerned.

It was agreed that I would accompany the Crow family group that welcomed Bush to the ranch, while Al-Bukhari stayed in the garden where the president would later give a speech to the assembled VIPs.

When the moment arrived, Crow gave me a few minutes' warning and we gathered at the front door. As the presidential limousine pulled up,

Bush's security guards jumped out and formed a cordon. Next minute I was shaking hands with the president of the United States and posing for photographs. How I wished my father could see me now. There was great excitement at the ranch as the line-up was arranged, and naturally everyone wanted to be next to the president.

I didn't feel it was my place to hog the limelight but then Bush said: 'Let me stand next to this beautiful lady.'

It was an unforgettable moment. My mind raced back to that first time I set eyes on Gaddafi, four years earlier, and felt his aura. George Bush, a tall, imposing man had the same sort of presence that comes from holding a position of great power. You try to act normally and tell yourself he's just a fellow human being but there's always something rather frightening about the first meeting, which was also the case when I was introduced to Gaddafi. Bush towered over me as we shook hands.

Crow and his family, plus Brent Scowcroft and Bush's campaign manager Bob Teeter, completed the group in the photograph. This picture still has pride of place on my office wall in Amman, alongside those of Gaddafi. Both men must be turning in their graves to be sharing wall space so closely.

After the introductions were over we moved indoors and, just before the fundraising dinner officially began, Bush gently took my arm and steered me away from the crowd. We were now standing in a large reception room, overlooking the terrace and garden of the ranch.

Fixing me with a stare, he said: 'How are you Miss Sharab? Tell your boss that if he wants to solve his problems with Lockerbie he needs to start with the British, not us. I think the King of Jordan would be a good intermediary.'

That was all he said, but I felt I needed to clarify one point. 'Who do you think is my boss?' I asked, assuming he believed Jordan was my master.

'Gaddafi,' the president replied. His message, delivered in a friendly manner, was short but clear. The Colonel was wasting his time focusing on America and should change direction.

With elections looming, Bush had to tread carefully and didn't want to be seen negotiating directly with Libya. Although his position on Libya had softened, in the past he'd described Gaddafi as 'an egomaniac who would trigger World War III just to make headlines'. So he could hardly backtrack and sit down round the fireside with his old foe.

At the time I was congratulating myself on having gained access to the president of the US, but later I came to realise that the whole episode in rural Texas was skilfully choreographed by Bush and his team. The call out of the blue inviting me to the ranch; a Libyan government minister able to travel unimpeded in the US; being hand-picked for the photo-opportunity; and my little chat with the president who knew my name. It was all too good to be true.

I believe now that that this trip to Trammell Crow's ranch was all carefully managed and, without wishing to underplay my abilities too much, I was a pawn. The Americans, who also wanted a breakthrough on Lockerbie, knew they had much to gain from opening a semi-official channel of communication with Libya. I wondered if even the rows on the phone between Trammell Crow and Scowcroft and Baker were all part of the theatre, or whether they genuinely didn't want Al-Bukhari there.

I also learned later that the CIA, the American intelligence agency, had a file on me. No doubt it was handed to Bush to read in the car before our encounter on the steps of the house.

Following our conversation, I joined the president and about 300 other guests inside for a buffet dinner. Later, people spilled outside into the garden to catch the last of the evening sun and listen to a speech by Bush. Our paths didn't cross again and that was also no coincidence. He was done with the messenger.

I also took the opportunity to speak to Brent Scowcroft, who was much warmer than I expected after the hostile phone call to Trammell Crow. We discussed Lockerbie and without giving too much away he made the right noises about finding some sort of compromise. He expressed regret for America's bombing of Libya in 1986, which was another gesture of conciliation. It was obvious to me that the Republicans wanted to solve the Libyan problem, which would be music to the Colonel's ears.

We stayed for two further days at the ranch, four in all, enjoying wonderful Texan hospitality before the arduous journey back to Tripoli via London, Geneva and Tunisia to report back to Gaddafi. He was fascinated when I showed him a copy of the photograph taken at the ranch, and listened intently as I delivered Bush's brief but important message.

'Good, we will continue working on Lockerbie but now you will negotiate with the British,' said Gaddafi, immediately grasping the significance of the message I'd just delivered from George Bush. My run of successful missions was continuing, but there was a hitch.

A week later I was summoned back to the Colonel's office, to find he had a frown on his face. Moussa Koussa from the intelligence office was claiming, with typical arrogance, that the photograph with Bush was a fake. He was insisting it was impossible for me to have gained access to the US president and that my entire account of the visit to the ranch was a pack of lies. I knew the snake-like Koussa would go to any length to try to discredit me but this was ridiculous and desperate.

The treasury minister, who'd seen it all first-hand, supported me and fortunately I didn't have to wait long to have the last laugh. A Dallas newspaper published an account of the meeting, with an accompanying photograph. There it was, plain as day, George Bush standing next to me. I arranged for a copy of the newspaper to be delivered to the Colonel's office and allowed him to draw his own conclusions about Koussa. It was further evidence that the intelligence office wanted to handle Lockerbie in its own twisted way, without me in the picture. Every time I got a result – with the Libyan prisoners in Britain, the leader's cousin and now Bush – it was embarrassing for them. I knew that Gaddafi used to taunt Koussa and his secret service colleagues, shouting at them: 'How can this little girl achieve all this yet you, with the big budget I provide, get nowhere?'

Part of me was also angry, because I knew that Gaddafi was basing many of his decisions on false information that was being drip-fed to him by his aides. Little wonder he made some bad calls. Tripoli was sinking in corruption. Everyone thinks that my unique relationship with Gaddafi made things easy for me in Libya, but that's not entirely true. Of course he gave me work but there was always someone in the background trying to derail me out of jealousy and spite, or because they thought I was the president's spy, or his mistress. Nothing went smoothly, although I also encountered many decent, clean officials such as Suleiman Al-Shahoumi, who was in charge of foreign affairs in parliament, and Mustafa Al-Zaidi, the minister of health.

Gaddafi decided in the aftermath of my meeting with George Bush to authorise Al-Montasser to take the lead on Lockerbie. I didn't have much confidence in the foreign minister, having already worked with him on the Lockerbie group, and joked with Gaddafi: 'You already have an air embargo. If you wait for this man to get out of his chair and reach the door you will also have sea and land embargoes.' Al-Montasser was a big man and despite the crisis engulfing his country as sanctions took a grip, Gaddafi couldn't help smiling at my rather unkind remark.

The UN had decreed that the sanctions would be reviewed every 120 days, but with the lumbering foreign minister in charge nothing changed. Gaddafi told me one day: 'You know Daad my people think I am going crazy, because when they just told me the embargoes were being renewed I burst out laughing. I was looking at the foreign minister and I remembered what you predicted.'

During this period I was spending much of my time in London, where I was still involved in trading oil and gas on behalf of the Libyans through my company Prime Oil. But if duty called I would travel to Tripoli, or anywhere else Gaddafi needed me.

Al-Bukhari had made a good impression on the Republicans and we were invited back to the Trammell Crow ranch a few months later in October 1992. This time we travelled separately, because I was attending my sister Reem's wedding in Jordan, and the treasury minister arrived two days ahead of me. The occasion this time was one of Trammell Crow's famous camp-outs. They were annual male bonding sessions at his ranch for government and business leaders, which involved sitting round open fires, trail riding and firing guns. If you have ever seen the Hollywood movie *City Slickers* you will get the idea. It was basically men playing at being cowboys, drinking beer and networking. Women weren't invited so I stayed well away. Not so much home on the ranch, but stuck in a hotel on my own while the Libyan treasury minister became an honorary Texan cowboy.

Given the restrictions on the minister's travel at the outset of the first trip I was curious to discover how he'd managed to get permission to fly to Texas at such short notice. It emerged that he'd been refused a visa, so he simply entered and exited the US illegally from Mexico by car. Maybe they should have built a wall to keep him out.

I felt it prudent not to ask any further questions, but it struck me as extremely risky. I knew the US authorities would take a dim view if they ever found out that the Libyan had been given assistance by his new American friends. As time went by I assumed they had got away with it, but four years later in a US court Henry Billingsley admitted his part in this subterfuge. He'd met the treasury minister at a hotel in the Mexican town of Matamoros, on the south bank of the Rio Grande River opposite Texas, where Al-Bukhari was provided with fake documents. From there they'd slipped over the US border to the town of Harlingen and jumped on a private aircraft to complete the 500-mile journey to Dallas.

'I made an error for which I am genuinely sorry,' said Billingsley after he was implicated. He claimed the Libyan was simply there to do a land deal, which was said to be worth $200 million. I detected the slippery hands of the intelligence office in masterminding the Libyan end of this murky plot, which could have jeopardised all the delicate negotiations that were going on around Lockerbie. Sometimes I felt like tearing my hair out, but this was just the way Libya operated, always looking for the short cut without thinking through the consequences.

Dealing with Libya in defiance of their country's ban also came back to haunt two of the lobbyists, Wade and Bodine. Both ended up with criminal records and Bodine, who was also part of the plot to smuggle Al-Bukhari into the US, was sentenced to twenty-one months in jail.

Not surprisingly the US media made much of the Crow-Gaddafi connection and Libya was accused of trying to buy favour in the US. To my knowledge the land deal was never done. The following month, George Bush lost the US presidential election to Bill Clinton, so Libyan attention turned to the Democrats.

There was one further postscript to these two very eventful trips to the US. I'm not usually one for collecting souvenirs, but I came home from Texas with a husband.

Chapter 10

A Wedding

I was the last to board and sensed the disapproving eyes of other passengers burning into my back.

In my haste to stow my cabin bag and settle in for the flight from London to Dallas, I barely noticed the only other Arab-looking person in the first-class section. Had I given him more scrutiny I might have made a mental note that he was tall, rather handsome and wearing smart, casual clothes.

In contrast I was dressed for comfort. I had a suit in my hand luggage, for changing into just before landing, but was wearing a baggy tracksuit which was less than flattering. My make-up and hair also needed some attention.

I was en route from my sister's wedding in Jordan to link up with the Libyan treasury minister for the second of our meetings with Trammel Crow. Tired from the celebrations I had overslept on the stop-over in London, ended up rushing madly, and barely got to the departure gate in time.

In those days the in-flight entertainment consisted of a library of video tapes, and soon after take-off I requested a movie from the flight attendant. I don't recall the title but she was very apologetic, informing me that another passenger had already chosen that one. It was Mr Handsome.

'If you'd like to watch it I don't mind,' he said, overhearing my conversation with the flight attendant.

'It's no problem,' I replied. 'I will sleep instead.'

Curling up in my seat I soon dozed off and did not wake until the announcement was made that we were shortly to arrive in Dallas. Then I dived into the aircraft rest room to freshen up and change into my suit, ready to meet the Libyan treasury minister at the airport as we had agreed. Mr Handsome clearly took note of the transformation in my appearance, giving me an admiring look but saying nothing. From my days in the bank I'd learned to deal with this type of male attention. It normally meant nothing but at the luggage carousel he approached me and began speaking in Arabic.

'How do you know I'm Arab?' I asked.

'Well, you don't look French and your necklace has an inscription in Arabic,' he laughed, and we made small talk until our bags arrived. I gave a few, vague details about the purpose of my visit and my Libyan connections. As we parted I handed him my business card, never one to miss making a potential new contact, then I was on my way. It was a diverting interlude but I didn't expect our paths to cross again, as he was heading to Austin while I was booked in at a Dallas hotel prior to the Trammell Crow camp-out.

So I was taken aback when the telephone in my room rang and it was my fellow passenger. I hadn't told him where I was staying, and demanded: 'How did you find me?'

He said: 'I know your name from your business card so I simply rang all the best hotels in Dallas until I was lucky. I need to talk to you urgently.'

He told me he would be at Love Field, an airport in the Dallas suburbs which handled a few internal scheduled passenger flights and private aircraft, at 9 p.m. that evening. My only thought was that he had information relating to the Libyans, or that the treasury minister was in some sort of danger.

I agreed to meet for an hour and, without giving a reason so as not to cause alarm, made my excuses to Al-Bukhari for missing dinner and commandeered his limousine for the 6-mile journey to Love Field. My main emotion was one of annoyance at going hungry and all the cloak and dagger behaviour. I had the feeling it was going to be a waste of my time.

Arriving just before 9 p.m., I watched the mystery man climb from the cockpit of a small private jet and jumped to the conclusion that he must be some sort of airline employee, or pilot. My tetchy mood didn't improve when he introduced himself and began giving me his life story. He was called Abdulhakim Al-Alawy and was a Saudi Arabian who lived in America. He had four children and was going through a divorce from his second wife. He was a businessman and it emerged during our brief encounter that the private jet, from which I'd seen him climb, was his own.

'Quickly,' I interrupted, still unimpressed. 'I don't have much time. Why are you telling me all this?'

He smiled and replied: 'Because I want to marry you.'

Perhaps I should have taken it seriously after my bizarre experience with Gaddafi's cousin. At least this man had set eyes on me before proposing, but I was convinced it was some sort of bad joke. My idea of a proposal of marriage did not include an airport coffee shop as the backdrop. I wasn't impressed and just wanted to escape back to my hotel.

'I will think about it,' I replied, simply to get rid of him and avoid an embarrassing public scene. I was preoccupied with the forthcoming meeting between the Republicans and the treasury minister, ensuring it went smoothly, so I pushed this apparently ridiculous proposal right out of my mind. It would be a nice line to say I fell in love at Love airport but, sadly, as far as I was concerned at that moment that was not going to be the case!

After finishing our business at the Crow ranch I did not return immediately to my flat in London because I had other matters to deal with in Switzerland and Spain, plus a prolonged trip to Libya. In fact it was many weeks before I set foot in England again.

To my surprise I arrived to find my flat bursting with fresh flowers. There were so many bouquets they were spilling into the corridor. The block had never smelled so good.

'They've been arriving every day for months,' said the bemused porter, who looked after the rented place while I was away and had been manfully dealing with all the wilted flowers as new bunches arrived daily. There were no cards attached and, even though I should have put two and two together, I was baffled.

All became clear a couple of days later when the door buzzer sounded. It was Abdulhakim Al-Alawy and it turned out he was deadly serious about marrying me. He invited me out for dinner at the restaurant of the Grosvenor House Hotel in Mayfair, where he was staying.

My sensible side was rather alarmed by a near-stranger tracking me down and turning up, uninvited, on my doorstep. My impetuous side was curious to know a little more about a man who proposed marriage, bombarded me with flowers and was willing to fly thousands of miles just to seek a date.

I was due to fly to Libya the following day but the sensible side lost the argument that was raging inside me. We had dinner after all.

Al-Alawy happened to be exactly my age, 31, at the time we met and the conversation flowed easily. He was well educated and seemed open-minded, agreeing with the idea of Arab women continuing to work after they were married. He'd studied in the United States and spoke very good English. I learned that he had been a fighter pilot in the Saudi air force before launching his own successful aerial photography company, which took him all over the world. A private jet was one of the perks.

I told myself that, although I liked him, it was nothing more than a harmless date. However, he had other ideas, persisting with the marriage proposal. He revealed he had fallen for me the moment I rushed on to the aeroplane for the flight to Dallas, unflattering tracksuit and all.

Stalling for time, I insisted I needed to speak to my father. As I've explained, in the Arab world the father's permission is paramount and my suitor asked for his details. Although I was drawn to this man I still fully expected it all to fizzle out but, yet again in matters of the heart, I was off the mark.

At the Al Mahary Hotel in Tripoli a few days later I received a phone call from Jordan. It was my father on the line, causing a stab of anxiety because he never bothered me in Libya unless there was some sort of family crisis or other emergency.

'Do you know a guy called Abdulhakim Al-Alawy,' he demanded to know. 'He's here in Jordan asking for your hand.'

I realised my feelings were changing. By approaching my father, according to Arab tradition, Al-Alawy demonstrated he was serious about me and I admired his very direct manner. I got the impression he was a man who was used to getting his way.

We didn't yet know each other well but many successful relationships start like this in the Middle East. When it comes to love and marriage you have to understand there are customs which may not make sense to people in the West. I know Arab marriages can appear a bit businesslike.

I realised I was warming to the Saudi Arabian, who seemed to share my outlook on life and have a modern approach to women's roles in society.

We were both Muslims, which ticked another box, because it would have been very difficult for me to marry outside my religion.

Besides, my biological clock was ticking and I had been thinking about having children. In the Arab world early thirties is very late in life for a woman to get married and start a family.

Mischievously I also realised that an added bonus would be to get my mother off my back, although I think she'd almost written me off as a lost cause by that stage. The recent marriage of my sister Reem, who was seven years my junior, appeared to underline that in her eyes I was destined for miserable spinsterhood.

I told my father: 'You still have a lot of connections in Saudi Arabia. Check him out and we will speak when I have finished in Libya.'

My father, who liked Al-Alawy, agreed and was already thinking ahead. He added: 'In any case, I've already explained to him that he must also have the approval of President Gaddafi, because he is like a godfather to you.'

Al-Alawy was now fully aware of my strong ties to Libya and Gaddafi. I relied on the Colonel's patronage for much of my income, through commission on oil deals. At that time I was making more than $1 million a year, and I also enjoyed my troubleshooting role for Libya. I'd just had successful trips to the US, where I'd made valuable contacts and got to meet the president. Yes I was attracted to Al-Alawy, but I wasn't willing to throw away my hard-fought financial independence. At the time it was rare for an Arab woman to be in this position. So I was not going to marry this man on a whim and end up getting fired by Gaddafi. I was pragmatic when considering marriage because I realised my entire future was in the Colonel's hands.

It was decided that Al-Alawy would accompany me on my next trip to Libya to meet the Colonel at his desert camp, near his home town of Sirte.

Again, I realise this approach must seem strange to Western eyes but by then Gaddafi was like a second father to me. Now, when we met he would ask: 'How is my daughter?'

I introduced Al-Alawy to Gaddafi, they shook hands, then sat down to talk. They spent about half an hour together in the Colonel's tent. As my future was being decided, I passed the time walking in the desert with my friend Naima. As we wandered in the baking sun in this tented village Gaddafi had created, we tried to predict the Colonel's reaction, but in reality neither of us had a clue.

That day I also saw another example of Gaddafi's eccentricity. He liked to portray himself as a Bedouin at heart, often dressing the part, and I don't doubt he was proud of his roots. But there among the tents was a small caravan, just like you see being towed behind cars in Britain. It was where Gaddafi liked to sleep, Naima told me, finding it more comfortable than being under canvas.

I discovered later that the leader interrogated Al-Alawy about his background, putting his mind at rest over potential security problems caused by me marrying a Saudi Arabian. Al-Alawy confided that his second marriage, to an American, had been a disaster and he now sought a suitable Arab bride. That must have delighted the Colonel and, finally, word came that Gaddafi approved of this man. When it was all over, the four of us sat in his tent, drinking coffee like old friends.

It was the third offer of marriage I'd received in my life, following the Palestinian engineer and Gaddafi's cousin, and this time I relented. The time was right for me to get married and I'd come to feel that the way we'd first met, on the flight to Dallas, was destiny.

I felt excited and I was thrilled to have Gaddafi's blessing, despite the poor relations between Libya and Saudi Arabia.

Would I have gone ahead with the wedding without it?

For me his approval was even more important than my father's, so the truth is no, I would not. At that stage of my life I still wasn't willing to sacrifice my career for any man. Thankfully, I did not have to make that choice as my future husband had assured Gaddafi during their meeting that I would continue to work.

Gaddafi is typically portrayed as a ruthless, insensitive brute, but this was a caring side that outsiders never saw. He could easily have blocked the marriage, keeping me to himself. I'd become an asset to the regime, but Gaddafi understood the importance of family, which is at the heart of Bedouin culture. It was yet another example of how he'd come to regard me as a surrogate daughter. I believe he genuinely wanted me to be happy and was genuinely pleased I appeared to have found a good man.

During the trip to Libya, I also broached the delicate subject of Sayed Gaddaf Al-Dam with my husband-to-be, because I did not want this earlier proposal to cast a shadow. I knew he was still on the scene in Libya and many people there still took his claim that we were married at face value. To my relief, Al-Alawy seemed to understand, and accept that I was blameless.

In January 1993 we threw a lavish engagement party. It's customary for this to happen six months before an Arab wedding and is a formal declaration of your relationship. All the marriage paperwork is signed and you are effectively man and wife. It's a sign that a woman is 'taken' and an important occasion for both families.

The bigger the engagement party the better and we really went to town at the five-star Le Meridien Hotel in Amman. Guests came from all over the world, including my old friend Adnan Khashoggi and Trammell Crow's daughter Lucy Billingsley.

Our wedding was also in Jordan, at the Intercontinental Amman Hotel, where the total bill came to $2 million. My wedding dress, with its long train and decorated with gold braid and pearls, had echoes of the gown worn by Lady Diana for her marriage to Prince Charles. It was designed by Tina Green, who had a boutique on Bond Street, in London, and cost $250,000. My gift from my husband, to wear on our wedding day, was a $700,000 diamond necklace set from the London jeweller David Morris, while my pearl tiara cost another $50,000. It was fun attending fittings with my mother, who flew over from Jordan.

Tablecloths were from Harrods and inscribed napkin rings, for guests to keep as a memento, were made from 24-carat gold. For the entertainment there was a star-studded line-up. My husband hired Hani Shaker and Amr Diab, who were among the most popular singers in Egypt, and the famous belly dancer Dina from the same country. Completing the list was Omar Abdullat, a renowned Jordanian singer. They all arrived on my husband's private jet.

It was extravagant but I intended our wedding to be a once-in-a-lifetime occasion. I felt I'd earned it and loved being the centre of attention.

This period was like a never-ending party as the engagement and wedding were followed by a three-month honeymoon, all arranged by my husband, to the US, Spain and Italy. In the gap between the engagement and the wedding we talked about our future plans. All my doubts were banished. I was in love.

We discussed setting up permanent home in London, where my business was based and my husband also had an office. I hoped for a little more time getting to know him before having a child together, but nature intervened.

When we returned from honeymoon I was pregnant and the dynamics in our relationship changed. Now I was carrying his child he began regarding me differently.

After a short time living in London he suddenly did a U-turn, insisting that we base ourselves in his homeland. Saudi Arabia was where he did most of his work and his family lived. I still had mixed feelings about the country, because of the oppressive atmosphere and the restrictions placed on women, but he persuaded me that we'd have a good life there.

So we rented a two-bedroom apartment in the diplomatic quarter of Riyadh, where he arranged for me to have an office so I could continue working during my pregnancy.

Despite the upheaval and my misgivings about Saudi Arabia, it was a happy time and we settled into married life. My husband was kind and attentive, although business often took him away.

In the compound where we lived I could walk outdoors without my face being covered but everywhere else it appeared to be just the same as when I was a child, with the Islamic religious police, who enforce morality, watching your every move. Worse, perhaps, because the capital was still less liberal than Jeddah where I'd grown up.

Occasionally I'd forget the rules and there would be the harsh shout: 'Cover your face, cover your face!' This would happen even when I was sitting next to my husband in the car. I respected the rules but I've made plain my views on this stripping away of identity.

Fortunately I had work to keep me occupied, but I longed for the freedom of London. When my husband was home everything was fine but Riyadh was a lonely place for a foreign woman. Salvation came from an unexpected source – the Saudi royal family. At a social gathering I met Princess Hessa, the Jordanian wife of Crown Prince Abdullah who was to ascend the throne in 2005. There was an instant spark between us and in next to no time we became firm friends. She introduced me to her six daughters and we would meet at the royal palace to chat, go shopping and drink coffee. One of the princesses especially, Abeer, still has a place in my heart. She was much younger than me but already had two children. Abeer's mother was Jordanian, which provided another connection.

Without the princesses, life in Saudi Arabia would have been insufferable but they too had to keep their faces covered in public and, like all women, were not allowed to drive. If we all went out to eat at a restaurant we'd always be ushered to a back room, which made the order in Saudi Arabia clear. Women second, always. Even shopping was a chore, because all the cloth covering your face made it impossible to see properly.

Nothing had changed since my childhood and if I wanted to travel abroad I needed my husband's written permission. Much as I enjoyed the princesses' company, and I owe them a huge debt for their kindness, I missed being able to socialise with male friends.

Fortunately, I also had the impending birth of my child to look forward to. For the delivery, my husband and I had agreed on a private clinic in London, where we spent the later stages of my pregnancy. I shopped for baby clothes, knowing we were having a girl.

However, at the last moment I panicked after being told she was not feeding properly in the womb through the umbilical cord and I would require a caesarean. All I could think of was having my family around me so, with my husband in tow, I jumped on a plane from London to Amman. Taking a flight when you are nine months pregnant is definitely not recommended but my head was spinning and I was scared. I was lucky that my baby bump wasn't too big, so no one at the airline stopped me flying. My husband wasn't keen on this course of action but I wasn't going to take no for an answer. It did cross my mind that my first child could be born in an aeroplane, but fortunately the five-hour journey passed without alarm.

We dropped off our luggage at my parents' home and went straight to hospital, giving my doctor a jolt.

'What are you doing here? You are booked in for a caesarean in London on Monday.'

My mother had assured me that the first baby always arrives late, but this one didn't get the message. The day after I arrived in Jordan our daughter Noor was born naturally, at five o'clock in the morning on 25 May 1994. I was in labour for eight hours at the Farah hospital, where she was safely delivered by Zaid Al Keelani, the country's most famous doctor.

Noor had a touch of jaundice but was otherwise healthy and beautiful. Her father witnessed her birth, insisting on cutting the umbilical cord because he'd been told it increased attachment between parent and child.

Noor was in an incubator for twenty-one days, when I didn't leave her side. For my husband it was a third daughter and he fussed around, putting flowers in the room and giving gifts of cash to the nurses to show his appreciation for their care.

When Noor was strong enough we moved in temporarily with my parents. It was wonderful to have my mother and sisters there, as I had no idea about how to be a mother. For that reason, when I first cradled Noor in my arms I felt a mix of joy and terror. At first my mother used to bathe her, because I was frightened I would drop her.

In the Arab world, I was old to be embarking on motherhood at the ripe age of 33 and I was fully aware that my priorities in life would have to alter.

When Noor was 2 months old, and strong enough to fly without any risk, we flew to London. I had a private nurse and my mother called every day.

Our stay there was brief, as Abdulhakim was intent on living in Saudi Arabia. I hoped the arrival of our daughter would be the seal on our happiness, now we were a little family, but there were storm clouds looming on the horizon.

Chapter 11

Divorce

They say you should never mix business with your personal life and I should have paid heed to those words of wisdom. My new husband accompanied me on my next trip to Libya and the whole expedition was a disaster from start to finish.

What with marriage, pregnancy and spending precious time with Noor at our home in the compound in Riyadh, eighteen months had flown by since I'd last visited Libya.

I tried to keep in touch with my friends and business contacts there but was conscious that I needed to show my face. I'd not seen or spoken to the Colonel and I feared that as more time passed I would be out of sight, out of mind.

I was enjoying motherhood but eventually the time came when I felt able to leave Noor with my mother in Jordan and return to Libya for a short trip.

My husband was wealthy, but I wanted to work like the career mothers I had so admired when I first went to Britain in the 1980s. They'd shown me that it was possible to enjoy the best of both worlds and I missed the wheeler-dealing of the business world and the unpredictable excitement of Gaddafi's missions. I also missed Libya, where I had so much more freedom than in Riyadh, and the friends I'd made there.

With hindsight I should have travelled to Tripoli alone, as usual, but my husband was keen to tag along and I thought: 'Why not?'

He seemed to have made a good first impression on the Colonel. It would also be an opportunity to show him more of the country I'd come to love and spend some quality time together, although Libya was going through a tough time.

The regime was still obsessed with the lifting of sanctions, but negotiations to hand over the two Lockerbie suspects Abdelbaset Al-Megrahi and Al-Amin Khalifa Fhimah were deadlocked. Gaddafi was offering to hand them over for trial in an international court, but the US and British governments of Bill Clinton and John Major had rejected the proposal. There was a feeling of mutual suspicion between Libya and the West. It was a vicious circle, as neither side was willing to budge an inch, and every few months sanctions were renewed. I could almost hear Gaddafi raging at the unfortunates who were tasked with engineering a breakthrough.

Before our marriage my husband had seemed enthusiastic about me continuing to work for the regime but, looking back, I think he quickly became jealous of my position there. His motive for accompanying me to Libya was not sightseeing, and he had no business interests there. He just wanted to keep an eye on me, which caused all sorts of problems in Libya because he insisted on sitting in on all my meetings. Tripoli regarded Saudi Arabia, which it considered to be hand in glove with the US, as an enemy – so you can imagine how my Saudi husband's presence at these sensitive meetings would have gone down. Quite correctly the Libyans didn't trust him with their state secrets and he didn't seem to understand that it had taken me, also an outsider, years to build up the trust I enjoyed. In the five days we were there it was just one problem after another and only added to the tensions between us.

Before our wedding my husband had portrayed himself as a modern, forward-thinking Arab man. But, first with his insistence that we live in Riyadh and now his controlling behaviour over my career and Libya, I saw a different side emerging. I didn't like it and I was increasingly worried that this was the real Abdulhakim, not the man who'd wooed me with flowers and assurances that we could be equals. It's the same the world over: men promise you the world before you are married.

It was odd because he was successful in his own right, and much richer than me. He struggled not with the money I earned but the reputation I'd built in Libya, other parts of the Middle East and London. He hated it when we went to a restaurant and people recognised me. Sometimes two or three other diners would shake my hand before we'd even sat down to eat, and he resented that. It was all about the balance of power in our relationship. He felt belittled, although to me it was no big deal. It is ingrained in the Arab culture for the man to be more important than the woman and my husband could not cope with the thought of a reversal of the traditional roles.

It was like being married to two different men. Sometimes there was the cultured, civilised, well-rounded businessman that I first met; at other times he behaved like a Bedouin who'd never left Saudi Arabia. He was at his worst in public and in front of his family in Saudi Arabia, where he no doubt felt peer pressure to have a dutiful Arab wife at his side. He also used Gaddafi as a stick with which to metaphorically beat me, always bringing up his name when we argued.

'Don't think that just because you know the big leader you can do what you want,' he'd sneer. I believe my husband was also a little afraid of the Colonel, because one day he revealed a snippet from the meeting with him in the tent in Sirte before our marriage.

Abdulhakim said: 'Gaddafi told me "You are marrying my daughter and if one day she comes to me with one tear in her eye because of you then I will bring you to Libya in boxes."'

I don't for one minute believe Gaddafi was being serious but it made me think of the famous interview Princess Diana gave to the BBC in 1995, about the same time as my marriage was unravelling.

'Well, there were three of us in this marriage so it was a bit crowded,' she said, referring to Camilla Parker Bowles who was then the mistress of Prince Charles.

My husband never accused me of being Gaddafi's mistress, but the Colonel's big personality still intruded on our marriage and Abdulhakim simply could not handle that. It was not sexual jealousy but envy of my connections and power that ate away at him.

There was a dramatic shift in his attitude after we were married yet I don't want to give the impression that he was ever abusive or cruel. In our home he was still the same, kind man I'd fallen in love with and he was a doting father to Noor, bathing her every night. If she ever woke in the night crying, he would rush to comfort her. We still planned for the future, including moving to a larger house. He spoke of his desire to have more children.

But rather than supporting me, it seemed like he always wanted me to fail. If I said 'right', he said 'left' without even realising what he was doing. If the phone rang he wanted to know who it was and if he called home and it happened to be engaged my husband would go crazy.

To make matters worse, Abdulhakim was having problems with his American ex-wife, who'd frozen his assets in the States and was denying him access to his other children.

In the first year of our marriage it began to dawn on me that I'd made an awful mistake, but what was I to do? There was our daughter to consider and it was not in my character to walk away, admitting failure, without a fight.

So I made a momentous decision, which flew in the face of everything I stood for and felt like a betrayal of my sex. For the sake of my child and my marriage I would take a step back from Libya and Gaddafi, for as long as it took. In years to come I didn't want to reflect on my life and conclude that I'd taken the easy option.

I tried to be more like his ideal wife by cooking his meals, looking after our child and the house. It was an unaccustomed role but I was so desperate to please that I even asked my mother to give me cooking lessons over the telephone and share traditional Arab recipes. I could see the funny side, because I was finally trying to become the daughter she always wanted. It was not what I'd hoped for but for three years I tried, really tried, hoping his mentality would change. I was determined to give our failing marriage every chance.

One further measure was to close my foreign exchange and oil companies in London, to give my husband and 2-year-old daughter my full attention. I didn't speak to Gaddafi during this difficult period, but his bodyguard, my friend Naima, kept him in the loop. The message came back that he understood and I must do whatever I felt was necessary.

Now I was the stereotypical Arab housewife doing nothing, just sitting there idly waiting for her husband to come home. If I wanted to buy anything it went on his credit card, so he even had control over my spending. It was just another erosion of my independence and it pains me that this is still often the norm in Arab countries. I felt a sort of emptiness inside.

I'd become a virtual prisoner and I used to go jogging in the compound at night, where at least I could run with my face uncovered, just to escape the drudgery. My husband's family was kind to me, particularly his mother, but there was a clash with one of his brothers, Ibrahim, who refused to bring his wife to their parents' home. He did not want my husband, his own brother, to see her face uncovered. Yet Ibrahim was happy to see my bare face. One day I lost my temper. 'You are a hypocrite,' I screamed at the brother.

It was a real kick in the teeth when I also discovered that Abdulhakim had tried to initiate an affair with his secretary. He just shrugged it off, as if it was all my fault for not being the perfect wife.

I couldn't go on living like this and felt like I was going to explode. If it had just been the oppressive laws in Saudi Arabia with a good marriage to compensate I could have coped, but there was nothing. It got to the stage when I kept telling myself: 'Give it one more month Daad, one more month.'

During this period there was one diversion from my marital troubles, when I was forced to go to court to sue a former business associate. Usama Salfiti was a well-known figure in the Arab business world who ran foreign exchange companies in Jordan and London. Hearing of my good connections with Libya, he contacted me in the late 1980s soon after I first began working with LAFICO. I introduced him to many of my clients, also helping him get a foothold in Libya where he met my contacts at LAFICO. We shared an office block in London and, through me, he made a fortune.

Salfiti owed me $2 million commission, but got into trouble playing the stock markets and never paid up. At one stage I was going to become his business partner but we ended up fighting one another at the High Court, in London. I won the case, and an appeal in 1996, but he sold all his UK assets and spirited the money away to Jordan where I also went to court successfully.

Salfiti is now dead, and his assets frozen, but I'm still pursuing his estate for my entitlement. Can you believe that it has now taken more than twenty years, I've won at every step, but haven't received a cent? At least the case taught me a lesson about the Jordanian civil courts which, one day, would prove very valuable. It pains me to admit this, but there is no fairness in my homeland.

While this was happening I was still fighting a more important battle: to save my marriage.

We talked and talked but nothing changed, then Libya got in the way again. My husband was unexpectedly invited to Sirte by Gaddafi, to help intervene in some fairly trivial dispute with the Central African Republic. The Colonel had got wind of Abdulhakim's friendship with the country's president Ange-Felix Patassé and wanted him to act as an intermediary. I hoped this trip might prove beneficial for everyone but it proved to be another nail in the coffin of our relationship. Sitting at home in Riyadh, I picked up the phone to hear my furious husband explain that he'd been received at the airport by none other than Sayed Gaddaf Al-Dam. By that stage my former suitor had a new role, trying to bring all the Libyan tribes together and keep them loyal to Gaddafi. The Colonel could have sent any other official but it was his idea of a joke to send his cousin, the man who'd wanted to marry me, to greet my current husband. Poor Abdulhakim was livid, interpreting this as a deliberate attempt by the Colonel to humiliate him.

It wasn't a nice touch by Gaddafi, and I can only think that he was trying to show my husband that if he let me down there was still a Libyan alternative waiting in the wings. Looking back, I realise he knew more about the state of my marriage than I imagined.

I couldn't help feeling sorry for my husband and the incident did nothing to improve the rocky state of our relationship, which was about to reach breaking point.

It all started with a devastating phone call from Jordan, in the middle of 1996. My mother, who was only 53, had suffered a cardiac arrest and was in a coma.

'Come quickly Daad, she could die at any time,' pleaded my father, throwing me into a frenzy as I tried to arrange a flight from Riyadh to Amman, 900 miles away.

Once again my dear friend Princess Abeer came to my rescue, not only volunteering to look after Noor but offering the use of a Saudi royal family private jet.

As I'd been led to believe, my mother was in a bad way. I could hardly believe it because she'd been in such robust health and seemed to have many more good years ahead. I sobbed uncontrollably the first time I saw my mother in her hospital bed looking so small, pale and lifeless. The doctors could give no reassurances and I was distraught as I contemplated the prospect of my daughter growing up without her grandmother.

My husband and Noor flew in a few days later and when he went home after two weeks our daughter remained with me. Little did I know then that I'd be at my sick mother's bedside for six months. I dared not leave Jordan, convinced that the moment I did she would pass away. A routine was established so that my husband would visit twice a month, but he had his business to attend to so he understandably couldn't stay permanently in Jordan.

Naively, I hoped the breathing space might actually improve matters between us, but then one day Abdulhakim called to say: 'You've been there long enough. If you don't come home we will be divorced.'

I was almost speechless at this ultimatum but managed to reply: 'What happens if I come home just for the weekend and my mother dies? I could never forgive you.'

He said, coldly: 'That is not my business, you've been away for six months now.'

Barely able to contain my anger I retorted: 'I don't care if it takes six years, I'm not leaving my mother. Divorce me if you wish, it's what I want anyway.'

In the heat of the moment, when everyone is under pressure, these arguments happen and can be forgiven after an apology. However, the next morning the fax machine at my father's office spluttered into life and began spewing out divorce papers. When I needed him to stand next to me, when my mother was on the brink of death, my husband let me down in the worst possible way.

I felt a mixture of dismay and relief but I didn't really want to expend any time on being angry with him, preferring to devote all my energy to my mother.

There was to be no going back, so I began court proceedings in Jordan to formalise the end of my marriage. I emerged from the wreckage with the greatest gift of my life, our only child Noor. For twelve years after our divorce my now ex-husband had no contact with her and provided no financial support. I paid for her private British school and dealt with her tears when her father was absent at parents' days.

He came back into her life when she was 14 years old, but there is still an awkwardness between them and Noor is hurt by the long gaps between his phone calls.

Over time I found a way to mend fences with my ex-husband Abdulhakim Al Bader Altamimi, who was president of the General Authority of Civil Aviation with a rank of Minister in Saudi Arabia from 2017–2019 in accordance with Saudi Law.

When he comes to visit our daughter now we all have dinner together and the atmosphere is friendly. He has told me many times that he deeply regrets his behaviour when we were married. He was, and still is, a good person but his all-consuming jealousy of my achievements dragged us down. He became obsessed with owning me and, although he remains the only man I have ever truly loved, that was never going to happen.

At least Gaddafi's threat to bring my husband back to Libya in pieces if he ever upset me did turn out to be a joke.

By early 1997, when the divorce came through, I was a single woman and free to run my own life. Although I don't rule out the possibility, I've never married again. If it ever happens it will not be to a Saudi Arabian!

My first task was to arrange for my mother, who was mercifully out of the coma but still far from recovered, to receive private specialist treatment in London. She'd undergone heart surgery in Jordan, which had saved her life, but had been left brain damaged. She required more neurological treatment, along with painstaking physiotherapy and speech therapy. I spent three months there, settling her in, before one of my sisters took over.

Then my attention turned to the one place on the planet where I was certain I could rid my mind of the jealous husband, all the rows, and the messy divorce. I confess I was also ready to flee the well-meaning but smothering attentions of my siblings, who all had their opinions on what should happen next. My mind was already decided. After three years away I was heading back to Libya, like the prodigal daughter.

I'd stayed in touch with my friend Naima as my marriage collapsed and she'd been to visit me and the baby in Jordan and London, so I still had social ties. But all my business links with Libya were severed and I was aware that in such a volatile country three years was a long time to have been away. I was apprehensive, and unsure about the state of the country.

There were reports of poverty, as sanctions took a grip, and inflation was running at over 30 per cent. Libyan hospitals were said to be short of supplies and schools and universities were reported to be without text books.

Above all I had no idea of whether I would be welcomed back into the fold, after such a long gap, by the Colonel. Everyone likes to think they are irreplaceable in their place of work, but it's rarely the case. Had I burned my bridges?

Chapter 12

Whispers

As the limousine wound its way through Tripoli to the Colonel's compound I gazed out of the window at the familiar sights and everyday street scenes. I immediately felt entirely at home in Libya and, superficially, not much had altered. In a vibrant, modern city you'd expect to see smart new office blocks and hotels spring up over three years, but the skyline was unchanged. I couldn't see any evidence of construction work and taking a closer look there was a run-down feel about the city, with men hanging idly round on corners. As I peered into the city's once bustling shops, all I glimpsed was row upon row of empty shelves. Libya wasn't exactly starving but it was obvious, even from this snapshot, that sanctions were biting hard. I worried about how that would affect Gaddafi's mood.

He'd made all the right noises about my doomed efforts to save my marriage and returning to work one day. Yet I feared he would consider me a deserter, and one more person to add to the long list of those who could not be trusted.

After my marathon two-day journey to reach Libya, via Tunisia because of embargoes on international passenger flights, I was expecting the cold shoulder, or a dressing down. Perhaps, to teach me a lesson, he wouldn't see me at all?

I needn't have fretted. Gaddafi greeted me with a warm handshake and offered me a coffee.

'Daad, how are you?' he enquired, as if I had only been away for a matter of weeks and making it clear from the outset that he did not consider our relationship damaged. Not sure whether to raise the subject of my divorce, I made small talk but I should have given him more credit.

'What's wrong, you seem upset,' he asked, and the whole sorry story of the end of my marriage came tumbling out.

Gaddafi waited until I had finished speaking, clapped his hands together and said: 'This is the best decision you've ever made. This man is not the one for you.'

And that was that. My husband's name was never mentioned again and as far as the Colonel was concerned it was business as usual.

'Go to LAFICO, sign a new contract and carry on as if nothing has happened,' Gaddafi instructed.

I offered up a silent prayer of thanks but I think the Colonel was just as pleased to have me back on board as I was to be received so enthusiastically. I represented stability and a calm approach, when so much around him was in a state of constant flux.

As if to demonstrate this he solved another problem that had been causing me sleepless nights. During my marriage I'd become financially reliant on my husband and, to put it bluntly, he'd left me a single parent and almost broke. There was the mortgage to pay on my flat in London, which my ex-husband was refusing to meet as some sort of pathetic display that he was still in control of my life. He was determined to leave me penniless and at the time I didn't have the stomach to go to court for maintenance or child support for our daughter. I just wanted Abdulhakim out of our lives.

Relief that I was back in business in Libya was tinged with concern that it would be a while before any cash, earned through commission on deals I arranged, landed in my bank account. I was still owed $3 million by the Libyan government for all the oil deals, but I knew it could be months, if not years, before the bill was settled and there would invariably be wrangles over the precise sum due. That was just par for the course in Libya.

I mentioned this to Gaddafi, who said: 'Don't worry, we will sort it out.' A few signatures later and the necessary legal paperwork was drawn up to expedite payment.

I began to express my gratitude but Gaddafi waved away my thanks, adding: 'This is your money, not a gift. All I've done is speed up the process.'

It was also a recognition that I never charged Libya for any of the special missions, including visiting the prisoners in Britain and opening the channels with the Bush administration. All this I did unpaid, just to maintain my unique relationship with the Colonel and show my commitment to Libya. I made good money in Libya on my other deals, so there was no need to be greedy. With his intervention $3 million was soon heading my way from the Central Bank of Libya, fixing all my financial problems instantly.

So far, so good, but some things never change. I was barely out of Gaddafi's office before the whispering campaign against me started again. It was orchestrated, of course, by my enemies in the intelligence office who were still circling Gaddafi.

I've referred many times to the special relationship I had with the Colonel and I knew that some people were convinced it went all the way to the bedroom. It was rarely said to my face, but I heard through Naima that some people simply assumed that I must be one of Gaddafi's mistresses. There was gossip everywhere I went.

'What do you do to keep the president so interested in you?' I would be asked, with a wink. 'What is the secret of keeping him so happy?'

I can fully understand why there were so many rumours because he protected me from the intelligence office, gave me a nice hotel suite every time I visited Libya and always put two official cars at my disposal. It must have seemed like I was treated like royalty, so no wonder conclusions were drawn.

I told everyone who cared to listen: 'Gaddafi can have any beautiful woman he wants. Our relationship is not like that. If it was just an affair it would be over within a year or two and I'd be finished, even if I am Brooke Shields.'

Even now, I know there will be those who read between the lines of my story and conclude that it was a sexual relationship. All I can say is that if I really was Gaddafi's mistress I would not have lasted in Libya for twenty-two years. No, he was looking for something else from me that the Libyans around him could not deliver. In me, I think he saw a woman who would take on any challenge and deliver what she promised. Unlike so many people in his circle, I never lied to him, or embezzled money from the state. Also, as I've pointed out, my Jordanian passport was a big asset when Libya was a pariah state.

In the end I got tired of denying all the rumours about an affair and tried to turn it into a joke. I couldn't really win, but if someone made a remark I'd say: 'I hope it's true.'

The visit to Libya following my divorce was my longest to date, lasting six months while I re-established my contacts and rebuilt my business. Fortunately, in addition to Naima I still had a good circle of friends and the arrival of satellite television meant I was not restricted to Libyan channels in my hotel room.

There was a personal cost, as I'd decided it would be for the best if I left two-and-a-half year-old Noor with my sister Linda in Jordan. There was the arduous travel to Libya to consider and I feared that if my daughter fell sick the medicines she needed might not be available because of sanctions. They grow up so quickly at that age and although I was able to speak to her every day on the phone I felt guilty about missing landmarks in her life. I made it a rule to make sure we were never apart for her birthdays. It was a near-impossible balancing act, as I was also determined to regain the independence I'd sacrificed during my marriage. There's no way to sugar coat it, I had bills to pay. Libya represented my best hope of getting back on track.

During that visit I was also reunited with Gaddafi's cousin Sayed Gaddaf Al-Dam. I knew it was only a matter of time before our paths crossed and I'd been dreading some sort of scene. Five years had elapsed since he'd proposed to me and I had accompanied him to the rehab clinic in Geneva. I had no idea whether he'd moved on, or still had the same feelings.

On that trip after my divorce, word reached me towards the end of my stay in Libya that Gaddaf Al-Dam was sick in hospital. He'd relapsed, so I agreed to visit him. Pushing open the door gingerly, I could see him lying on the bed. He looked terrible and it seemed to be a tremendous effort even to open his eyes. A smile passed his lips and he said: 'It cannot be true. Is this really Daad? Punch me to make sure I am awake and not dreaming.'

He was delighted to see me and we spoke about what had happened in Switzerland when I'd fled, leaving him at the clinic, when he still hoped to marry me.

'I hope you read my letter and understand?' I said, referring to the note I'd scribbled and dropped off on my way to the airport.

'I know everything and I appreciate all you did for me,' Gaddaf Al-Dam replied. I felt a huge weight lift from my shoulders, because I'd been carrying guilt about my behaviour for five years. I was pleased that we were able to draw a line under the whole episode and he bore me no ill will. We parted warmly, but Gaddaf Al-Dam had one more surprise.

He told me solemnly: 'I want you to know that whenever you visit Libya I always arrange for men from my military base to stay on your level of the hotel to protect you.' That cleared up another mystery – I had been puzzled by the fact that I always seemed to be the only foreigner. Now I knew I had my very own guardian angel and felt touched by his kindness.

During that six-month period in Libya, I paid off the arrears on the mortgage on my flat in London. I also bought a house in a residential area of Amman and after leaving Libya began dividing my time between Jordan and London.

My company, Prime Oil, was one of the casualties of my disastrous marriage as I'd elected to close it down. So now all my business was initially done under the umbrella of LAFICO, the state-owned company which handled all Libya's foreign investments. It felt good to be back in the thick of it, acting as a middle woman in multi-million dollar deals. I clinched agreements for Libya to invest in hotel chains in Jordan, taking 15 per cent control. Through me, Libya also bought stakes in several Jordanian banks. In all, after returning to Libya in 1997 following the break-up of my marriage, I estimate that I had a hand in deals totalling more than $1 billion. I also opened a new consultancy firm of my own called Trans Arab World for Commercial Mediation, or TAWCO for short. It was an extension of my work for Libya, using my contacts and knowledge of how business works in the Middle East and the West to broker deals. It meant I wasn't entirely reliant on Libya for my income, and Gaddafi was happy for me to retain a degree of independence.

The deals between Libya and other Arab countries had a much wider significance. Gaddafi was still intent on overcoming the impasse over Lockerbie and, against the odds, was making progress. Despite the stubbornness of the US and Britain there was growing sympathy for Libya in other parts of the world, and he was winning the propaganda battle in the Middle East. Images of hospitals running out of supplies always make an impact and the feeling in the Arab world was that Gaddafi was bending over backwards to find a workable solution.

The willingness of Arab countries to deal with Libya, flying in the face of sanctions, suggested the blockade against Libya was beginning to crumble.

Russia and China were also supporting an end to Libya's isolation, which could not come soon enough for the Colonel. Historically, Libya had good relations with the Soviet Union in the 1970s and 1980s. This continued with Russia, which obviously did not play well with either

Britain or the US. It was one of the reasons why Gaddafi was never really trusted by the West, even when he later claimed to be set upon rapprochement.

There were lots of small steps towards the end of sanctions and one contribution I made was to smooth the path for America's prestigious *National Geographic* magazine to send a writer to Libya, to report on the state of the country and how ordinary people were suffering. That sort of coverage, changing opinions in the US, was priceless for Gaddafi and I persuaded him that it was a good move to meet the writer. He liked the resulting piece, which was broadly sympathetic.

When Nelson Mandela threw his hat into the ring, negotiating on behalf of the Colonel, the writing was on the wall and it became a matter of when, not if, sanctions were lifted. Mandela was revered almost everywhere in the world and his friendship with Libya, against the wishes of the US, delighted the Colonel.

'How can America have the arrogance to dictate to us who our friends should be?' said Mandela about his controversial state visit to Libya in 1997. He rubbed the Americans' noses in it by awarding Gaddafi a medal.

It's a big regret that I didn't get to meet the charismatic South African, who became a close friend of Gaddafi and never forgot Libya's assistance in the early days of his fight against apartheid. The closest I got was a brief glimpse of him leaving the Al Mahary Hotel, in Tripoli, which was my base. He was engulfed by cheering Libyans.

All that remained was thrashing out the details of where the two Lockerbie suspects Al-Megrahi and Fhimah would be tried. The breakthrough came in 1998 when the Americans and British came up with a plan to try the pair in a special court in The Hague, in the Netherlands, in front of three Scottish judges. By that time Britain had a new prime minister, Tony Blair, who was much more willing to compromise on the thorny Lockerbie issue than his predecessor John Major.

Six years earlier, Gaddafi had offered to hand the suspects over to the Arab League for trial so he could claim, with some justification, that the deal now on the table was very similar. He could deliver the two Libyans without looking weak, or losing face.

He was willing to sacrifice the pair, but exploited the situation until the last minute. 'I am not sure America and Britain have the good intention to solve this problem,' said Gaddafi. 'I am not assured they are serious.

'More details have to be clear. You cannot say give us these two people quickly; they are not tins of fruit. They are human beings. Their destiny must be assured. What is the destiny of the suspects if they are convicted or acquitted?'

It was all posturing and I already knew it was a done deal. In early April 1999, Al-Megrahi and Fhimah boarded a chartered United Nations plane to Europe. As agreed, sanctions were suspended.

The key men in the regime who helped get the Lockerbie deal over the line were Moussa Koussa, from the intelligence office, Mohamed Al-Zwae the Interior Minister and future ambassador in London and Abdul Ati Al-Obeidi, a former prime minister and ambassador in Rome. In contrast to the untrustworthy Koussa, both Al-Zwae and Al-Obeidi were good men who worked selflessly for Libya and weren't interested in lining their own pockets like so many around them.

After every meeting in London they were under instructions to brief me on progress, so I'd been beavering away in the background for months in anticipation of this historic day for Libya, which I knew was near.

As you can imagine, when Libya finally came in from the cold there was a bun fight among companies in foreign countries who wanted to trade. One day no one would touch Libya with a bargepole, the next, everyone was scrambling for Libyan cash. Defence and communications companies, especially, were falling over themselves to get a foot in the door because Libya's infrastructure was badly out of date after seven years of isolation.

My telephone was red hot, and even before sanctions were suspended I was poised to draw up contracts with multinationals such as VT Group, specialising in defence, and Racal, the telecoms and electronics provider. Rather than spread myself too thinly, my policy was to take on a few good companies and work hard for them, as their agent in Libya.

In my opinion, the deal that was done between the US, Britain and Libya over Lockerbie was all about money, not justice. In the end, money made Lockerbie go away. Gaddafi went along with the charade because he was worn out and the sanctions were crippling his country.

I don't think Tony Blair was really interested in justice. He wanted his place in history as the man who solved the Lockerbie problem. He also wanted to take credit for opening the door to Libya for British companies.

They made billions of pounds after sanctions were at first suspended then later lifted entirely. Blair was like a vulture hovering over Libya.

For some of the families of the victims I also believe, sadly, that it was all about getting as much compensation as possible. Others just wanted revenge and someone to blame, which I completely understand. They swallowed whatever version was put in front of them by their government. I met Jim Swire, the British doctor whose daughter Flora died on the Pan Am flight, and I had more respect for him because he wanted to know the truth, however long it took to uncover.

Four years later, in 2003, Libya paid $10 million to the family of each of the 270 poor souls who perished. The compensation was a drop in the ocean when compared to the money Libya was able to recoup through international deals. The Libyan government didn't even foot the bill, which I know was paid by businesses in Libya who were in line to benefit when sanctions were lifted.

Although I am still cynical about the motives, I won't pretend that I wasn't grateful that the embargoes were gone. Now I was free to broker the deals that were my speciality.

The day after sanctions were suspended I was part of the official delegation on the first passenger flight from Amman to Tripoli, which was greeted with great fanfare at Tripoli airport. It was a relief to be able to hop on a plane again rather than endure a tortuous drive through the desert from Tunisia every time I visited.

Chapter 13

On the Road

When Libya came in from the wilderness following the suspension of sanctions, Gaddafi was determined to change his country's image. No longer would he tread an isolationist path – but instead reach out to the rest of the world. He'd sacrificed the two Lockerbie suspects to appease the West and now dreamed of becoming a sort of elder statesman in Africa, like his great friend Mandela. The Colonel wanted to expand his horizons, encourage other nations to invest in Libya and show that he had changed his ways.

A top priority was to improve relations with his neighbours, which had been volatile to say the least. It was decided to organise a series of state visits and there was no shortage of nations wanting to hold out the olive branch. Say what you like about Gaddafi, he was a charismatic figure and always aroused a good deal of curiosity and attention. After being shunned for years he was in demand like the latest pop star, and it was a question of drawing up an itinerary which pleased him. As this was under discussion, I received a call from my homeland.

'We would like to invite President Gaddafi to Jordan,' said my contact in the office of the government, who was aware of my strong relationship with the Colonel. 'He has not been here for twenty years and it would be a good opportunity to sign some trade agreements. Can you convince him to come?'

I considered it to be an excellent suggestion, but persuading Gaddafi might not be easy because Jordan was West-leaning and this was a constant source of irritation to him. Gaddafi had a long memory and I worried that he might try to use his new-found popularity to settle a few old scores.

I know the exact nature of my role has been questioned, so I would like to elaborate. To put it simply, Gaddafi was a proud Bedouin who didn't like being told what to do and I believe this was at the root of many of his problems with the US and Britain. Dignity was a word that often cropped up during our conversations. Treat him with dignity, show him the respect he thought was due to a leader, and you had an excellent chance of making progress. The Lockerbie problem got solved when the Americans and the British stopped barking orders and took a softer negotiating stance. Initially, they made a strategic mistake by being confrontational and the breakthrough only came when they negotiated on equal terms. America, especially, is still very arrogant when it comes to foreign policy and dictating how other countries are run. There appears to me to be ignorance of cultural difference.

I like to think I came to understand what made Gaddafi tick and quickly realised that if you wanted him to do something it was all about the approach. I don't claim I wrapped him round my little finger, but he said yes more often than no! In fact, I came to realise that if he meant no, he would tell me: 'I need time to think about that.'

Regarding the Jordan trip, I could easily have barged into his office and told him: 'You must go to Amman, it will be good for the economy.'

But I'd learned to take a more indirect route, so I began: 'You know, on the wall of my office in Jordan I have a portrait of you. My brother was there the other day and asked 'who's that?' Can you believe that he doesn't recognise you? It would be nice for the new generation in Jordan to get to know you. Maybe you should arrange a visit, because there are also lots of Palestinians living there who will be overjoyed to see you.'

It was as if a bell sounded in Gaddafi's head. 'Yes, I will go,' he replied. 'Tell your king.'

I have shared this exchange to try to show the doubters that my so-called special power over Gaddafi was not sexual but, along with the trust I built, an ability to get inside his head.

So, in October 2000, Jordan became part of his mini-tour, also encompassing two other countries with which he'd had many disagreements: Saudi Arabia and Syria.

It fell to me to help organise the Jordan leg and I was inundated with questions from the protocol office about his likes, dislikes and what sort of programme should be arranged. I knew Gaddafi was interested in women's rights, so I suggested some sort of meeting with the Jordanian Women's Union as well as the usual trade talks.

I was also asked about his dietary requirements, which were quite simple. He was a light eater, who liked to start the day by drinking camel's milk and eating dates, then enjoyed vegetarian food for lunch. He also had a taste for Libyan-style pasta, a throwback to the days of Italian occupation. In the early evening he would perhaps eat grilled meat. Twice a week, on Mondays and Thursdays, he fasted for religious reasons and he prayed five times a day. I never saw alcohol, which he banned soon after he came to power in 1969, pass his lips. After his death, all sorts of claims were made about Gaddafi being a cocaine addict. I never saw any evidence of drug taking – on the contrary he was very health conscious and had a treadmill in his compound. Another of his ways of keeping fit was hunting rabbits and deer, on foot, in the desert near his camp in Sirte. When the pressure got too much Gaddafi would always seek sanctuary there.

All these insights into Gaddafi's lifestyle and habits I provided to the Jordanians, in advance of his first official tour after the suspension of sanctions.

The Colonel decided to do it in his own inimitable way, travelling by land rather than air. It was agreed that he would enter Jordan from Egypt, to meet King Abdullah and the prime minister, Ali Abu Al-Ragheb, at Aqaba, on the Red Sea. From there he would travel by car to the capital Amman.

When the time came, I received a phone call from the Jordanian chief of protocol who sounded panic-stricken.

'I have counted them, and President Gaddafi has arrived in a convoy of 600 land cruisers,' he said, gloomily. 'If he brings them all to Amman it's going to bring the entire place to a standstill. Can you speak to him?'

The number didn't really shock me, as earlier that year he'd taken a 1,000-strong entourage on a land trip to Togo. But I agreed to have a quiet word with Gaddafi, deciding on the same softly-softly approach as previously.

'You told me that you wanted to meet ordinary people on your trip to Jordan,' I said, after knocking on the door of his room at the king's palace in Aqaba.

'Do you want the people of Amman to say "get President Gaddafi out of here, because we cannot reach our homes or workplaces because of him"? So many cars in the city will upset them.'

The Colonel paused for a moment and enquired, with the flicker of a smile: 'Is this your king speaking, or your idea?'

I replied: 'It's mine.' I'd broken my rule to always be truthful but on this one occasion it was necessary.

Gaddafi shrugged, then said: 'OK then, tell them we will reduce the number of vehicles to 200. Leave the rest in Aqaba.'

That minor diplomatic crisis averted, we set out by road to Amman with the intention of arriving before sunset so that the crowds could see Gaddafi. Roads had been closed so we could travel at speed on a pre-agreed route and I was travelling just ahead of the Colonel's vehicle. Our first stop was to allow him to lay a foundation stone for the new Al Disi project, to pump water from an aquifer beneath the desert. Through me, the Colonel had agreed to finance the scheme.

Everything went smoothly until there was a sudden flurry of activity and I could see the military helicopters, which were escorting the convoy, swooping down. For an awful moment I thought there had been an attack, but it soon emerged that Gaddafi had ordered his driver to take a different route into the heart of the desert. In the chaos that followed, a huge dust cloud was created as other cars, at the head of the convoy, backtracked to catch Gaddafi and those who had followed him. To an observer it must have had all the hallmarks of a comedy movie, but at the time I was far from amused. If anything had happened to Gaddafi in Jordan it could have started a war.

It took ten minutes to find him, not far up the rough desert road, where he had stopped and made his way to a small tent on a hill. He'd spotted it from the main highway and it was the reason for his unscheduled detour, ruining all our timing.

The Colonel was deep in conversation with the occupants of the tent, a poor Bedouin woman and her family. She had no idea who Gaddafi was, assuming he was some sort of Jordanian government official.

'Mother,' he said to her. 'How do you live here in such conditions?'

The woman began ranting: 'We have no water or electricity and it's all the government's fault.'

Realising she did not recognise him, Gaddafi said: 'Don't you watch TV?'

She replied: 'My son has a pick-up truck and for half an hour each evening we connect our TV to the battery to watch the news. That's it.'

Finally, I decided to intervene. 'Mother, don't you realise this is President Gaddafi in front of you?'

She stared at him then clapped, hardly able to believe that he was visiting her tent. I looked on as the woman clasped the Colonel's hands in her own, prompting his security guards to try to shoo her away.

Gaddafi swore at them, took her hands and kissed them. He said: 'Do you know my own mother's hands were dry like yours because of all the hard work? It is a pleasure for me to touch them.' Finally, he took a wad of US dollars from his escort, placed it under the woman's pillow and we all carried on our way to the capital.

You might well dismiss this episode as a stunt, but when we arrived in Amman one of his first conversations with the king was about the plight of the poor Bedouin woman.

'I want you to arrange a better house for her with water and electricity,' said Gaddafi to his bemused host. His wish was granted. The Colonel was very affected by this woman, because of the memories she evoked. Can you imagine any other leader behaving in that way?

There was another incident involving a singer called Omar al-Abdalat, who had performed for Gaddafi in the past in Libya. The poor guy had moved the leader so deeply that he ended up hoarse, having sung for hours. This man was also a Bedouin and happened to live in Jordan, so the Colonel insisted he must hear him sing again. Somehow the Jordanians managed to track him down quickly and he entertained a delighted Gaddafi the same evening.

Knowing that the Colonel enjoyed mixing with ordinary people, we also arranged a meal in a well-known, but quite modest, restaurant in Amman. I'd once mentioned the place, called Reem Al Bawadi, or Deer of the Deserts, to him when we were talking about my home city. The Colonel made it clear that other diners were not to be disturbed on his account, so just one small table was set up for him. He loved to feel normal, connecting with people from a similar background and was delighted when some of the Jordanians came to his table, unprompted, to shake his hand.

The four-day state visit to Jordan was a resounding success, but I breathed a sigh of relief when Gaddafi crossed the border into Saudi Arabia and his whims were someone else's responsibility.

During this period after sanctions ended I was very busy, because there were so many new business opportunities, and divided my time equally between Tripoli and Amman. I always had a bag packed.

There is no doubt the Jordan trip resulted in improved relations between the two nations, but it seemed that some of the good work might be undone a few months later. There was an Arab League summit in Amman and Jordan was anxious that its new friend, Gaddafi, attend as a show of unity. However, he had other plans.

His absence from the Arab meeting could be interpreted as a snub. The King of Jordan's office called me, seeking my intervention.

'Did you ask Gaddafi's office officially?' I said.

'Yes we did, but we have been told he has another engagement, in Benghazi,' came the response.

I managed to convince Gaddafi that the summit was important and he agreed to change his plans. I relayed this to the king, but the Jordanians were still being told by Gaddafi's people that he would not be attending.

'Believe me, he will be there,' I replied. Sure enough Gaddafi flew to Jordan, even arriving two days before the conference so he could hold talks with King Abdullah.

The Colonel expected the red carpet to be rolled out and was delighted to find he was being accommodated in the royal palace, whereas other delegates were in hotels.

But after such a good start, including a personal greeting by the king, matters soon took a turn for the worse.

Gaddafi felt he wasn't receiving sufficient attention as the busy royal attended to other pre-summit duties. Eventually, in a fit of pique, he decided on the eve of the event that we were all going back to Libya. On this occasion I think he was right to feel slighted as, up until he suddenly lost his cool, he had done everything to please his Jordanian hosts.

The entire entourage began heading for the airport in convoy but, as we were passing through the Abdoun area of Amman, Gaddafi spied an ice cream shop and ordered a stop. Everyone piled out of their cars, causing chaos in the evening rush hour, and a crowd gathered while the Colonel held court inside.

The Jordanians were horrified that Gaddafi was leaving and I received a call on my mobile, informing us that the king was at the palace and at his Libyan guest's disposal.

I relayed the information and a Libyan official whispered in the leader's ear. He calmly continued eating his ice cream, making no sign of moving despite the pleading of his aides. Stepping in, I told Gaddafi: 'The king is waiting for you and as a Bedouin it is not polite for you to leave him standing there.'

The Colonel nodded, climbed back into his limousine and the roads were cleared for us to make our way back to the palace complex. We found King Abdullah, wearing ceremonial military uniform, standing outside Gaddafi's guest quarters. He began walking towards the Colonel, as if to shake hands, but when he got within about five paces the king suddenly halted, turned on his heels and began striding away.

I was shaking, wondering if this was some attempt to humiliate Gaddafi, but then the king took off his belt which held a pistol in a holster. He walked slowly back to the Colonel and shook his hand. I was very impressed with how the king, who was still quite young at the time, handled the tricky situation. He realised that approaching the temperamental Gaddafi while armed could be misinterpreted, and this little gesture saved the entire trip. After that the pair sat down and spoke amicably for more than two hours, before heading to the following day's summit.

There was further evidence of Gaddafi's eccentricity when, after all the business was over, we arranged for him to visit the Dead Sea. He was obsessed with Palestine, which can be seen in the distance from the Jordanian side and we chose the part-Libyan-owned Movenpick Hotel as the perfect vantage point. At the time LAFICO had a 10 per cent stake (worth $29 million), in the chain's holding company, through a deal arranged by me.

It was no surprise when Gaddafi threw the plan into turmoil, by stopping to buy tea from a roadside seller. He was fascinated by the man's charcoal burner, which heated the water, and spent a few minutes chatting. As everyone got back into the fleet of cars, Gaddafi handed the man a bundle of US dollars. It was a life-changing amount and the man could hardly believe his good fortune.

A few miles further on the Colonel stopped again, to eat barbecued meat from a stand, then for a third time to join a kickabout with a group of boys playing football next to the beach.

It was all unscheduled and Moussa Koussa, who was in charge of security, was screaming that it was unsafe. He was terrified about the close proximity of Israel, telling Gaddafi that we were within range of missiles.

'My life is in the hands of God,' said Gaddafi. 'Let me enjoy this game of football.'

By the time he was done, a journey that should have lasted half an hour had taken three times as long.

Finally we reached the hotel and Gaddafi was able to gaze over the water to Israeli-occupied Palestine.

'How can Jordan be so close yet do nothing to return this land to the Palestinians?' he asked loudly. I urged him to keep his voice down, or risk upsetting his hosts but he simply replied: 'I don't care.'

To try to lift his spirits I suggested that Gaddafi might enjoy a massage in the hotel spa, using the famous Dead Sea mud, but this plan was quickly vetoed by Moussa Koussa and three of his other top security men because the area had not been checked in advance.

Instead the Colonel went to rest, before having a meal and getting ready to return to Amman. To my amazement, Koussa and his henchmen headed to the supposedly unsafe spa, for a mud massage, and I couldn't resist causing some mischief by running to Gaddafi.

'Do you know your security men are enjoying themselves in the spa?'

The Colonel paused for thought for a moment, then said: 'OK, get everyone together. We are going back to Amman but leave them in the spa.'

Just as we were setting off Koussa, who'd finished his treatment, saw what was happening and jumped in my car.

'I know you told the president,' he said, darkly.

Of course, I denied all knowledge but I couldn't help laughing when we got back to Amman. Waiting for us was Nouri Al-Mismari, Libyan chief of protocol, who'd somehow managed to find a taxi and arrive before us. In his haste he was still covered in Dead Sea mud, which was oozing from beneath his clothes. That night Gaddafi gave all four of them hell!

During this period, my role was more like an unofficial diplomat than a businesswoman. Frequently, I was asked to be the mediator in some dispute or other involving the Colonel. The temptation was to bang heads together, but I learned to tread very carefully. There were all sorts of political games going on as Libya jockeyed for position in the Middle East and Africa. Relationships with other countries were always fragile and a misplaced word, a perceived insult, or slight could set back months of diplomacy.

I recall another trip Gaddafi arranged, to Sudan, to attend an Arab League summit.

He was due to fly to the capital, Khartoum, in a few days' time so I'd seized the opportunity to fly home to Jordan to spend some time with Noor.

When I landed in Amman, there was a short message waiting for me: 'Return to Libya immediately.'

Naturally I was worried there had been some sort of emergency, so I took the next flight back to Tripoli and called Gaddafi's office. I sat in my hotel waiting for instructions, but the hours passed and there was no word. Early next morning, while I was still asleep, there was a loud knock on the door and I was confronted by two men in military fatigues.

'Come with us now,' said one of them. 'You are flying with the president to Sudan.'

Without further explanation they picked up my half-unpacked suitcase and indicated I should follow to their waiting car. In my haste I forgot my passport, which was in the hotel safe, but was assured: 'Don't worry, you don't need a passport. You are with Gaddafi.'

Sure enough we breezed through immigration at Khartoum airport and I was soon at the Hilton Hotel, still completely in the dark about the reason for my presence. I was not normally involved in these summits.

At about 10 p.m. that evening I was, at last, summoned to see Gaddafi who was staying in a private villa. In the yard was the colourful Bedouin tent that he insisted on taking on foreign visits, and he was seated inside. Entering, I could see an overturned television set on the floor and the Colonel was clearly furious.

The reason for my sudden flight to Khartoum became apparent, as he raged: 'They have announced that your king is not coming. Call him now.'

For once I made the mistake of directly questioning Gaddafi, telling him: 'It's late. I will call in the morning.'

Gaddafi almost bit my head off, shouting: 'Call him now, or I will cut all Libya's relations with Jordan.'

It mattered so much to the Colonel because he was counting on Jordan's vote on some issue. I managed to cool him down and began punching telephone numbers, desperately trying to raise someone. Eventually I managed to get hold of an old friend, Haitham al-Mofte, who was the manager of the King of Jordan's private office.

All this was happening in front of Gaddafi, who told me to keep the phone on speaker. Now I was terrified that my contact would say something unguarded and set the Colonel off again. So I began: 'I am sitting here with President Gaddafi in Sudan and he has seen on television that King Abdullah is not attending the summit. He is very angry and would like the king to be here.'

Although taken aback by the call, interrupting his dinner at a restaurant, my friend understood the sensitivity of the situation and promised to do all he could.

Gaddafi insisted I wait with him in the tent for some sort of outcome, but as the minutes ticked by the atmosphere became steadily more tense. Fearing the Colonel would erupt if he had to wait until morning, I managed to persuade him to allow me to return to my hotel so I could make more calls.

Not long afterwards my prayers were answered when my friend rang to say: 'The king was not planning on attending, but out of respect for President Gaddafi's personal wishes he has agreed to attend the opening then fly home.'

I had a skip in my step as I returned to Gaddafi's side to pass on the good news. I emphasised that the change of heart by the king was a favour to Gaddafi and his mood changed, as quickly as the click of thumb and finger.

Now he was all smiles, so I asked him: 'Why did you put me in such an impossible situation? You know I have no official status in Jordan and I know his Majesty the King and one of his Majesty's sisters. I am a bridge between your countries but I have no power.'

Gaddafi gave one of his shrugs and replied: 'Daad, I knew you could sort this. That's why I had you flown here.'

I was unsure whether to feel flattered or infuriated by this faith he had in me. How would the Colonel have reacted if I had not managed to catch my friend in the restaurant that evening? I'd seen Gaddafi angry many times, but the smashed television was a violent side I'd not previously witnessed. It was growing evidence of his unpredictability and mood swings.

Chapter 14

The Prince and the Jet

One of the first items on the Colonel's shopping list after he was welcomed back into the fold was that must-have item for world leaders: a big private jet.

While Libya was under pressure to hand over the Lockerbie suspects, and still burdened by sanctions, Gaddafi was effectively a prisoner in his own country. But now he was free to travel, not just in the Middle East but also much further afield.

As I have stressed, he was not driven by status symbols or luxury goods. I remember once returning from a successful trip to Europe and presenting him with a beautiful military-style hooded jacket, by Versace, to wear in the desert. It cost $8,000 but might as well have come from a charity or thrift shop, as Gaddafi had no concept of the value of designer labels.

His motivation for owning his personal version of the US president's Air Force One, a huge converted passenger aircraft, was partly for practical reasons but mainly for his own security. Primarily, the Colonel did not trust scheduled passenger services, with good reason after Lockerbie, or private flights organised by outsiders. The latest jets were equipped with missile protection and other high-tech security wizardry. This was what he had in mind. As his wish for his own jet became common knowledge, an array of aircraft that were up for sale began arriving in Tripoli. Brokers from Europe, Lebanon and Qatar were crawling all over the airport, desperate for their commission. They were like used-car salesmen, except their wares carried a much heftier price tag. The going rate for one of these aircraft, refitted to Gaddafi's specifications, was over $100 million.

Jets were not my area of expertise, but one of my contacts was Prince Al-Waleed bin Talal, a billionaire entrepreneur and grandson of the first king of Saudi Arabia. His modus operandi was buying shares in companies with strong global brands but depressed share prices, then prospering as markets recovered. He invested in everything from hotels to banks and when we first met, in 2000, he owned stakes in EuroDisney, Apple, and the Saks Fifth Avenue chain of stores. He's been described as 'the Arabian Warren Buffet', and one rich list published in that year placed him as the world's sixth wealthiest man with a fortune of $20 billion.

Prince Al-Waleed originally approached me just before sanctions were suspended, with the idea of building luxury hotels in Libya. As it happened he was also looking to trade-in two of his private jets, to raise funds to buy a new model. He was exactly the type of well-connected individual that Libya was seeking, so I approached the Colonel to suggest a meeting.

'Who is this man, I've never heard of him,' replied Gaddafi, with a dismissive wave of his hand. Whereas he had an encyclopaedic knowledge of world political leaders, it was typical that he hadn't the faintest clue about the identity of one of the planet's richest businessmen. The Colonel had no real interest in commerce, but I managed to persuade him that forging links with Prince Al-Waleed would be beneficial. If the influential Saudi was seen to be investing in new Libya, then other money men would surely follow.

Having won Gaddafi round, I set up a meeting between the pair, in Sirte, and also arranged for Prince Al-Waleed to take a whistle-stop tour of the country. In Tobruk he inspected some land where a new resort was proposed. In Tripoli he visited the preserved ruins from the 1986 US raid on Gaddafi's compound and signed a book of condolence for the victims. This bombed out 'house of resistance', from which the Colonel had so narrowly escaped, was kept as a permanent reminder of the evil ways of the US. Many visiting dignitaries were taken there, to see his bedroom just as it was in 1986. Another feature was a statue of a giant gold fist, clutching an American fighter plane.

It was at the memorial that I had my first encounter with the prince, then in his mid-forties, who was also a renowned philanthropist and had a well-oiled PR machine to ensure he was always portrayed in a favourable light.

My first impression was of a smooth, rather vain, but charming man. However, the more time I spent with him the more I noticed how uncomfortable he was when dealing with people one-to-one. In a business situation, surrounded by advisors and lawyers, Prince Al-Waleed was in total control but remove all the hangers-on and he was a different person. He wasn't shy but seemed to be on edge all the time, always fidgeting. I found it slightly unnerving to deal with someone who was so hyperactive and it took all my powers of concentration not to focus on his eyebrows, which moved up and down constantly.

He gave the impression he wasn't concentrating, rarely making eye contact, but that was not the case. He was a clever man with an excellent business brain.

I was never entirely comfortable around him and, although nothing was ever said, I wondered early on if he had an issue doing business with women. If that was the case he must have realised his luck was out if he wanted to work with Libya, because all foreign investment had to go through LAFICO and he was my latest pet project.

Also in Tripoli I helped him negotiate a contract to build a resort on the coast. The Libyans were so keen to attract tourists that the prince got a free lease, but he never went ahead with the scheme.

We became better acquainted while flying to Benghazi for the final leg of his Libya trip, and my next meeting with Prince Al-Waleed was in Riyadh, where he lived. It was my first visit to Saudi Arabia since the break-up of my marriage but, thankfully, it passed uneventfully and I did not bump into my ex-husband.

In the summer of 2001, the prince invited me to his private yacht, which was moored in Cannes, in the south of France. The plan was to discuss business in general and talk more about the two second-hand planes for sale.

As I left the Carlton Hotel, where I was staying, and made my way to the harbour, I felt like movie star. Prince Al-Waleed's 85-metre yacht, boasting its own helipad, had in the past been owned by Adnan Khashoggi and Donald Trump. It also had a starring role in the James Bond film *Never Say Never Again*, released in 1983, when it was used as the villain's headquarters.

The five-storey yacht was far too big to berth at the quayside so I was shuttled out on a small launch. I was dressed for the scorching Mediterranean weather in a simple skirt and blouse and I had to stifle a laugh when the prince welcomed me aboard. He was wearing shorts and a casual shirt with a button too many undone, showing a vast expanse of chest hair. Perfectly coiffured hair and sunglasses completed the look. Had I travelled back in time to the 1970s?

I enjoyed his hospitality but was also struck by his temper. The prince could lose his cool over the slightest irritation, such as a coffee cup being out of place.

We parted on good terms, with Prince Al-Waleed offering me generous commission if I arranged for Libya to buy one of his two surplus jets. My contract with Gaddafi and LAFICO allowed me to take a percentage if I brokered the deal, but the understanding was that I would take nothing from the Libyans. The purchase was verbally agreed with the prince's personal representative, Fouad Alaeddin, over dinner at Ayoush, a Moroccan restaurant in Mayfair, London but still required the Colonel's stamp of approval.

So far he hadn't shown much interest in the procession of private aircraft flying into Tripoli for his consideration.

Now, though, he suddenly came to life declaring: 'OK, where is Prince Al-Waleed?'

Caught off guard I replied: 'I believe he is doing business somewhere else in Africa.'

This didn't please the Colonel who ordered: 'Get him here right now with both aircraft and I will choose one.'

I made some calls, tracing Prince Al-Waleed to Algeria. Two days later he and his planes, an Airbus A340 and a Boeing 767, were on the tarmac at Mitiga airport in eastern Tripoli and the three of us were sipping coffee in Gaddafi's Bedouin tent.

To break the ice I made a joke, telling the Colonel: 'You know President Gaddafi, when Saudis get rich they become very spoiled. They need two private jets! We went to the airport to greet your guest, the prince, and when we put out the red carpet the first plane was empty. Fortunately the second plane landed with him on board.'

The Colonel could see the humour in haggling with a billionaire over which jet to buy and had just one question. It was nothing to do with the layout, the on-board Jacuzzi or the colour scheme.

He asked: 'Which one has four engines?'

The prince looked puzzled but replied: 'The Airbus.'

Gaddafi said: 'In that case leave the Airbus here for me and take the Boeing away with you. Daad will handle the price with you.'

I knew what was going through the safety and security conscious mind of Gaddafi. In the event of a bomb on board, or some sort of technical failure, he reckoned the additional engines would give him more chance of surviving. He didn't even want to see either aircraft before deciding on the 5-year-old Airbus.

The deal was clinched in a matter of minutes, leaving the other brokers who'd flown to Tripoli furious. Yet again, jealousy reared its head as everyone assumed my special power over Gaddafi was the only reason for my success in clinching a sale. They were stupid because the real explanation was that Gaddafi did not trust them and feared the aircraft that each offered was bugged, or worse. That was why he wanted Prince Al-Waleed's two planes flown to Tripoli at such short notice, with as few people as possible in the loop. Gaddafi also knew all along which aircraft he would buy, but insisted on both being available to build in another layer of security. If there were to be any skulduggery then both jets would have to be rigged.

All that remained was to fix the price and my commission, which we did on the Airbus at the airport before the prince flew home on the unwanted Boeing. The final figure agreed between LAFICO and him for the Airbus was $120 million, which included $10 million for my commission. As he cleared his personal possessions from the Airbus, I seized the opportunity to give it a quick inspection. It was certainly presidential, with silver-coloured sofas in the main living area and separate bedrooms and showers.

The prince's Airbus was later modified for Gaddafi, although the silver and burgundy interior remained. An aircraft of this size would normally carry more than 300 passengers but the Colonel's private version had just fifty first-class style seats, tucked away at the back for his entourage. The Airbus, in Libyan presidential colours, later became a familiar sight at the world's airports.

When all the paperwork was complete it would represent the single biggest deal of my life. Without my intervention it would never have got off the ground and the prince was extremely grateful.

So impressed, it transpired, that he decided to add to my growing collection of marriage proposals. One day, out of the blue and about a month before we closed the deal, he offered me his hand in that now familiar businesslike Arab manner.

'You are a strong woman,' the prince began, while we were on the jet making a few final checks. 'I need a woman like you alongside me to help run my life.' He was a married man, but the Muslim law allowed him to take up to four wives and he knew I was divorced.

'I need time,' I replied, giving my stock answer because I didn't want to derail the aircraft deal at such a sensitive stage. 'Let's finish the business first then talk about marriage.' Of course, I wanted my money.

In subsequent telephone calls he repeated his declarations of love, but no one believed me when I told them I was being pursued by a Saudi prince. That is until I allowed my sister Linda to listen in!

I was never going to accept this proposal, because I knew he treated women like toys to be discarded when he got bored after a few years. When Arab men get rich they think they can have any woman they want. It's a pattern of marry and divorce, marry and divorce. I won't be a commodity for anyone and I suspected the real motive behind this unexpected offer of marriage was my excellent contacts in Libya.

I witnessed his attitude towards women for myself during one of our many meetings. We were at the exclusive brasserie Fouquet's, on the Avenue des Champs-Élysées, when he introduced me to a young, dark-haired woman called Ameerah, who was part of his small group. One of his staff told me she was the prince's wife and as we all left the café I waited politely for her to gather her coat and handbag, so we could all walk together.

'Why are you standing there,' Prince Al-Waleed asked me.

'I'm waiting for your wife,' I said, taken aback by his abruptness.

He became angry, denying she was his wife and wanting to know who'd given me this information.

Then, before I could answer, he summoned the poor woman, demanding: 'Did you tell anyone I am your husband?'

She replied: 'No, I didn't say anything.'

The prince told her harshly: 'Stay away from Daad.'

So Ameerah was forced to walk a few metres behind as we strolled along the street. I was sorry I'd unwittingly been responsible for this humiliating treatment. It only reinforced my belief that I could never marry a man who disrespected a woman like that.

Whether or not the prince and Ameerah really were married at that time, as I suspect was the case, I still can't be entirely sure. There's no doubt they did become man and wife at some stage, but the official announcement came a few years later.

I was pleased to learn that she became a powerful voice in the women's movement in Saudi Arabia, including fighting for the right to drive. Sadly, the marriage did not last.

Although we'd shaken hands with Prince Al-Waleed on a price of $120 million for the Airbus, Gaddafi was adamant that he did not want to be seen to be paying more than $85 million. This was the sum President Hosni Mubarak of Egypt had reportedly paid for his private jet a few years earlier. The astute Gaddafi realised that his image as a man of the people did not sit comfortably with this type of lavish spending, and this was his way of cushioning the impact.

The solution was to draw up paperwork showing that the Airbus falsely cost $70 million and that another $70 million was to be invested in an ambitious desert reclamation and agricultural project the prince was organising in Egypt's Nile Delta. In reality, it was $120 million for the jet and $20 million for the scheme, called Toshka. It was just another example of the Libyan people having the wool pulled over their eyes. In any language it was corruption on a grand scale, but that was the way the regime often operated. Nothing could be taken at face value.

The first instalment, of $70 million, was paid by Libya to Prince Al-Waleed in 2003. I immediately sought the first half of my commission from the prince but, ominously, he refused, stating that he would not pay anything until he'd received the final balance. I hoped this was simply the prince being a hard-nosed businessman, rather than a warning sign that my deal with him was unravelling. Unfortunately, that was precisely the case because, behind the scenes, some Libyan officials were trying to block the second payment. By then Gaddafi had pulled out of the reclamation scheme, so the prince was still owed $50 million.

My involvement hadn't gone down well in the usual quarters, and no doubt these men were in line for a backhander if a certain other jet was purchased.

Unsurprisingly, the prince was angered by the delay and took matters into his own hands.

The aircraft, which was still registered in Prince Al-Waleed's company name, Kingdom Holdings, had been taken to Germany for routine maintenance. The Libyans had approved this but then I received a frantic telephone call from Moussa Koussa in the intelligence office, informing me that the Gaddafi Airbus was in Saudi Arabia. I had no idea what was happening but managed to contact the prince, who was in Syria.

'Don't worry,' he reassured me. 'We have just taken the jet to Saudi Arabia so we can re-register it.'

I made the mistake of trusting the prince, who promised the Airbus would be returned within two weeks. But I knew it was a foolish move by him to allow the jet to land in Saudi Arabia, which had strained relations with Libya.

Gaddafi had visited the country in 2000 to try to build bridges but cordial relations did not last. At the Arab League summit of 2003 there was a public slanging match between Gaddafi and the Saudis. The acrimonious exchange, which was broadcast live across the region, began when the Colonel addressed the delegates. He said Saudi Arabia's King Fahd had been ready to 'strike an alliance with the devil' when American troops were deployed to protect the kingdom after Iraq invaded Kuwait in 1990. The two countries' differences had not been patched up and there was simmering mistrust. The security of the Airbus was now compromised and I feared this could jeopardise the entire deal.

Although Gaddafi frequently drove his guards mad by making unscheduled trips to markets, where he liked to check the prices, in other ways he was paranoid when it came to personal safety. Just one example was his refusal to touch papers with original ink, in case they were poisoned. So, naturally, he wanted the aircraft under watchful Libyan eyes and not in the hands of his enemies the Saudis.

Weeks, then months, passed and there was no word from Saudi Arabia to inform me that the aircraft had been re-registered. Finally I managed to speak to the prince who had been avoiding my calls. He said bluntly: 'I'm not returning the aircraft until the Libyans pay the outstanding $50 million.'

This was a disaster. Not only were the Libyans livid about being hoodwinked, but people jumped to the wrong conclusion that I had colluded with the Saudi Arabian. It was me who'd brought him to Libya in the first place after all, and there were attempts to have my contract with LAFICO scrapped. I tried to explain to Gaddafi, who was not only refusing to pay the balance but said tersely: 'The aircraft deal is finished. I want our initial $70 million back.'

Prince Al-Waleed's hard-ball tactic, designed to force the Libyans to settle the whole bill, had backfired and LAFICO threatened him with legal action. Realising he had made a terrible mistake, he called me when I was in London and begged me to come to Paris to try to negotiate a solution.

'There is only one way forward,' I told the prince. 'You must come with me to Libya to apologise, in person, to the president and convince him the aircraft is safe for his use. That is the only way we can solve this.'

The prince agreed, but it was a fraught trip. His visit in 2005 happened to coincide with Revolution Day celebrations to mark the overthrow of King Idris. These were always vibrant affairs, with lights strung up in trees, dancing and military parades. Revolution Day, held on 1 September, was the biggest event in the Libyan calendar but there was no party atmosphere in Gaddafi's tent. We'd barely arrived before the Colonel's office manager, Mohamed Hijazi, more or less accused the prince of being a hijacker and began berating the stunned man in front of Gaddafi.

It was obvious that this was the Colonel's position, otherwise the outburst would never have been allowed in the presence of a guest. Prince Al-Waleed was not used to being treated like this, but he must have been expecting trouble because he had flown into Tripoli on a rented jet rather than his own brand-new aircraft. It was obvious he did not trust the Libyans and feared his own jet would be impounded if the dispute was not solved.

Thankfully, the tense atmosphere soon subsided and the apology was duly made. Gaddafi got his private jet, Prince Al-Waleed got the outstanding $50 million a few months later and that should have been the conclusion of the matter. All that remained was my not insignificant commission.

I'd set up the deal and bent over backwards to resurrect it when the prince made the big error of trying to force Gaddafi's hand. Yet the ungrateful royal refused to recompense me. I was shocked because I did not think the prince, who had other business deals with Libya, would choose to incur the wrath of Gaddafi for a second time. I was left asking myself if the marriage proposal was all a plot to avoid paying me $10 million. Maybe he thought I was part of the deal.

My many calls to his office were ignored and I pondered what to do next. Taking one of the world's richest men to court is not a step to be taken lightly but, although I suspected it would be a long, drawn out process, I was sure I had right on my side.

I decided to sue Prince Al-Waleed bin Talal but, just as I feared, it would be many years before I had the pleasure of seeing him squirm in the witness box. The delay was not only due to the slow turning of the wheels of justice, but also events that would threaten my life in Libya.

Chapter 15

The Lockerbie Bomber?

A prison guard ushers me into a small room, containing only a table and a couple of chairs. Already seated is a bespectacled man, in his early fifties and with grey flecks in his brown hair, who is wearing a baggy tracksuit. Before him there's a large file of documents and as I enter he stands to shake my hand. His grip is gentle and he appears a little nervous. When he speaks it's almost in a whisper, although we are not being overheard.

During my time working for Gaddafi, the Lockerbie bombing and its aftermath provided a constant backdrop. It was the single issue that most occupied the Colonel's mind and in 2003 I was summoned to the leader's office, to be told he was sending me to Scotland to meet Abdelbaset Al-Megrahi. As far as most people were concerned this man had the blood of 270 innocent people on his hands. Outside Libya he was better known simply as the Lockerbie bomber.

Al-Megrahi spent the first three years of his sentence at Barlinnie, a high security prison in Glasgow, where he was incarcerated in a purpose-built unit. Other than family members and lawyers, Nelson Mandela was one of his few visitors. Barlinnie has the reputation as 'Scotland's toughest jail' and is also the country's largest, holding more than 1,000 inmates.

The Libyan government had a small office in Glasgow, solely to support Al-Megrahi, and one of the five staff greeted me at the city's airport. Next day we drove the short distance from my city centre hotel to Barlinnie, where memories of my previous prison visits came flooding back as I passed through security.

The prisoner was expecting me and had been briefed that I was representing Gaddafi directly. Al-Megrahi resembled a mild-mannered accountant but, if the Scottish justice system is to be trusted, he still remains the biggest mass killer in British history. He didn't look like a murderer, but how do you tell? Of course, Libya always had a very different view and regarded him as a sacrificial lamb. The West needed a figure to blame and to be able to claim justice had been done; Gaddafi needed to find a way out of the mess of sanctions. Everyone benefited except Al-Megrahi and his family. He already had one failed appeal behind him, but when we first met was working on another. In the West there was growing unease about the safety of his conviction, and the expectation in Libya was that he would soon be coming home. Britain wanted rid of him but, unusually, was in disagreement with the US which was taking a much harder line.

My brief was simple: to check-up on Al-Megrahi and offer reassurance that he had not been forgotten. He was pleased with the new trainers and two tracksuits that I brought, and over the next two hours we spoke openly about his case and prospects for release. Al-Megrahi told me that he had not been coerced by Gaddafi to hand himself in for trial, but I couldn't help wondering: how could he have refused? The pressure must have been unbearable because Libya's future relations with the US and Britain, not to mention the entire issue of sanctions, were hanging on finding a solution to the Lockerbie problem. It took years to find a compromise, which entailed handing over Al-Megrahi and another suspect for trial at a neutral venue, and agreeing to pay $2.7 billion compensation to the families of the 270 victims. The final piece of the jigsaw was a carefully worded statement. In it Libya 'accepted responsibility for the actions of its officials' but did not admit guilt for bringing down Pan Am Flight 103 in 1988. It was often wrongly interpreted as a full admission, but anyone reading the words closely could see that was not the case. It was a fudge and, in my view, represented diplomacy at its most cynical. Libya bought peace with the West, which framed an innocent man. When the Lockerbie verdict came through in January 2001, delivered by three Scottish judges, I was in Tripoli. The second suspect, Al-Amin Khalifa Fhimah, was acquitted and I remember Gaddafi telling me: 'It's what I expected. They could not lose face by releasing both men.' The Colonel was determined to secure Al-Megrahi's early release but, speaking to the prisoner, it was clear that he felt let down by his country. Al-Megrahi urged me to use my connections with the royal family of Jordan, handing me a letter addressed to King Abdullah in which he protested his innocence and pleaded to be transferred to a prison in any Arab territory until his innocence was proved. Here is an excerpt:

'Your Majesty, I am an Arabic Libyan citizen who was unfairly convicted in the case of what is called Lockerbie on a false accusation based on the allegation that I was the suspect who bought the clothes from a storekeeper in Malta that were found in the remains of the suitcase bomb that was the cause for the plane crash over Lockerbie, and that I was available in Malta and that my colleague the second suspect who was acquitted by the court is the one who put the suitcase on the flight from Malta.

'Your Majesty, I am a rational Muslim; I am not an extremist at all. I have a family and children who I do love more than any other thing. I swear to Allah the One, the Almighty, the Most Gracious, the Most Merciful, the Holy, the Bestower, the Alive, The Lord of Majesty and Bounty, I swear with all the beautiful tributes of Allah that I have never in my life bought any clothes from any store in Malta. I have never seen the clothes, nor the storekeeper in my life except during the trial when the witness presented his deposition. I have never dealt in my life with a suitcase that contains an offence at any airport in the world. My presence at Malta, if it were really the beginning of this crime, as claimed by the allegation, was merely to get some necessities.

'Your Majesty, I beg you on behalf of my family and my children to raise my problem with those concerned in the United Kingdom and the United States of America to be transported to a prison in my homeland, or in your country or in any other Arabic country (as I consider any Arabic country as my own homeland) until the time when Allah Almighty will show my innocence to the entire world.

'Your Majesty, I conclude my letter with this verse: By the name of Allah, the Merciful our Lord! Rescue us from this town, whose people are oppressors; and raise for us from thee one who will protect, and raise for us one who will help.'

In 2005, Al-Megrahi was transferred to the more relaxed surroundings of Greenock prison, where he served the rest of his sentence. I wasn't surprised to find that he was depressed. In the early days of his captivity his family relocated to Scotland to be near him, but they encountered hostility from locals and soon moved back to Libya. The separation from his loved ones had clearly affected his mental health and he was not sleeping well. Al-Megrahi, who had five children, was most upset about missing the wedding of his only daughter. He told me that she'd come to Scotland with the marriage papers, for him to sign according to Arab custom. He'd cried for a week after her visit, he told me, adding: 'Every day I spend here my children are growing up. My daughter was a child when I left Libya and now she is a woman. Please remind President Gaddafi.'

We spoke about Al-Megrahi's journey from Malta, where he worked for Libyan Arab Airlines, to the special court at Camp Zeist in The Netherlands where he was convicted in 2001. He was alleged to have used his position to evade lax security and smuggle the bomb into a suitcase on a flight which connected with Pan Am 103. At the prison I was interested to learn that he'd never met Gaddafi face-to-face and all his dealings, prior to being handed over for trial, had been with Abdullah Senussi in the intelligence office.

Al-Megrahi told me: 'Senussi came to see me and said to me: "There is an agreement with the West to send you for trial, which the leader says you are free to accept or reject. No one will force you to go and you will be protected by us."'

He gave himself up for his country but at the time he was sure he would not spend long behind bars, and this was eating away at him. He did not believe he'd received the fair trial that had been promised.

From what I observed, Al-Megrahi was well treated and, in return, was a model prisoner. He was able to cook his own Halal food and sometimes used the prison gym, although he devoted most of his spare time to reading and researching his case. Satellite television was installed in his cell so that he could watch Arab stations, delighting other inmates who also had access to a host of new channels. Rather predictably, his unit became known as 'the Gaddafi café'.

I was allowed to take a camera into my meeting with Al-Megrahi at Barlinnie. Returning to Libya to present my report, I first showed Gaddafi photographs of myself with the prisoner. Until I explained his identity, the Colonel seemed to show no recognition of the man at my side. For anyone who still believes Gaddafi personally instructed the Lockerbie bomber, interpret that how you will.

I told Gaddafi of his countryman's dismay about the passing years and apparent inaction by the Libyan government. He replied: 'Meet him again. Tell him that I received his message and I will find a solution. Tell him that I promise he will be home soon.'

From that moment, the Colonel did everything possible to keep his case in the spotlight, also funding lawyers for his appeal and paying for investigators to gather new evidence.

When I next visited Al-Megrahi, he was a frightened man. He'd become convinced there was a plot to assassinate him, by deliberately leaving the doors to his secure unit unlocked.

'The other prisoners hate me,' he told me. If what he was saying was true I knew he had good reason to be terrified, because the Lockerbie bomber was a prize scalp. I promised to pass on his concerns and, to the best of my knowledge he never suffered any harm in either prison.

In Libya he was regarded as a martyr. The Colonel's wife, Safia, took Al-Megrahi's wife, Aisha, under her wing. She was treated like a VIP, often appearing at functions and on Libyan television. I liked Al-Megrahi and we kept in touch. He had my mobile telephone number and occasionally I'd receive calls. We'd speak for a few minutes about the case and we exchanged letters. I used to urge him to keep his spirits up, and reassure him that he was always in Gaddafi's thoughts. Al-Megrahi was ultimately granted a second appeal, which I'm convinced would have cleared his name. The already weak case against him was gradually being dismantled, as it emerged key witnesses had been paid millions of dollars to testify. Tony Gauci, the Maltese shopkeeper who picked out Al-Megrahi as the man who bought the clothes which were found in the suitcase containing the bomb, was discredited. There was doubt he was even in Malta at the time, which would have blown the entire case out of the water. Few people who have studied the evidence in any depth truly believed Al-Megrahi was the bomber, or that Libya was behind the attack. Had the appeal gone ahead it would have been very embarrassing for the West and there was a good chance Al-Megrahi would have ended up receiving compensation for wrongful imprisonment. There was also talk in Libya of suing Britain for the economic damage caused by the years of sanctions against Libya. Can you imagine that?

I was shocked when he was diagnosed with prostate cancer in 2008. He was released by the Scottish government on compassionate grounds on 20 August 2009, when he was said to be terminally ill. Six days earlier he withdrew his appeal, explaining: 'I have been faced with an appalling choice: to risk dying in prison in the hope that my name is cleared posthumously or to return home still carrying the weight of the guilty verdict, which will never now be lifted. The choice which I made is a matter of sorrow, disappointment and anger, which I fear I will never overcome.'

It was just one more political deal over Lockerbie and his early release, after eight and a half years in prison, brought condemnation from the US. 'We think it is a mistake,' said President Barack Obama. Many of the relatives of the Lockerbie victims were also angry but the decision was welcomed by Jim Swire, the doctor whose daughter was among the dead. As usual he gave a measured response, stating: 'I feel despondent that Scotland and the West didn't have the guts to allow this man's second appeal to continue because I am convinced that had they done so it would have overturned the verdict against him.'

A survey in *The Times* revealed that 45 per cent of British people believed his release had more to do with oil. I don't disagree. I'd urge anyone who is interested in the case to look at Dr Swire's website, Lockerbietruth.com.

As he was released, Al-Megrahi said he bore the people of Scotland no ill will, and thanked the prison staff at Barlinnie and Greenock for their kindness. He received a hero's welcome back in Tripoli. I was in Jordan at the time but watched on television, noticing that Al-Megrahi flew home on the same jet I'd helped Gaddafi buy from Prince Al-Waleed bin Talal of Saudi Arabia. Also on board was the Colonel's son, Saif, in his white robes and holding Al-Megrahi's arm aloft as he stepped on to Libyan soil. Saif was basking in the glory of the triumphant homecoming, although in reality I knew he'd barely been involved. I was seething inside as I watched him steal all the credit, while the real hard workers were nowhere to be seen. Saif regularly went to London, but he never once bothered to hop on a domestic flight to Glasgow to visit Al-Megrahi in prison at either Barlinnie or Greenock. The jubilant scenes didn't go down well in the West, which had requested a restrained welcome, but this was too good an opportunity to pass up. It was rare that Libya got the upper hand against America.

However, when he came home I hardly recognised Al-Megrahi who was walking with a stick and had to be helped down the steps of the aircraft. He looked nothing like the healthy man I'd last visited a few years earlier. It was said at the time of his release that he would die within three months. In fact he lingered on for another three years, even outliving Gaddafi which no one could have envisaged at the time. I found the outcry from the West over Al-Megrahi's failure to die sooner distasteful. I always felt very sorry for him and never doubted his innocence. What reason did he have to lie to me, an agent of the regime?

In a moment of desperation, he once told me in prison: 'They would be very happy for me to die here.'

There is a suspicion in my mind that Al-Megrahi did not receive very good medical attention in prison, because prostate cancer usually responds well to treatment if it is caught early. He died at his villa in the suburbs of Tripoli, in May 2012, aged 60. I hope he found peace and was able to enjoy precious time with his family. In my eyes Al-Megrahi was the 271st Lockerbie victim.

By then the final compensation cheques had been paid to the families, much to the dismay of Gaddafi. Although he appreciated the importance of keeping up the instalments, he often railed against the unfairness and how the handing over of compensation would be interpreted.

'Why should I do this when Libya is innocent?' he asked many times. For those working behind the scenes it was a constant battle to persuade the Colonel to take a pragmatic approach. Finally Abdul Ati Al-Obeidi, one of his key advisors on Lockerbie, spelled this out in very direct terms. At one of our regular Lockerbie briefing meetings with Gaddafi, he told the leader: 'Look, we don't want to see you suffer the same fate as Saddam Hussein. If the cost is money, then we have a lot of money. Let's just pay them, get rid of this issue, open up our country and keep it stable. America can do anything it wants. Do you want us to end up watching you on TV like Saddam Hussein?'

It was a very blunt reference to Saddam's capture and humiliation by US forces, which had so rattled Gaddafi. For all his bluster he knew that America and its allies could topple him at the drop of a hat. The bombing of his compound in 1986 by the Americans was a constant reminder of the West's power. After Al-Obeidi's intervention the Colonel didn't make such a fuss about the blood money.

The burning question remains: if Al-Megrahi was innocent, as I firmly believe, then who brought down the Pan Am flight?

At the time of the Lockerbie bombing there were loose alliances between various states and organisations. They were generally opposed to the ideals of the West, and pooled resources. Bombing an aircraft is no easy matter, so if one country didn't have the expertise to carry out an attack it simply funded a group that did. I don't carry a smoking gun but Al-Megrahi, who knew the case inside out and had access to Libya's files on Lockerbie, was convinced that it was a joint enterprise between Iran, Syria and The Popular Front for the Liberation of Palestine. The shooting down of the Iranian passenger jet by the American warship *Vincennes*, six months before Lockerbie, was too much of a coincidence.

It was the crucial link, but by the time the evidence began to stack up no one wanted to point the finger at Iran or Syria, who had helped Western coalition forces in the first Gulf War. My time on the fringes of international diplomacy taught me that politicians are like shifting sands in the desert.

Sadly I never got the opportunity to see Al-Megrahi following his release but I know he intended to present fresh evidence at his appeal, insisting he had nothing to fear or hide.

'I had most to gain and nothing to lose about the whole truth coming out,' he said.

I am sure the British intelligence services know the truth about Lockerbie, but it has been covered up. Al-Megrahi's early death was convenient, although his family did eventually get a posthumous appeal. It came as no surprise to me that it was rejected, or that Al-Megrahi's family have called on the British government to release secret files which implicate Iran. Justice has not been done and, for political reasons, I fear we may never learn the truth.

In another recent development the US has named and charged another so-called suspect, Abu Agila Mohammad Masud. I don't claim to know every member of the Libyan intelligence services but I can tell you I never encountered him during my many years in Libya, or heard his name mentioned by Gaddafi. Why did the Americans choose to make this announcement on the 32nd anniversary of Lockerbie? In my opinion it is nothing more than another crass political stunt.

In that period Lockerbie grabbed most of the headlines but there was another barrier to Libya rejoining the international community.

Previously I've also briefly mentioned the case of UTA Flight 772, the French airliner that was brought down by a bomb over Niger in September 1989 with the loss of 170 lives. Ten years later, six Libyans were convicted of the attack by a court in Paris. Among them was Abdullah Senussi, my enemy from the intelligence office and one of Libya's key Lockerbie negotiators.

The parallels between the two bombings were obvious: the finger of blame pointing at Libya; Gaddafi refusing to accept responsibility; and wrangles over compensation. The big difference was that the UTA 772 suspects were not handed over for trial and were convicted in their absence.

Whether Senussi was involved in the UTA bombing, or not, I don't know. However, I will repeat that I believe this man was capable of anything.

Most of those on board the aircraft, which was flying from Congo to Paris, were French and the court fixed the compensation at up to 30,000 Euros to the family of each of the victims. Compared to the $10 million Gaddafi reluctantly agreed to hand over for each of the Lockerbie dead it was a trifling amount, and the French felt insulted. 'Is the life of one of our citizens worth less than that of an American or a Briton?' it was asked.

Legally, France didn't have a leg to stand on as its own court had set the compensation, but it felt Libya had a moral duty to increase the sums to the French families.

Negotiations had been going on for years, but the waters were muddied when Gaddafi's son, Saif, became involved. He flew to Paris and signed an agreement which would see an extra 185 million Euros ($1 million per victim) paid to the families. The money was to come from a charitable foundation, run by Saif, but, according to the agreement, Libya would not accept responsibility for the bombing.

It was still a long way short of the compensation paid to the Lockerbie families, but France was satisfied and the deal was announced in Paris with great fanfare.

All hell promptly broke in Libya, where the Colonel appeared to have no idea of his son's involvement. Foreign Minister Abdel Rahman Shalgham was wheeled out on state television, claiming that Saif had no official authority so the agreement was worthless. To make matters worse, it emerged that Saif had persuaded Crown Prince Mohammed bin Zayed Al Nahyan, of the United Arab Emirates, to underwrite the payment. The Crown Prince, who had been approached by a wealthy friend of Saif called Hassan Tatanaki, was furious at being dragged into this diplomatic spat. It was just one more example of the chaos around

Gaddafi, who couldn't even control his own son. Saif had a big ego and no doubt hoped to impress his father, but his unauthorised negotiations with Paris backfired disastrously.

The incident was highly embarrassing for French President Jacques Chirac and potentially damaging for Libya, which did not want to make an enemy of France when talks over Lockerbie were so delicately balanced.

As all this was unfolding, I received a call from Jean-Paul Perrier, the chairman of the part state-owned Thales defence and aerospace company. I'd met him at an arms show in London soon after Thales took over the British electronics firm Racal, which I had represented throughout the Middle East. I was hoping to enjoy the same arrangement with Thales but Perrier had been non-committal, saying only: 'We will see.'

Now he wanted me to intervene in the farce involving Saif and Tatanaki.

'Can you speak to Gaddafi?' pleaded Perrier. 'Public opinion is growing against our president and he has an election coming up. Chirac needs your help.'

I also agreed to meet Tatanaki, whom I knew through a common Egyptian friend, Shereef Husain. Mr Tatanaki was an opponent of the Gaddafi Regime and was only allowed back from exile abroad back after Saif's intervention. The Colonel did not like the man, so I was wary. However, when I met Perrier and a French intelligence official called Allan Juliet both men supported Tatanaki's version of events.

A panic-stricken Tatanaki told me that from the moment the row erupted he had been trying to contact Saif, and Abdullah Senussi at the Libyan intelligence office, but neither was answering the telephone. Crown Prince Mohammed bin Zayed was understandably angry and seeking answers from Tatanaki, blaming him for the crisis. Tatanaki also begged me to intervene with Gaddafi, telling me that the Crown Prince had requested my involvement.

I agreed to fly to Tripoli, where I sat down with the leader. Initially he seemed uninterested, until the name Mohammed bin Zayed Al Nahyan was mentioned and the Colonel suddenly began to listen.

'What do you think?' he enquired, realising the importance of a fall-out with the United Arab Emirates. Twice he asked me if the Crown Prince was still willing to underwrite a deal to pay the 185 million Euros if the mess involving Saif and Tatanki could be resolved. I assured the Colonel that I understood this to be the case, and that it would be good for Libya to keep the UAE onside. There was also great political mileage in appeasing France.

'Look, Chirac cannot force you to pay but he is a politician who often supports Arab states and has great influence over French-speaking African countries,' I told Gaddafi, conscious that the French president was also a long-time advocate of a Palestinian state. 'He could be a very useful ally in future and you should take care not to upset him and France. If he chooses, he could make your mission in Africa very difficult. Do this as a personal favour to Chirac. It is not a huge amount of money for you.'

The Colonel took all this on board, then delivered his verdict. First he instructed me to invite the Crown Prince, Jean-Paul Perrier and Hassan Tatanaki to Libya, in ten days' time. Gaddafi made sure that his chief of protocol Nuri Al Mismari made the call to the Crown Prince's office in the UAE using the mobile telephone network Thuraya, not a Libyan landline, because he didn't want Abdallah Senussi or Moussa Koussa eavesdropping.

The Colonel added: 'Go back to Paris tomorrow and tell them I will solve the problem.'

I waited for more details but none were forthcoming.

'Please don't send me back to France then make an announcement that will upset them,' I said, wondering what was in the Colonel's mind as I prepared to return to Paris to brief Perrier.

"You will have your answer in the morning," I told the Frenchman, keeping my fingers crossed.

The following day, at 9 a.m., it was announced on Al Jazeera news that Libya was sending its foreign minister, Shalgham, to France to make the agreement official. When the legal paperwork was drawn up it bore the signatures of Libyan government officials, not that of his son. That was a very public slap on the wrist for Saif.

A few days later the Crown Prince, Perrier and Tatanaki arrived in Libya to meet Gaddafi to shake hands formally on the deal. At the last minute, in a deliberate snub to his former opponent, the Colonel refused to greet Tatanaki. However, despite this, Tatanaki was relieved to be off the hook. Later, he called to express his gratitude for my intervention. Whether or not he ever told the Crown Prince that I'd helped save the day, or simply took the credit for himself, I still don't know.

Perrier was delighted and did not waste his new connection with Gaddafi, he was on board the first French private Jet to land in Tripoli after sanctions were lifted, enabling Thales to steal a march on its rivals. My reward for stepping in was to become Thales's consultant in the Middle East.

It was a very lucrative arrangement but the flip side was the certainty that I'd angered Gaddafi's son, who did not take kindly to being humiliated.

Chapter 16

Dark Days

Despite his support for Iraq in the first Gulf War, the Colonel was no friend of Saddam Hussein. He regarded him as a bully and a tyrant. To my knowledge, Gaddafi never invited his Iraqi counterpart to Libya and the contempt was mutual. On the occasions their paths crossed on neutral territory there were invariably angry clashes. The bad blood between the pair dated back to Gaddafi's support for Iran in its protracted war with Iraq in the 1980s. So, on a personal level, the Colonel shed no tears when his old sparring partner was overthrown by US-led coalition forces in 2003.

Yet, looking at the bigger picture, this was also very worrying for Gaddafi. Deep down he had grudging respect for how Saddam had clung on to power for so long. He was in his twenty-fourth year when he was toppled and, like Gaddafi, had survived despite daring to stand up to the West. Like it or not, there were parallels between the two regimes and the Colonel was not blind to that. The fall of Saddam convinced Gaddafi, more than ever, that seeking better relations with the US and Britain was the right path. The premise for the invasion of Iraq was its supposed programme of weapons of mass destruction. The Colonel was shaken when the West called Saddam's bluff and invaded after he refused to disarm. At the time, Libya had its own nuclear weapons programme and the British Prime Minister Tony Blair made it his crusade to persuade Gaddafi to give it up. At that stage sanctions against Libya were only suspended and Blair dangled the carrot of full lifting if Gaddafi toed the line. The pair developed a very warm relationship, although I never fully trusted the British leader's motives. I never met Blair, but one day, late in 2003, I happened to be in the Colonel's office when a call was put through from London. Gaddafi, who was suffering from a bad back at the time, was lying prone on a couch so spoke to his friend Tony on loud speaker. I was standing there with a sheaf of papers, ready for the leader's signature, and overhead the start of their conversation. This was not long after Saddam's capture and, before the usual pleasantries were exchanged, Gaddafi said he had something to tell the British prime minister.

'I don't like the way the photographs of Saddam being humiliated are all over the British media,' complained the Colonel, referring to images of the Iraqi leader's medical examination after capture by US forces. Saddam was shown being searched for head lice, and his mouth was held open while his teeth were checked.

Speaking through translators Gaddafi told Blair: 'This is not right. Saddam is a military man and the head of the army. He should be treated with respect and saluted by the most senior soldier. He should not be paraded on television.'

Before I retreated from the room, I heard Blair reply: 'The prime minister of Britain does not control the media.' This did not seem to satisfy Gaddafi, who said: 'I don't want to see anything like this happen again. Treating an Arab leader in this way only builds anger against America and Britain.' As I've stressed, respect and dignity mattered a lot to the Colonel even when it came to dealing with an enemy.

This ticking off for Blair didn't seem to cause any harm, as in March the following year their so-called 'deal in the desert' was signed. There was a sincere handshake between the Colonel and the British prime minister, who was making his first visit to Libya. Gaddafi confirmed his pledge to give up his quest for weapons of mass destruction. In exchange, Libya took another leap towards international redemption. A further outcome of the meeting in Gaddafi's tent was a gas contract, worth $200 million, for the British-Dutch company Shell. Another lucrative petroleum company deal, for BP, followed a few years later. Blair hailed the 'new relationship' between their countries and they agreed to fight together against extremism and terrorism. In many ways this unlikely alliance between Libya and the West made perfect sense, because both were afraid of the rise of the terrorist group al-Qaeda and Osama bin Laden. After the 9/11 attacks the almost unthinkable had happened: Gaddafi expressed his sympathy for the Americans. In the past, this devastating strike against the powerful West would have been a cause for celebration. Blair became a regular in Tripoli, continuing to visit even after he left office. The Colonel liked him a lot, and I never heard him say a bad word about the British prime minister.

One of the men who helped negotiate this historic deal was my nemesis Moussa Koussa, head of the intelligence office. He was suspected of having organised the supply of weapons and explosives to the Irish Republican Army for its terror campaign against Britain. It was barely twenty years since he'd been thrown out of Britain for threatening the lives of Libyan dissidents, but his shady past seemed to be forgotten. The visit by Blair opened the floodgates for other important political figures to come to Tripoli over the next few years, including Condoleezza Rice, the US Secretary of State, Italian Prime Minister Silvio Berlusconi and Nicolas Sarkozy, the president of France. Sarkozy and his first lady, Cecilia, took it upon themselves to intervene in the bizarre case of a group of Bulgarian nurses who were held in Libya accused of deliberately infecting children with HIV. Cecilia and Gaddafi became very close.

Another high-profile visitor was Vladimir Putin, whose visit came about after I mediated in a row between Russia and Libya over arms. It related to a 12-year-old old deal for Russian tanks, which were never delivered because sanctions got in the way. After the embargoes were lifted, Russia insisted on sending the tanks, in exchange for $4.5 billion, but Libya wanted to rip up the agreement because the armoured vehicles were by then outdated. It seemed that simmering resentment over the deal would sour relations between the two countries, but I managed to thrash out a compromise which involved the scrapping of the original deal and the signing of a $6 billion military and civilian contract for Russia, which included the supply of new tanks. As a gesture of goodwill it was also agreed that Putin would make a short visit to Libya, which was a huge coup for Gaddafi and a sign to the West that his compliance could not be taken for granted. Publicity shots of Putin and the Colonel standing in front of the monument of the American fighter jet being crushed in a giant Libyan fist left that in no doubt. Among all the politicians, I most admired Putin because he was a straight talker. The Americans could promise something and change their minds the next day, but Putin always delivered. Unfortunately, I never got the opportunity to meet him.

The year of Blair's visit, 2004, is memorable for different reasons. It should have been a time of great personal happiness but, instead, was one of the darkest periods of my life.

It just happened that two of my brothers, Firas and Ezalden, were getting married in the same year so we decided to arrange a joint celebration at The Four Seasons Hotel, in Amman, for 600 people.

Although he was only eight years younger than me, Firas was like a son. I mollycoddled him when he was at school, while our father was often away in Saudi Arabia for work, and gave him a home at my flat in London when he was studying Business Administration. There were many distractions in London and I tried to keep Firas focused on his studies. At the time we sometimes fought like cat and dog, as he rebelled against my interference, but there was always a close bond.

After graduating, Firas spent a couple of years in the United States before setting up a company selling supplies, such as blankets and uniforms, to the military. I introduced him to my contacts in Libya, including Gaddafi, and he used my office in Tripoli as his base. The Colonel liked Firas and had promised to travel to Jordan for the wedding.

With four days to go I was staying with my parents in Amman, so that I could help with last-minute preparations. I was enjoying the party atmosphere with the rest of the family and the two brides, Noora and Lana.

Their dress designer had flown in from Lebanon and there was great excitement as everyone got a first glimpse of his creations. The two brothers and a cousin were in Libya, where Firas had many friends, delivering invitations and staying out from under our feet.

I was due to try on my own outfit for the wedding, but a little incident during rehearsals unnerved me. Noora's tiara kept slipping to the floor and the hairdresser told me this was a sign of bad luck. A sense of foreboding swept over me and, making some excuse, I left the party early to return to my own home.

In the early hours of the following day, my niece Cecilia, who'd flown in from America for the wedding with my sister Linda, answered the phone at my house. It was my brother, Ezalden, calling from Libya and asking for me. Still half asleep, I heard crying then a scream and the words: 'Firas is dead.'

Next the line disconnected, leaving me wondering if I could trust my ears. I didn't want to believe what I'd just heard, because Firas was 31 years old and appeared to be in perfect health. He was into bodybuilding and spent many hours working out in the gym. Immediately I dialled the president's office, although it was 3 a.m.

'This can't be true,' I was told. 'We saw him only a few hours ago, but we will make some calls.'

About fifteen minutes later the phone rang again. It was Gaddafi's office confirming the terrible news. I swear, I felt the earth tremble beneath my feet.

I was in blind shock, but also in denial. My sisters were wailing around me. When I called Noora and Lana who were still at my parents' home, the two young women collapsed.

Over the next few hours, by speaking to our cousin Aehab in Libya, I was gradually able to piece together what had happened. It emerged that they were all enjoying a barbecue at their villa in Tripoli the previous afternoon, when Firas began complaining about a sore hand. He set out with a driver to go to a pharmacy and pick up some painkillers but waved away offers by the others to accompany him, insisting it was nothing to worry about. They'd barely left when my brother began suffering chest pains and diverted the car to hospital. Even then it did not seem too serious – the driver later described how Firas was able to walk into the building unaided and lie down in an examination room. My brother was being checked by a doctor when he suddenly stretched out his arms, detaching the monitors that were on his body, and cried out. He'd suffered a massive heart attack and, despite being in hospital, could not be saved. The main artery was blocked and the only explanation the medics could give was Firas's high protein diet, along with the supplements he took for his bodybuilding. How was I going to tell my poor parents?

My mother, who never really recovered from the heart attack and brain damage she'd suffered when I was married, had memory loss. Sometimes there would be a spark and she'd recognise us but often she just sat in a wheelchair, in her own world and unable to communicate, until her eventual death in 2007. It was a blessing that Firas's death just washed over her, but my father was a different matter.

Baba, as we all called him, was also in bad health following a serious road accident a few years earlier. Travelling home from work, his car was involved in a head-on collision which killed his driver. Baba was in hospital for six months, where his entire face was rebuilt. He also had diabetes and high blood pressure, but his brain was still sharp. I feared that suddenly learning of the death of his son could kill him. So I gave instructions for the telephone line at his house to be disconnected. Then I went to my father's home, told him I felt unwell, and asked him to come with me to hospital where I'd arranged for the family doctor to be waiting to treat me.

My eyes were red with crying and Baba asked: 'What's wrong?'

I brushed away his concern, telling him I had allergies and begged him not to ask further questions.

Arriving at hospital, I initially told my father only that Firas had been gravely injured in an accident. We persuaded him to take a sedative then, as it took effect a few minutes later, the moment could be put off no longer.

'Baba, I have to tell you Firas has died,' I said, holding his hand as my shattering words sank in. 'Pray for him.'

It's not the natural order for a child to die before his parent, and my father had waited so long for a first healthy son to carry on the family line. I have never witnessed such raw grief, as Baba began screaming and fell to the ground. I had agonised over deceiving him, but as I watched him being given oxygen and morphine I knew that preparing him gradually for the loss of his son was the right course to take. He never got over the death of Firas. Gaddafi offered a private jet and before dawn the following morning I was waiting at Amman airport, with my sisters, when Firas came home in circumstances no one envisaged a few days earlier. Our father insisted on being present, arriving by ambulance. Ezalden, who was on the flight from Tripoli, was in a terrible state. My brother's body was taken to hospital, where we were still clinging to the forlorn hope that it was all some sort of terrible mistake. The screams and uncontrollable sobbing of my sisters when the coffin was opened and they saw Firas lying lifeless told me everything.

From helping to arrange his wedding, now I was organising my little brother's funeral. Hundreds of people who had received invitations to the celebration now had to be contacted and, like us, they could not believe Firas was dead. Among the mourners at the funeral were a Libyan government delegation, and many of my brother's friends from the country.

The funeral was followed by forty days of mourning, as is traditional in the Muslim world, and throughout them all I tried to stay strong. When I was a young woman my father made me head of the family in his absences and I still carried this heavy burden, trying to take everything on my shoulders. That's just the way I am, but sometimes the load becomes too much. On the forty-first day I could bear the loss of my brother no longer and collapsed, worn out with grief. You are not meant to have a favourite sibling, but among all my brothers and sisters Firas was most dear to me. His death, at such a young age and so unexpected, destroyed me. I felt utterly lost, and did not know where to turn. My brother's picture was everywhere in my father's house and the time came when I had to escape.

When my marriage broke up I fled to Libya, but this time I retreated to London. For eight months I didn't work, passing my days in a haze. I took long walks, usually in Hyde Park, sat alone in coffee shops or watched television for hours on end. Occasionally I'd burst into tears for no reason, or when something triggered a memory. I hoped to clear my head, but my brain was flooded with the happy times I'd spent in London with Firas when he was studying. At night I couldn't sleep and eventually I sought help from a psychiatrist. Talking helped, as did the arrival of my daughter Noor from Jordan in the summer holidays, but finally the time came when I felt able to return to Libya.

I wanted to be busy again, and regain some sense of normality, but as soon as I arrived in Tripoli I had the very painful task of clearing my brother's villa. Gaddafi had ordered that the place be sealed after Firas died, so nothing had been touched since he enjoyed the barbecue with his brother and cousin on his final day alive. With a heavy heart and more tears I packed his possessions, for carriage back to Jordan. It's strange how an entire life can be consigned to a few boxes.

Meeting the Colonel for the first time since Firas's death, and still dressed in black for mourning, I was touched by his compassion. As I entered the room, Gaddafi stood, embraced me and placed his hands on top of my head. 'You have lost your brother, which is God's wish, but now you can consider me your brother and father,' he said.

I noticed his eyes were brimming with tears. This was the other face of Gaddafi; the side that no one talks or writes about. It's this memory, of the man who cried for my dead brother, that I try to keep.

There was always something to keep me occupied in Libya and I remained there for three weeks, before returning to Jordan.

Chapter 17

The Colonel and his Lovers

Fending off the unwelcome attention of amorous men went with the territory in Libya, but in all my years working for Gaddafi he never once made a pass at me.

That might come as a surprise, because he has a reputation in the West as an out-of-control womaniser, serial rapist and abuser. You might assume that no woman was safe in his company.

My intention is not to defend, or judge, the Colonel. I cannot pretend to know everything about his life, or what happened behind closed doors. I can only share what I saw, heard or was told. However, this common portrayal of Gaddafi as a sexual predator troubles me. It does not tally with the man I knew.

He was no angel – far from it. Gaddafi had affairs, but that does not set him apart from prime ministers and presidents of Western countries, or princes in the Middle East. He was not the first, and will not be the last, world leader to use his power in that way but his relationships with women were complex.

Under Gaddafi's rule, female literacy improved dramatically in Libya as he increased the number of years girls spent at school. Women were encouraged to attend university and take professional jobs, such as in medicine and the law.

The more I came to understand Gaddafi's personality, the more I realised that he put women into two distinct compartments. In the first were those he respected and who would not be touched; in the second were women he treated as his playthings.

On one of my early visits to Libya in the late 1980s I was introduced to a woman of about my own age. She was another of Gaddafi's bodyguards and offered to show me the sights. We'd chatted a few times and, by then a little bored with my own company and the sight of the walls of my hotel room, I was open to making new friends.

We passed a pleasant afternoon together, driving in the Tripoli suburbs and the surrounding countryside. Afterwards I thought little more about her until Naima, my friend from the Women's Union and also one of Gaddafi's guards, took me to one side. She warned me to be wary of this woman, claiming that my new friend was the president's lover. Apparently she'd met Gaddafi while studying and he'd later arranged coveted membership of the Revolutionary Nuns. By the time I met her, she and the Colonel had been in a relationship, which was an open secret among his inner circle, for about five years. She was attractive, with long dark hair, and clever. It was easy to see why a man would be drawn to her.

Despite the warning from Naima, I liked the woman and we became close. She told me that while she was studying, Gaddafi used to pay for her books. On the morning of an exam, for good luck, he would play music down the phone line. It was always by the same female singer, called Fairuz, who was very popular across the Arab world at the time.

Over time I became a confidante of Gaddafi's lover, although I was not blind to the risks. One day she revealed to me that, earlier in their relationship, she'd become pregnant by him. She told me that the Colonel wanted her to keep the baby, but refused to marry her. Muslim custom allowed him to have up to four wives but taking a mistress was another matter, so the relationship was kept hidden from the Libyan people. Furious at his refusal to take the honourable course, she terminated the pregnancy.

I can't verify her story, but I have no reason to disbelieve her. I think she confided in me because I was an outsider, and she just wanted someone to turn to. On my next visit I was told that she had fled the country.

I heard that she was living in Egypt, where she'd got married to another man and had a baby girl. Much later she returned to Libya, when she tried to rekindle the relationship with Gaddafi but he wanted nothing to do with her. We picked up our old friendship, but eventually lost touch. I have no idea where she is now; some say she is in Paris.

I don't draw any conclusions, good or bad, about Gaddafi's behaviour towards this young woman but hope the story provides a little more insight into his character.

It has been claimed that the whole idea of the Revolutionary Nuns was nothing but a front. The women have been described as Gaddafi's hand-picked harem and, following his death, there were allegations by some that they were sexually abused by the leader and his aides.

The bodyguards, including Naima, never complained to me about Gaddafi's behaviour. I got to know many of them, because if you wanted access to Gaddafi you first had to get past the formidable Revolutionary Nuns.

The myth has been created that the job description included good looks, but that was not the case. He surrounded himself with these women because they were loyal, trustworthy and could not be bribed. It just happened that Western newspapers, which were obsessed with Gaddafi's troupe of female guards, only published photographs of the most attractive.

The same went for his nurses, usually from the Ukraine. Gaddafi was obsessed about his health and they were always on hand to check his cholesterol, his blood pressure, and his diet. From what I observed, he kept relations with the nurses professional for security reasons. Why would he take a nurse for a mistress and risk her poisoning him with an injection if she became jealous?

I spent a lot of time around his office, in the compound, which was separate from his home. He had a bedroom there, so that he could rest for a few hours during the day or sleep overnight if he was working late.

I can say, hand on heart, that I never witnessed Gaddafi force himself on any woman, but that's not to say he didn't take advantage of his position. There was a procession of women who threw themselves at Gaddafi. Delegations would arrive from Africa and women, dressed provocatively and with their breasts on display, would flock to see him. By behaving like hookers these women, who were half his age, hoped Gaddafi would look favourably upon their countries. I don't doubt he used them for sex, because it was put on a plate, and they exploited him in return.

Officially, Mabrouka Sherif had responsibility for organising visits by female dignitaries, but her unofficial role was to arrange women for Gaddafi's pleasure. She's been described as the madam of his brothel and, sometimes, I'd see five or six women arriving together so that he could take his pick. I don't think he cared, or was embarrassed, that I witnessed this. I didn't interfere in this aspect of his personal life, although in the last years of Gaddafi's rule I became increasingly worried about the growing influence of Mabrouka. She was poorly educated, and could barely sign her own name, but in the last ten years of his rule she steadily exerted a greater hold on him.

She practised black magic, which she learned on visits to southern African countries. Although Gaddafi had no interest in her witchcraft he tolerated it because she was totally without scruples and did his bidding – no questions asked. She operated mainly at night time, working from the Colonel's office which, along with her dark hair, black eyes and pale skin, only added to her air of menace. Mabrouka, who was in her thirties when I first met her, never wore make-up and usually kept her head covered. She wore traditional Arab dress, invariably black, and was said to have a fondness for diamonds. The Colonel kept a supply to give as gifts to the wives of African leaders and rumour had it that a few ended up in Mabrouka's pockets.

Like Abdullah Senussi she had family ties to the leader, having been married to one of Gaddafi's cousins. Another trait she shared with Senussi was jealousy of anyone whom she feared was getting too close to the Colonel. I never felt comfortable around her and she made it perfectly clear she didn't like me either.

I despised the way in which she procured women for the president, who gave her the meaningless title 'head of his private office'. Everyone knew exactly what she did. It was dirty work and I wanted nothing to do with Mabrouka. She used to phone Gaddafi all the time, saying: 'I have a new girl for you.' When she was around, the Colonel had no interest in running the country.

There was one woman the Colonel desired who did not reciprocate his strong feelings. He adored the former US Secretary of State Condoleezza Rice, describing her as his 'African princess'. The Colonel kept a scrap book full of photographs of Rice and composed a song in her honour. He was always drawn to powerful women with black skin and Condoleezza Rice made him weak at the knees.

'I admire and am very proud of the way she leans back and gives orders to the Arab leaders... Leezza, Leezza, Leezza,' he said in an interview with Al Jazeera in 2007. 'I love her very much. I admire her very much because she's a black woman of African origin.'

It was more like a schoolboy crush, and I noticed that Gaddafi was not entirely comfortable around the opposite sex. When he was first introduced to a woman he would sometimes look at the ground, avoiding eye contact.

One incident sticks in my mind, which began innocently enough when a businessman came to Libya from Switzerland at my request. I managed to arrange a meeting with Gaddafi at his desert camp near Sirte, which finished late in the afternoon.

As we were wrapping up a currency deal, the guy said out of the blue: 'My wife is back at the hotel and she is dying to meet you.'

My reaction was one of annoyance. Why didn't he simply ask to bring his wife along in the first place, and she could have shaken hands with the president when the talks were over?

Gaddafi, however, was used to this type of request and took the inconvenience in his stride. He agreed to see the wife briefly the following morning, at a military base, and I accompanied her.

The Colonel greeted her warmly, while I slipped away to the adjacent kitchen to arrange drinks. When I returned the pair of them had vanished, leaving one of Gaddafi's female bodyguards to explain that he'd taken her to the library to show her some book or other.

She returned alone, about thirty minutes later, smiling and laughing. The woman, who was Iranian, gave her earrings to the guard as a gesture of thanks. She was obviously delighted to have been granted this special audience with Gaddafi and flattered by his attention.

Then, as we left the base in an official limousine to return to her hotel, she began crying.

'What's wrong?' I asked, wondering if she had fallen ill.

'President Gaddafi raped me and I'm scared what my husband will say,' she replied, to my absolute astonishment.

To this day I have no idea what happened while she and the Colonel were together, but I clearly recall her good mood and the gift to the bodyguard. It was not the behaviour of a woman who'd just been attacked.

Nothing more was said and the following morning I met the couple at Sirte airport, from where we were due to fly to Tripoli in the businessman's private jet. Also on board the jet were Mohamed El Huwej, the LAFICO chairman, Nuri Al-Mismari, head of the Libyan protocol office, and five of the businessman's assistants.

Of all my experiences in Libya, nothing prepared me for what happened next.

We'd hardly taken off for the short flight to the capital when the businessman pulled out a gun, pointed it at us and accused Gaddafi of attacking his wife. He was demanding $70 million compensation, which would also guarantee our safe release.

It took a few seconds for it to sink in that we were being hijacked! He was in his sixties and I couldn't imagine a more unlikely hostage-taker. This was so ludicrous that I didn't even feel frightened, as we were told we were heading for Germany.

It didn't take long for the unauthorised change of course to alert air traffic control, and we were soon being shadowed by two Libyan fighter jets. All the time negotiations were continuing with a remarkably calm Al-Mismari, who soon managed to persuade our hijacker that he had no hope of escape. I think the sight of the military jets brought him to his senses, and he really had no intention of killing everyone by firing a gun in the pressurised cabin. His plan was insane.

The hijacking was over almost as quickly as it began and we landed safely in Tripoli, where police and security services swarmed over the aircraft.

Looking back I am convinced the entire episode, including the alleged rape, was a clumsy plot to blackmail Gaddafi. This unscrupulous couple assumed he would be willing to pay millions of dollars to protect his reputation.

In any other country a hijacker would have been locked away for decades, but this was Libya. He was simply disarmed, his plane refuelled and he and his wife were sent on their way home. The Libyans took the view that throwing a Swiss citizen in jail, at a time when the focus was on mending relations with the West, would only undermine all the hard work. They did not want a diplomatic crisis and knew that the claim about Gaddafi attacking a woman would have been reported globally without question.

It was a crazy episode which I share only to show that not everything you have heard, or read, about the Colonel should be taken at face value.

Chapter 18

The King of Kings

The years after sanctions were lifted was a golden era for Gaddafi. World leaders were beating a path to his door, Libya was prospering as foreign investment poured in, and he was finally getting the respect that he felt was due to an elder statesman.

It all went to his head, as his sense of self-importance became over-inflated. There was a growing arrogance, which seemed to stem from a belief that now he'd made peace with the US and Britain he was untouchable. I've remarked that in many ways Gaddafi was a humble man, who never forgot his Bedouin roots, but I saw this quality less and less. The Colonel counted Tony Blair among his friends, Berlusconi of Italy was photographed kissing his hand, and he toured European capitals. He'd never had it so good.

In 2007, I was part of the 400-strong delegation with the Colonel on the first leg of his European trip to France and Spain. Gaddafi delighted Parisians by pitching his Bedouin tent near the Élysée Palace. The French were equally fascinated by his posse of female bodyguards, who drew more headlines than the lucrative trade and arms deals agreed between France and Libya. The Colonel added to the theatrics by dressing in his desert robes and bringing a camel. He visited Versailles, sailed down the river Seine and dined with dignitaries at the Ritz Hotel. The tent was largely for show as he stayed in the sumptuous Hotel Marigny, a nineteenth-century mansion close to the president's palace that serves as an official guest house for state visits.

The first official visit to France for thirty-five years was further evidence of his rehabilitation. He was being warmly embraced by European leaders who'd recently shunned him. By that time Nicolas Sarkozy was in power and it has since been alleged that Gaddafi, who had previously entertained Sarkozy in Tripoli, helped fund the French president's election win.

The icing on the cake was the visit of Condoleezza Rice to Tripoli in 2008. The Secretary of State was the most senior US official to visit

Libya in more than half a century and the Colonel was convinced it was only a matter of time before an American president followed to Libya, or he was welcomed to the White House. His days as an outcast were over, and he must take credit for engineering the remarkable transformation. However, he let a great opportunity slip through his fingers.

During this period, I recall an unguarded conversation with some of his closest aides, including Moussa Koussa.

We were discussing the change in the Colonel's behaviour and I told them: 'You have to wake him up. The path he is taking is dangerous and will finish him. You have to tell the president that his ego will kill him. He is behaving like a god.'

Gaddafi became ultra-sensitive to criticism and I recall one incident from this period, involving a magazine called *Al-Majaleh* which was owned by the Saudi government. The Colonel took exception to an article about him and his daughter, which he considered to be offensive. Unfortunately for me, the author happened to be Jordanian and I was woken in the middle of the night by Nuri Al Mismari, the chief of protocol, who informed me that a furious Gaddafi wanted to summon the Jordanian ambassador in Tripoli for a dressing down. I happened to be in Libya at the time, so was given the duty of organising the meeting –immediately. The official, Al Sherif Fawaz Al-Zaben, was roused from his bed and hauled in front of the angry leader at 2 a.m. The ambassador tried to apologise, but the Colonel was so furious that he insisted on raising the issue with King Abdullah who visited Libya two days later. My king also tried to calm matters with an apology for the behaviour of his citizen but Gaddafi was in no mood to back down. I heard much later that the journalist was handed over to Libya by the Jordanian intelligence office, for 'questioning'.

The Gaddafi I first encountered in 1988 had the same revolutionary verve that had swept him to power in 1969. He cared about women's rights, fought to solve his country's differences with the West and was a popular leader. Gaddafi loved to think he had everything in common with his heroes, such as Nasser and Castro.

He'd often tell me: 'Don't call me a politician. I am a revolutionary.'

But gradually, from about 2005 onwards, he began to take his eye off the ball. The Colonel lost touch with his revolutionary side.

George Bush Snr., Mr Trammell Crow, Mrs Crow, and his son and daughter with family at Mr Crow's house.

Hanan Ashrawi (the former Minister of foreign affairs of the Palestinian Authority) and Mohammad Bukhari (the former Libyan Minister of Treasury) and I, at the IMF meeting in New York.

Photographs of Shimon Peres and I in Tel Aviv.

Trammell Crow, his wife and I.

Trammell Crow, Mohammad Al-Bukhari (the former Libyan Minister Treasurer) and I at Trammell Crow's office in Texas.

My wedding crown, designed by Angela Kelly, the Personal Assistant, Adviser and Curator to Queen Elizabeth II.

At the airport in Amman, reunited with my daughter Noor after one year and nine months of detention in Libya.

His Majesty King Abdullah of Jordan and I at his office in Jordan.

Another photograph of His Majesty King Abdullah of Jordan and I in his office in Jordan.

My daughter Noor when she was nine years old, with Prince Al-Waleed Bin Talal on the plane during his last visit to Libya.

Prince Al-Waleed Bin Talal and I on his boat in Cannes where we agreed on the plane deal.

Salmeh, head of Military Security Guards for Gaddafi, and I.

Gaddafi and Salmeh.

Muammar Gaddafi, Fathieh from the Revolutionary Guard and I during his last trip to Paris.

Mohammad Al Zwai, his wife and I in London. Al Zwai was handling the Lockerbie negotiation case and he was the ambassador to Libya in England.

My barrister Clive Freedman, my lawyer Richard Waller when I was meeting the reporters after I won the case against Prince Al Waleed.

Mrs Hillary Clinton and I.

Photographs taken when I was reunited with my father after I was released from Libya, with my uncle and my daughter's nanny at Amman airport.

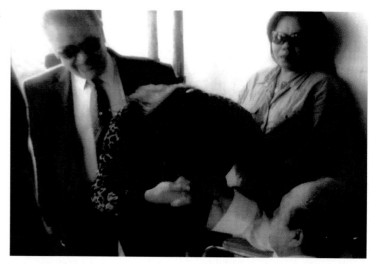

Mrs Hillary Clinton, Oshwal, Amar Singh and I with other guests at dinner.

Me with my daughter Noor when she graduated from UCL university in London.

Chief of Indian Muslims Community at his house in India, when I handed him a letter from Gaddafi.

Members of my staff and I, at my company in Jordan. They were with me for over twenty years and they played a big role in my success. From left to right; Mr. Sharab (Development Manager), Mr Awajneh (private colleague), Ms Noor (Marketing Manager), Ms Lina (Secretary), Mrs Huda (Office Manager), Mrs Nuha (Deputy), and Mr Khashman (Lawyer and Legal Advisor).

Muammar Gaddafi during his trip to Jordan when he stopped to drink coffee from a street man.

Muammar Gaddafi during his visit to Jordan when he stopped to play football with a child.

Muammar Gaddafi, kissing the hand of the child who played football with him. Salmeh also appears in the picture.

My daughter and me.

Gaddafi had grand designs on southern Africa, scattering Libyan oil revenue across the continent in an attempt to buy favour. Cash which would have been better spent solving problems at home was lavished on mosques, named in his honour, in Uganda and Tanzania, and a host of other questionable schemes.

He was frequently absent at African Union events, but the crowning glory of his delusions of grandeur was when he accepted the ludicrous title 'King of Kings'.

It was bestowed by 200 traditional African leaders at a ceremony in Benghazi, in 2008. A preening Gaddafi sat on a throne while they danced around him. It was a ridiculous spectacle, but convinced the Colonel that he was right to pursue his dream of creating a new superpower – a sort of United States of Africa, with its own currency, army and passport. Millions of dollars were sent from Libya to prop up the proposed new currency, the gold dinar, which never materialised. As far as I know the cash never returned to Libya and is still floating around somewhere in Africa. Someone got very rich at Libya's expense.

Gaddafi began meddling in the affairs of state of other African nations, by removing politicians who were not sympathetic and encouraging uprisings. He was completely obsessed with Africa and would drop everything to deal with any problem that arose on the continent. He proposed marriages between Libyans and people from other African countries, with the idea of making his country 'more black'.

Many years earlier, he had a similar dream for a pan-Arab state which also came to nought. He didn't learn his lesson: that countries valued their independence too much to throw in their lot with the unpredictable Libyan leader. Despite his improved image there was still mistrust of his motives.

Gaddafi tried to move the headquarters of the African Union to his home town, Sirte, and paid a large chunk of the organisation's running costs. He even got to redesign the AU flag in his favourite green.

In my opinion, Gaddafi lost the ability to make sound judgements in the last four years of his life. It has been suggested that he was mentally ill, and although his mind appeared as sharp as ever, I believe he was suffering from depression. He was reflecting on his life and resented having sacrificed his best years. On several occasions he told me that the goals of the revolution had not been achieved. He'd set out to fight imperialism but ended up bowing down to the West. He was a bitter man, also believing he didn't get the gratitude he deserved from his people.

Everyone around him could see it was going to end badly, but either he wouldn't listen or his advisors were scared to question the leader.

Once I told Gaddafi: 'You have always been opposed to titles and now they put a crown on your head and call you the King of Africa. This is wrong. Now when I see your name written in the newspaper all the titles before your name fill half the page.'

His response? Nothing but an enigmatic smile.

The following year he achieved his ambition of becoming chairman of the African Union, further fuelling his ego. Africa was his vanity project.

It's academic, but I wonder now whether the solving of the Lockerbie issue and the lifting of sanctions actually sealed his fate? All the time Libya was an outsider there existed a siege mentality which united the country. When the embargoes were gone there was nothing to keep him busy and bind the different tribal factions in Libya.

I never got any sense at that time that people were turning against him, but you could hear the grumbling in the background. Libyans could travel abroad after air embargoes ended and compared their own country, often unfavourably, with other nations. Foreign companies were welcomed by Gaddafi with open arms, makings fortunes, but corruption and bureaucracy prevented ordinary Libyans from thriving. A few people became very wealthy, but the majority continued to struggle.

I also warned Gaddafi about corruption, which was still rife, but he didn't act. Perhaps naively, after sanctions were lifted I expected Libya to follow international laws and become more civilised but little changed.

The Colonel became more short-tempered, and would frequently storm out of meetings if matters weren't going his way.

I got the impression that he was becoming tired. Don't forget that by the mid-2000s he'd been in power for almost four decades. He was 65 years old, the pensionable age in many countries, and he seemed to care less and less about what was happening in Libya.

Gaddafi gave his best years to his country, made many sacrifices, and I think he woke up one day and felt old. He'd been in power since man first landed on the Moon and during his rule there had been seven US presidents.

In 2007, life expectancy in Libya was 72 years, compared with 78 and 79 in the US and Britain. The Colonel tried to fight against the ageing process, by dyeing his hair, but it was a sensitive subject. All the money in the world could not make him young again.

He had power, but he craved ordinariness. In Libya he couldn't visit a restaurant or a market without being mobbed. He used to ask me very innocuous questions about how I passed my spare time and I might answer that I'd been to some restaurant or other.

His eyes would light up and he'd demand: 'Tell me about it. What did you eat? Describe the food. Did you enjoy it?' They were the sort of questions a child would ask.

It was as if he wished we could swap places, even just for one night. There's no doubt Gaddafi lapped up the adulation that came with his power, but sometimes he just wanted to be normal.

It was also obvious to me that he was struggling to control his children, who took advantage when he was out of the country on African Union business.

He wasn't blind to the threat they posed, telling me once: 'If you have a relationship with me, you don't have a relationship with any other member of my family. If you are a friend of my children then you are not my friend.'

I'm often asked what Gaddafi's children were like but, for the reason I've outlined, I never really got to know any of them. The Colonel often despaired of their outlandish behaviour and extravagant habits. In Libya it was possible to keep a lid on their antics, but they left a trail of chaos in their wake when they travelled abroad. There were reports of fights in nightclubs, drinking, mistreatment of domestic staff and drug-taking. I know that Gaddafi resorted to imprisoning his own sons to try to bring them under control.

At one stage there were rumours that Gaddafi was grooming his second son Saif to succeed him as leader. Born in 1972, Saif tried to cultivate an image as a moderniser. In contrast to his father's Bedouin robes, he preferred designer suits and was a regular at Annabel's nightclub in London. He kept a pair of pet Bengal tigers, which he took with him to Austria when he was studying there. He was also educated at the London School of Economics, but there was a scandal over a £1.5 million donation from his charitable foundation, with some alleging he'd bought his qualification.

I'd seen at first-hand how Saif tried to take credit for the UTA and Lockerbie breakthroughs. He was close to Abdullah Senussi in the intelligence office.

I considered Saif a very dangerous and untrustworthy man. The row over his degree was typical of his approach, which seemed to be to buy his way out of any problem.

Tackling the Colonel on the persistent whispers I'd heard about Saif becoming leader, I said: 'If this is the case then let me brief the King of Jordan, so he can prepare the US.'

I felt that King Abdullah, who had very good relations with the West, could help smooth the path of succession.

Gaddafi was adamant it was not happening, but I persisted, asking: 'After you die, who is going to handle Libya?'

I was shocked by his reply. 'I don't care,' he said. 'Me first, then to Hell afterwards. I don't care what happens.'

Another of his sons, Mutassim, had a very public affair with a Dutch model who'd once appeared in *Playboy*. Gaddafi despaired of the lot of them but took pride in the achievements of his only daughter, Aisha. She was nicknamed 'the Claudia Schiffer of North Africa' because of her dyed blonde hair and elegant clothes but became a lawyer and goodwill ambassador for the United Nations. Aisha never caused me any problems.

Incidentally, I can also shed light on one of the enduring mysteries of Gaddafi's reign. He always claimed that his adopted daughter, Hana, was killed in the US bombing raid on his Tripoli compound in 1986. However, doubt was cast on her death with a series of reported sightings in following years. Some insisted this was a different girl, but I can confirm that Hana is alive. She was injured in the US attack but continued to live in Gaddafi's house after she recovered. It was no secret in Libya that she'd survived.

I believe Gaddafi loved Hana more than his own daughter, which was a source of friction. Gaddafi's children would tell her: 'You are not our sister. Never forget that.'

Hana kept a low profile, not only to try to continue the propaganda myth of her death at the hands of the Americans but because Gaddafi's children were jealous of the attention he lavished on her.

I met her on several occasions, including once at the theatre where she was attending a concert when she was about 15 years old. The musician was Hani Shaker, who'd performed at my wedding, and I happened to be sitting next to Hana. She was a simple girl and at the end of the show she handed me her diary, which she asked me to give to Shaker to sign.

By the time I'd arranged this Hana had disappeared, so I took the diary back to my hotel. She kept a daily journal and I couldn't resist reading a few of the entries. It was obvious she had emotional problems and was affected by the death of her genetic parents when she was a baby.

Hana, who became a doctor, is now married with her own children. I was told the marriage was arranged by Gaddafi's wife, Safia. Following the fall of her father Hana spent time in Algeria, before settling in Cairo where she still lives.

Chapter 19

An Unlikely Peacemaker

One day in the summer of 2008 I was sitting at my desk in Amman when my mobile rang. The caller announced herself as a secretary from the office of Shimon Peres, the president of Israel.

My first instinct was that this was some sort of practical joke, or dirty trick by Gaddafi's intelligence office, so I ended the call immediately. In all my years in business in the Arab world I'd had zero dealings with Israel, and that suited me just fine. Given my Palestinian heritage, it doesn't take a genius to conclude where my sympathies lie. What on earth could Israel want with me?

However the caller was persistent, ringing twice more, and eventually my curiosity got the better of me. I agreed to listen although, if she was genuine and word got back to Gaddafi that I was so much as speaking to a sworn enemy, I had much to lose. My numerous Arab business contacts would doubtless also take a dim view of any perceived collusion with Israel. It did cross my mind that I was committing career suicide, but I pressed on.

A meeting was proposed, with two Israeli government advisors, and I now felt it was prudent to inform the Jordanian intelligence office. First, I wanted to confirm this was not an elaborate hoax; second I needed to cover my own back. Nothing had been said but I was certain this involved Libya and was nothing to do with my own business interests.

I was surprised to discover that not only was the Jordanian intelligence service aware of Israel's interest, but had also handed over my telephone number! It was all very cloak-and-dagger. However, now I had the blessing of the Jordanian government I was a little less on edge.

The meeting place was Amman airport, where the two Israeli officials were still giving little away. I gleaned only, as I'd suspected, that my Libya connections were behind the approach and it was proposed that I fly to Tel Aviv for talks.

My next step, the moment Libya was confirmed as the subject matter, was to inform Gaddafi, but I had no intention of alerting the likes of Mabrouka Sherif, Abdullah Senussi or Moussa Koussa. Bypassing the Libyan intelligence office I called Salma Milad, another of the female bodyguards and someone I trusted with my life. The Colonel appeared to share my opinion because, at the time, Salma was one of the most senior women in the Libyan army, holding the rank of colonel. Almost as tall as the Colonel, and beautiful with it, Salma fitted the Western stereotype of the guards. However she wasn't selected by Gaddafi for her looks, having been trained by the Soviet military. When she was not clad in her customary camouflage fatigues, Salma loved European clothes. Unlike the three characters I've just mentioned, she was totally honest and possessed a good heart.

Word soon came back from Salma that Gaddafi, sharing my sense of curiosity, was content for me to meet the Israelis and find out what they wanted.

It was made clear, however, that I must not give any indication that Gaddafi either approved or knew about the meeting. I would not be representing Libya, merely acting in a private capacity, which was not unusual under the terms of my arrangement with LAFICO.

The flight time from Amman to Tel Aviv, by private jet supplied by Israel, is a mere forty-five minutes, but I was entering new territory.

Never in my life did I think I'd have any reason to visit Israel, and on arrival the subterfuge continued. No passport, no visa, no stamp. Officially this July visit wasn't happening.

From the airport I was driven by limousine, with blacked-out windows, to a city centre hotel which was crawling with security men. In a suite on the third floor I was introduced to Shimon Peres, the ninth president of Israel, who extended his hand in greeting. You know by now that I am no diplomat and emotions got the better of me.

'I cannot shake hands with you, because you are killing Palestinians every day in Gaza,' I said.

The smile did not leave Peres's face. 'Sit down Mrs Sharab, I am pleased to meet you,' he replied, calmly. If he took offence, the veteran politician was wise enough to show no outward sign.

Finally the reason for Israel reaching out to me was explained, and it took all my powers to prevent my mouth gaping open in disbelief.

'The intermediary between Israel and the Palestinians is President Mubarak of Egypt,' Peres began. 'But we feel a fresh approach is required. It is my intention to solve the Gaza issue by signing some sort of agreement with the Palestinians. We believe that President Gaddafi would be an ideal middle man. Will he help us?'

It was an extraordinary request. Gaddafi the terrorist. Gaddafi the pariah. Now, if I could believe my ears, Gaddafi the peacemaker.

Continuing, Peres explained that the Colonel was perfectly placed to take this role because Libya had no border with Israel. Old animosities between the two nations were ideological, not over land. Furthermore, Libya was a wealthy nation which did not need financial favours from anyone. In brief, Peres was confident that the Colonel could not be bribed or blackmailed. Last but not least was Gaddafi's new status as a serious statesman.

His popularity in the Arab world was also cresting a wave so, despite his erratic behaviour, Peres was sure that Gaddafi would be acceptable to the Palestinians.

'We think he is the right man,' concluded President Peres. Whether or not that really was the case, the Colonel's stock had never been higher and Peres added: 'We are willing to fly to Libya, or meet him in a neutral country. At this stage we are simply testing the water. What do you think?'

The notion of Gaddafi welcoming Peres, or any other Israeli dignitaries, to Libya at that time was a non-starter but I didn't rule out the Colonel's involvement. Privately, I knew it would be a huge boost for his already swollen ego.

We kicked around a few possible venues and decided my own country, of which Gaddafi had fond memories, might be a good compromise.

The meeting with Shimon Peres lasted two hours.

When it was time for me to leave we both stood and said our farewells. In spite of myself I found myself warming to Peres, who'd shown an interest in my family background.

I believed he was sincere in his attempt to find a solution to the Gaza issue, and I liked the idea that I could be a force for good for the Palestinian people.

As we parted I made the first move to shake hands and kiss both his cheeks in the traditional Arab way. I felt I'd made my point when we were first introduced and a further slight would be churlish.

My next step was to report back to the Jordanian intelligence office and float the suggestion of a peace camp, with Gaddafi at its heart.

Jordan, which would gain kudos for taking the initiative, was happy to proceed but I knew that getting the Colonel on board would be much trickier. In some quarters, any negotiating with Israel would be interpreted as a sign of weakness and I feared Gaddafi would reject the Peres proposal entirely.

I briefed Salma, the bodyguard, by telephone and a few days later she called back with the Colonel's response.

'The president is willing to do this under one condition,' she said. 'The talks must be held in secret. If there is a successful outcome and a peace accord between the Palestinians and Israel is signed then he is happy for all the details, including his role, to be made public. But if there is no agreement then everything must remain secret.'

The Colonel did not want to take the risky step of sitting round a table with Israel, which would be bound to upset many Libyans, only to end up being associated with failure. In contrast, if the talks proved to be a triumph he took the view that the plaudits that would come his way for helping to broker a deal would outweigh the criticism.

It wasn't an unreasonable demand, but Gaddafi, clearly terrified of leaks, added a caveat. He decreed that if the talks ended in stalemate and details of the failed summit subsequently emerged then King Abdullah of Jordan must break his country's peace treaty with Israel.

The agreement, signed in 1994, had opened border crossings between Jordan and Israel. Full diplomatic relations had been restored, land disputes settled, precious water resources shared and trade deals agreed. Tourism between the two countries was encouraged, enabling holidaymakers to Israel to tack on a visit to the ancient stone-carved city of Petra, in Jordan. The agreement was a milestone in Jordanian history and my heart sank when I heard of this draconian condition imposed by the Colonel. It was near impossible to rule out leaks, and I knew Jordan would never agree to ripping up the peace treaty.

I reported back to my countrymen and it was just as I feared – such a condition was unacceptable.

Sadly, the proposed peace summit between the Palestinians and Israel, hosted by Jordan and with Gaddafi as the conduit, was already dead in the water.

There was a postscript a few weeks later when I was enjoying a few days' holiday in Wadi Rum, a beautiful desert valley in southern Jordan. My phone rang and it was Shimon Peres on the other end of the line, attempting to revive the plan. I promised to speak to Gaddafi when I was next in Libya, but both men went to their graves with no further progress on the matter.

Only a handful of people were ever in the loop, in Israel, Jordan and Libya. At the conclusion of my one and only meeting with Shimon Peres we posed together for a photograph, which was never intended to be made public. Until now I've always kept it hidden away and never discussed my visit to Israel with anyone. Yet I feel sufficient time has elapsed for me to reveal, for the first time, the remarkable story of how Gaddafi was once lined up to become a Middle East peacemaker. A leak can't harm anyone now.

It came to nothing but the Israel approach was more fuel for the Colonel's ego. He was suffering from a full-blown case of megalomania.

Also in 2008 he dispatched me to India, almost 4,000 miles distant from Tripoli, to forge new alliances.

The sub-continent and world's largest democracy might, at first glance, appear a strange target for Gaddafi but there was some method in his madness. India is home to 172 million Muslims and, at the time of my visit, there were more than 18,000 of its nationals working in Libya. Many of them were employed in the health sector, or laboured on Gaddafi's great man-made river – a vast irrigation scheme which carried water underground in 1,700 miles of pipes to northern Libyan cities. Libyan oil found its way to India, while machinery and electrical equipment flowed back in return.

I was handed a list of about forty prominent Indians, from many walks of life, and told to seek introductions. The plan was to invite them to Libya, to further strengthen links between the two countries. Way back in 1984, Indira Gandhi had visited Libya, so there were historical ties. Gaddafi also proposed making an official visit to India, which he regarded as the next frontier in Libyan expansion, after Africa. However, like many other countries, India viewed him with an equal mixture of fascination and suspicion. He did his cause no good by speaking in favour of independence for Kashmir, while a visit by his son Saif in 2001 had ended in controversy when a cheque for $800,000 to an Islamic centre bounced.

My trip, lasting a month, was exhausting but eventually I was able to pass on all the invitations. Among the recipients was a well-known politician, Amar Singh, who proved to be a very useful contact. He had the ear of former US President Bill Clinton and his wife Hillary. Singh reportedly donated $5 million to their charitable fund, The Clinton Foundation, and that scale of largesse buys access. The Clinton's fund was supposed to change lives around the world, but sceptics claimed it was all about politics and opening the right doors in powerful corridors.

Singh was a regular dining companion of Mrs Clinton, and I couldn't overlook this wonderful networking opportunity.

At the time she'd just lost out to Barack Obama for the Democratic nomination in the 2008 US presidential election. It was widely anticipated that she was going to be offered the post of US Secretary of State, if Obama won the forthcoming election against John McCain.

Gaddafi was keen to open channels of communication, not least because Mrs Clinton was still also being tipped as a future US president despite her setback against Obama. It was a travesty when she eventually lost to Donald Trump, because if you compare their two CVs there should have been a different winner. Trump is not a politician. He is a casino operator.

Through Amar Singh, I managed to arrange an invitation to a private dinner at the Manhattan apartment of an Indian businessman in New York. It was to be an intimate evening with only six of us on the guest list including Hillary Clinton and our host Sant Chatwal, who owned several hotel chains and was another big donor to Clinton good causes.

Mrs Clinton was aware of my background and keen to discuss future US-Libya relations in an informal environment. Gaddafi was also excited about the prospect of Hillary visiting Libya. Politically, he had much more in common with the Democrats than Republicans such as Bush.

The Colonel instructed me to pass on the simple message: 'Libya harbours no hard feelings towards the United States despite what has happened in the past. We want to build strong ties with the US and the Democratic Party.'

I spent two hours in Mrs Clinton's company and found her to be warm, polite and engaging. I was impressed that she didn't try to patronise me by wasting time making small talk. We spent every moment discussing politics.

She wanted to know all about life in Libya following the lifting of sanctions, and attitudes in the country towards the US. I raised the possibility of her and Bill making an official visit and, as we ate delicious Indian food, she told me: 'I would like to meet Gaddafi. He is a man with great charisma.'

Aware of my heritage, she also sought my views on the ongoing problems between Palestinians and Israel in Gaza. I explained to her that most Palestinians did not hate the Jewish people, but they detested the government of Israel for occupying their land and failing for fifty years to find a solution. Mrs Clinton also wanted to know Libya's position on Palestine, and how the rest of the Middle East currently regarded Gaddafi. I gave my opinion that his popularity was high in the region, where the explosion in satellite TV channels allowed much greater access to his public speeches than in the past.

I'm sure she had also been briefed about my Saudi Arabian connections, because she asked one rather odd question: 'Mrs Sharab, do you think the royal family of Saudi Arabia will continue ruling?' I wondered if the US was keen on regime change in the country, but nothing more was said on the subject.

I formed the impression that Mrs Clinton had a very sound understanding of the Middle East. Of course we were having an informal dinner, not sitting around the negotiating table, but she was also very diplomatic about Gaddafi. There was none of the angry rhetoric often favoured by US politicians, which so raised his heckles.

I was glad Hillary Clinton met my expectations, because I was predisposed to like her. She had succeeded, against the odds, in a male-dominated world. I identified with that.

As the evening drew to a close, she shook hands with the other departing guests then made a point of returning to me and requesting my business card. I kept in touch with her office by email. Had Gaddafi survived, I have no doubt she would have visited Tripoli.

The following year, Gaddafi became chairman of the African Union. Also in 2009, he shook hands with Barack Obama, at a G8 summit in Rome. It was the first time a serving US president had extended this courtesy to the Colonel. Another box ticked was his maiden speech to the United Nations General Assembly, lasting one and a half hours instead of the allotted fifteen minutes. In it, he defended Somali pirates and claimed that swine flu was designed for military purposes. He was introduced as 'leader of the revolution, the president of the African Union and the king of kings of Africa'. It was ridiculous, but the Colonel loved all the attention and his growing influence in world politics.

By the end of 2009 I had three bulky dossiers in my briefcase – on my arduous visit to India; my productive dinner with Hillary Clinton; and the clandestine trip to Tel Aviv to meet Shimon Peres – ready to present to the Colonel.

Normally, whenever I was holding important information like this I would hop on a flight to Tripoli straight away. However, as I've described, Gaddafi seemed preoccupied with other issues outside Libya and our relationship was about to take a turn for the worse.

The tipping point was the wedding of my brother Ezalden. His relationship with Lana had lasted only a matter of months, blighted by the death of our brother. He eventually fell in love with another girl, Rasha, and there was great joy when he announced they were to marry. At last we all had something to celebrate.

The Colonel promised to attend the ceremony, an honour for my family, but finding a date that suited him proved difficult. Three times the wedding was pushed back to accommodate his busy diary, until finally a date was agreed. We considered Gaddafi to be one of the family and it would have been impolite not to extend an invitation. We were all thrilled that he was willing to fly to Jordan to join the festivities, and Ezalden was happy to work around the Colonel's schedule. After all, not many people get the chance to welcome a president to their wedding!

The venue was again the Four Seasons Hotel in Amman, but Gaddafi didn't show. His absence cast a shadow over the day. We all knew he was a busy man, but if he couldn't attend then all he had to do was politely decline and send a family member in his place.

He blamed his office for failing to remind him, but he and I both knew that was nonsense. I'd called his office two days before the wedding and there was no problem, so what suddenly changed? I was angry at the Colonel's behaviour, because everyone knew I'd served him loyally for more than twenty years and his empty chair was interpreted as a deliberate snub.

I always showed respect to Gaddafi. All I asked for was the same in return, and a little attention. A few months earlier he'd sent a huge Libyan delegation to the wedding of a Jordanian politician, yet this guy had not achieved half as much for Gaddafi or Libya as I had over the years. Other officials from Libya, including the interior minister Mohamed Hijazi and Gaddafi's head of security Joma Al-Marfe, were at my brother's wedding, but although Al-Marfe was one of my best friends in Libya that was scant consolation.

I didn't set out to provoke Gaddafi but for months after the wedding I ignored calls from his office to return to Libya.

I don't regret taking this stand, but I'm sure my enemies in the intelligence office used it against me to try to poison Gaddafi's mind. Looking back, I'm certain it played a part in my eventual downfall.

Among those pestering me was Mabrouka Sherif, which should have rung alarm bells. It was usual for me to deal with the Colonel's information director Ahmad Ramadan or one of the bodyguards, and I had no intention of being seen to do Mabrouka's bidding. Her reputation for corralling women for Gaddafi's amusement was well known, and I didn't want to be associated with this woman or her dubious methods.

It was never my intention to stay away from Libya permanently, but I had plenty of other business in the region to occupy my time. I was never an employee of Gaddafi, only an advisor with a contract, so Libya didn't own me. I needed space to cool down.

Time slipped by until, early in 2010, I was in the United Arab Emirates on my own business when I received a call from Eid Al-Fayez, the interior minister of Jordan.

He told me: 'We have an important guest here in Amman, wanting to see you.'

Intrigued, because I was not expecting anyone, I asked: 'Who is it?'

It turned out to be Abdul Hadi, a nephew of the Colonel, who'd flown from Libya without an appointment to try to persuade me to return. For twenty-two years I'd dropped everything, jumping to attention when Gaddafi snapped his fingers. For once, I stood my ground.

'I'm not altering my plans,' I said, also a little annoyed that the Jordanian government was acting as an intermediary in our squabble. Hadi was someone I knew well, so there was no need for this indirect approach.

'I will see Abdul Hadi when I get back to Jordan the day after tomorrow,' I added.

Keeping my word, I met Gaddafi's nephew in an office at the home of the interior minister.

Hadi got straight to the point, beginning: 'My uncle, the president, would like to know why you are not happy and why you didn't come to Libya?'

I replied: 'I have nothing against your uncle, only that he didn't even send flowers to my brother's wedding. This doesn't look good after all I have done for Libya. It was his chance to show just a little appreciation.'

Continuing to get everything off my chest, I went on: 'Why has Mabrouka Sherif got all my telephone numbers – my mobile, my home in Jordan, my flat in London? She is calling me all the time. I don't want to deal with her, or take orders, because I know her reputation for making trouble. She is someone I cannot work with and if the president is relying on her then I cannot work in Libya.'

For a few seconds there was a hush in the room, and I wondered if I'd crossed a line. I was well aware that dissent wasn't tolerated within the regime, but Hadi seemed to be in conciliatory mood.

'OK,' he sighed. 'You know my uncle regards you like his daughter. If your father makes a mistake, you forgive him. Gaddafi needs to see you in Libya as soon as possible, because he is flying out of the country soon on African Union business and would like to read the files on India and Hillary Clinton before he goes. It's been a while since you carried out these missions.'

I'd shown Gaddafi that he couldn't just take me for granted. Now it was time to bury the hatchet, but there was a genuine reason for me to delay my return to Tripoli a little longer. My brother Ezalden and his wife were expecting their first child, a son, in a week's time, and I wanted to be there when I became an aunt.

'This is my time, family time,' I told Hadi. 'I have made enough sacrifices for Libya, so this is all I ask.'

He appeared to accept this and the following day flew back to Libya.

Then the calls began again, with even greater frequency. Four, five times a day. 'When is the baby arriving? When will you come to Libya? The president wants to see you as soon as possible and his trip is approaching. He must have your reports.'

On and on it went, incessantly, then I woke one morning to find one of the female bodyguards on my doorstep in Amman. It wasn't one of the women I knew and trusted, but she was insistent I accompany her back to Libya.

'The president gave me an order not to return without you,' she said, sternly.

I wasn't surprised. It was part of the culture in Libya that if Gaddafi wanted something badly enough everyone ran around in circles, shouting and showing their muscle, until his wish was fulfilled. Yet I had no intention of being one of his obedient puppies.

'You can wait here a day, a week, or a month,' I told the shocked girl, who was not used to anyone defying the leader. 'I will go to Libya but, as agreed, only when the baby is born.'

The following day Ahmad Ramadan, a man I highly respected, was on the line. The message was the same: 'Gaddafi wants you here, tomorrow.'

Although nothing was spelled out, I realised it was time to climb down. Refusal would not only jeopardise my arrangements with LAFICO but could also undermine my entire relationship with Gaddafi. So, not for the first time, I put family second.

I told the Libyan information director: 'I will fly to Tripoli tomorrow, under one condition. I will stay two days, present my reports, then come home.'

The birth was already scheduled, by Caesarean, so this would get Gaddafi off my back and allow me to be home in time. I began making hasty plans to travel to Tripoli, including my sister Reem in the arrangements. Completing our small party was, as usual, an assistant from my office whose job was to help with paperwork and shuttling documents back and forth from my hotel to various government offices for signature. My sister had recently separated from her fiancé and I thought the short trip might raise her spirits. It would be her first visit to the country, and she'd be good company.

On 10 January 2010, we packed our bags and set off for Queen Alia Airport in Amman, to catch a flight to Tripoli. I had been away from Libya for nine months. Maybe I should have picked up on the warning signs – the involvement of the dangerous Mabrouka Sherif, the increasing urgency of the calls on behalf of Gaddafi and the bodyguard descending on my home – but as I settled back into my aircraft seat I had no inkling that I was about to step into hell.

Chapter 20

Prisoner

Every time I arrived in Tripoli there was a set routine. Quickly through immigration, meet my driver from the protocol office, then straight to my suite at whatever hotel happened to be flavour of the month. This time we were staying at The Corinthia, run by a Maltese chain and a relatively new addition to the growing array of five-star accommodation in the city's burgeoning business district.

While I was unpacking it was my habit to flick on the television to catch up with the news in Libya, which was always dominated by Gaddafi's accomplishments and latest speeches. I felt a flicker of annoyance as I happened to catch a segment about elections and saw that the Colonel was in Sirte. I had been led to believe he would be in Tripoli for our meeting, but it appeared he was less desperate to hear my reports than the frantic efforts to secure my return to Libya suggested. It also meant a 600-mile round trip the next day if I was to keep to my forty-eight-hour deadline and get home for the birth. I called the leader's office to put plans in place for the following morning, not unduly concerned because the Colonel would often take off for some place or another on a whim.

After a good night's sleep, I was called at 9 a.m. to be informed that a private jet was ready to take me to Sirte. It would wait at the airport, then return to Tripoli immediately after the meeting with the Colonel was finished. It seemed everything was going like clockwork.

Knowing I'd be back within the day, I didn't bother to pack an overnight bag and the three of us headed to Sirte. My base there, as always, was The Palace Hotel and again I turned on the television.

One of the channels was broadcasting a live speech by Gaddafi, who'd already been on his feet for three hours. My assumption was that I would be taken to him the moment the address ended, so I informed the relevant officials of my arrival in Sirte. All perfectly normal. It wasn't the least bit out of the ordinary to be kept hanging about by the Colonel.

At last his rambling address drew to a conclusion and I waited for the call. And waited. Silence.

As time went by, dragging into the early afternoon, it became obvious to me that the likelihood of meeting Gaddafi that day was diminishing. He was normally tired after long speeches and would spend the rest of the day resting.

Just as I'd given up hope, there was a knock at the hotel room door. It was one of the president's minor officials, but instead of arranging to take me to the leader he had a nasty surprise for me. Mabrouka Sherif, the woman I despised and had insisted I wanted no dealings with, was downstairs asking to see me.

'She just wants to say hello,' said the aide, unconvincingly.

The motive was not to exchange pleasantries, of that I was sure, and it bothered me that my refusal to have anything to do with her was being ignored. It also meant that she was still very much a part of Gaddafi's inner circle. That was also worrying.

I saw no advantage in agreeing to see her, so sent word that I preferred to remain in my hotel room. She would not take this well, but by that stage our working relationship was already untenable. I figured that I couldn't make things much worse.

To my relief, I discovered that she had left the hotel after receiving my message and I resumed my long wait to be summoned by Gaddafi. Still silence.

By now I'd reluctantly accepted that our meeting was not going to happen that day. I knew he was flying off to Ethiopia on African Union business at 11 a.m. the next day, but this still left time for an early morning rendezvous. In the past, when time was against us, we'd met at the airport where private rooms were available. I was used to working round his schedule and sudden changes of mind.

The knock came at 2.30 a.m. It was one of Gaddafi's new bodyguards, a young woman I'd never met, and she informed me that the Colonel would see me at his desert camp not far from the city.

When we arrived he was sitting alone outside his tent. He was wearing a white shirt. I'm not sure why that sticks in my mind – maybe because it was the last time I ever set eyes on the Colonel.

We shook hands but I sensed some hesitancy, which I attributed to the time apart and my obstinacy after my brother's wedding. I didn't want to cause any embarrassment, so the subject wasn't mentioned as I opened my briefcase and prepared to get down to business.

I began by showing him photographs from my dinner with Hillary Clinton and meeting with Shimon Peres. Just as I was about to produce the accompanying reports, he raised a hand and said: 'We will do this later. Let's wait until I get back. I will meet you in Tripoli when I have time to do your work justice.'

Then, out of the blue, he began ranting about King Abdullah of Jordan and his queen.

'I know what your king is planning against me with the president of Egypt,' he said.

I didn't have a clue what he was talking about and, unhappy with the direction our meeting was taking, reached for my bag.

He stood to get up from his chair, which fell over in the soft sand. It was a trivial incident but Gaddafi began screaming: 'Why has no one put wood beneath my chair to stop this happening?'

There was no reasoning with the Colonel when he was in this sort of foul mood, so I began to walk away. From past experience I knew his tantrums passed quickly, but instead of cooling the atmosphere I only inflamed it.

'Where are you going?' he shouted.

'I am going to walk in the desert until you finish insulting my king,' I replied.

Gaddafi's rage continued: 'I've supported you for twenty-two years and now you are more loyal to your king than me?'

This was ridiculous and I tried to calm him, saying: 'Just tell me what the problem is between you and King Abdullah. I will talk to him. Maybe someone is making mischief, or your intelligence office has provided incorrect information. I've solved this type of misunderstanding in the past.'

This seemed to strike the right note with the Colonel, who strode off to his caravan. When he reappeared ten minutes later he was more like his old self.

'Forget what I just told you,' he said. 'Go back to Tripoli, don't meet or show anyone the reports. I will be gone for two days. Wait for me in your hotel.'

Our meeting in the Sirte desert lasted half an hour. With that he was gone, and I returned to the hotel. Although we parted on good terms, I was slightly puzzled by his behaviour. I still don't know what the problem was between him and the King of Jordan. Now, trying to make sense of everything that followed, I wonder if it was all just an excuse to manufacture a row with me.

Eight hours later we landed at Tripoli airport where two official cars were waiting: one to take Reem and my assistant to The Corinthia Hotel; the other to take me to the office of Ahmad Ramadan, so that I could deposit my briefcase containing the three reports for safe keeping before rejoining my sister. Inside the car was a man in military uniform, who told me he was from the intelligence office.

It was dark and raining heavily as we pulled away from the airport, heading towards the city, but I knew Tripoli well enough to realise we were taking a strange route. About twenty minutes later we were pulling into some sort of compound, which I'd never previously visited. The back door of the car was opened and I was ushered into a building, with long corridors. Next I was shown to a small room with a thick metal door. My first thought was that it resembled a bank vault but it quickly dawned on me, as I noticed the absence of any windows, that it was more like some sort of cell.

'You will stay here,' said the military man. 'You are under arrest.'

My initial reaction was that he must be joking, but his manner made it clear that he was deadly serious. He tried to take my briefcase, but I folded my arms around the bag, clutching it to my chest, and he did not persist.

I was utterly confused. Although there had been an awkwardness during my short meeting with Gaddafi, at no stage did I detect that he bore me any serious ill will. Certainly nothing had happened during that thirty minutes in the desert to warrant arrest, and I knew I'd done nothing else wrong unless you include my pique over the wedding. If I'd had any inkling that there was any threat to my personal safety I would never have returned to Libya, let alone exposed my sister to danger.

At that moment I didn't feel very bold, but rather than submit meekly I came out fighting.

'I am not staying here,' I screamed. It was a combination of fury and hysteria, as I genuinely feared I could not cope with the stress of being cooped up in that room.

There was a hushed conversation and I was escorted further along the corridor to something resembling an apartment, with a bedroom, living area and shower room. It wasn't five star but a lot better than the alternative. An old man brought me coffee and settled down on one of the seats in the living room. He didn't say much but I deduced that his job was to keep an eye on me. It was clear I was going nowhere.

I was trying to make sense of what was happening. Was the Colonel pulling the strings, or one of my enemies in the intelligence office operating behind his back? At the time I favoured the latter explanation – and the prime suspect was Mabrouka.

This created another pressing problem: the reports I was carrying. My briefing document and a copy of the photograph of my meeting with Shimon Peres was especially sensitive, and potentially damaging if it fell into the wrong hands. Libya's official stance was anti-Israel, pro-Palestine. No one but Gaddafi knew of this secret mission and I feared I could be accused of spying.

I made my excuses to the old man, went to the bathroom, pulled a lighter from my handbag and burned the reports and the Peres photograph in the sink. Then, as best I could, I flushed the ashes down the toilet.

The bed was not comfortable and I didn't get much sleep that night, my second back in Libya.

At 9 a.m. the following day I was told I was on the move. It was a short journey, also through unfamiliar streets, to another compound. In the daylight I was able to get a better idea of my surroundings. The high walls, watchtowers and armed men in military fatigues filled me with a sense of foreboding. In terms of the geography of the city, I was still disoriented.

Mentally, I gave up hope of getting back to Jordan for the arrival of my new nephew. Little did I know that this grim military base would be my 'home' for the next twenty-one months.

On the compound was a two-storey office block. I was taken to the second floor where, in a second-floor room, was a man sitting behind a desk. He was wearing civilian clothes, but introduced himself as General Abdul Hameed Al Saeh. I later discovered that he was the head of anti-terrorism.

Politely, he said: 'President Gaddafi sends his best wishes. Before he left Libya, he gave instructions that you should be our guest here until he returns. We have a villa ready for you.'

He might call it a villa and refer to me as a guest, but this was going to be no holiday.

Suddenly, a flashbulb went off in my mind. In Libya it was common for the regime to place senior people under house arrest, as a warning if they got too big for their boots or upset the Colonel in some way. As I've explained, even his sons suffered this indignity to try to bring them under control. The villas were reserved for VIPs, not common criminals. It appeared this was to be my fate and I felt a mix of emotions.

On the one hand these stays were normally a short, sharp shock lasting a few days. On numerous occasions I'd been involved in having men released after someone, usually a friend or family member, asked me to intervene. In fact, although I'd never seen the villas and didn't know their location, they'd become a standing joke.

Long ago some official had been held there and his disappearance had been falsely explained away. Anyone asking after him was told he was on a business trip to Geneva. From that moment Geneva became a euphemism.

'Where's so-and-so?' someone might ask.

'Oh, he's in Geneva,' would come the reply. Nothing more needed to be said.

Now the joke was on me it didn't seem so funny, and more concerning was the mention of the president. If the general was being truthful, then Gaddafi himself was behind my imprisonment.

My initial reaction was to explode in anger, but I realised it would be futile. General Al Saeh did not appear to be relishing what was happening and, if I was to be held here only until the Colonel returned from his African Union trip, I didn't want to upset my jailor in the meantime. Al Saeh could, after all, make my life a misery.

I complied with his request to hand over my mobile telephone and business bag. We drove a short distance to a group of nine small villas. If they had been on the beach, the box-like little grey houses might have looked quite appealing, but on the military base they were not at all welcoming. Al Saeh explained that some of the villas were 'occupied' but I had my pick of the others. There was little to choose between them so, of the three or four I was shown, I opted for the cleanest. It also happened to be the closest to the heavily guarded compound exit, although I wasn't thinking of staging an escape attempt.

'It's a nice choice,' said Al Saeh, without a hint of irony. 'In fact Gaddafi's son Mutassim has just moved out.'

I had no reason to doubt him but didn't ask for further details as I surveyed my new surroundings.

The entrance had a floor-to-ceiling iron bar gate, which the general unlocked, then a more normal wooden door. It opened into the Arabic-style living room, where there were a couple of low leather sofas and a television. Off the living area was an office with a desk and chair, small kitchen and, to the other side, a modest bathroom. Not a bad prison, all in all, but a prison nonetheless. When that outer gate was locked there was no way out, as the windows had security grilles.

After the guided tour, Al Saeh said: 'Now, we will send your driver to your hotel to pick up some clothes and toiletries.'

Soon a small bag arrived. Containing underwear, pyjamas and a couple of tracksuits, it had been packed by my sister.

Much later I learned that they lied to ensure her co-operation, telling Reem that some important matter had come up and I would be busy for a day. When I didn't show after twenty-four hours she reported me missing to the Jordanian embassy in Tripoli and my case became a diplomatic incident between the two countries. Of course, I knew none of this at the time.

It became apparent that I was going to have a housemate, called Dohaiba. She was a young policewoman in her mid-twenties and was friendly enough, although she didn't have much to say.

The metal gate was locked for the night and she took the sofa in the living room. So began our routine, with the gate only opened for food to be delivered.

That first night I had plenty on which to reflect, with my main emotion still one of bewilderment. I was being well treated and didn't feel threatened, taking comfort from the usual use of the villas for short stays but was still at a loss to comprehend what was going on.

In my twenty-two years at Gaddafi's side he must have heard many awful falsehoods about me, but never allowed a hair on my head to be touched. What had happened now to turn him against me? I felt sure someone had poisoned his mind against me, and concluded that whatever I was accused of must be serious to warrant imprisonment. All the time I was glued to the satellite television, hoping to see a report about Gaddafi's return from Ethiopia.

My first interrogation was the following morning in a nearby office. A military man, sitting behind a desk and claiming to have been appointed by Gaddafi, spent an hour bombarding me with questions. There was nothing subtle about his approach.

'Why did it take so long for you to return to Libya? Where else did you travel during that period?'

It was no secret that I'd been to India, London, Dubai, UAE and the US. My passport was in the hotel safe if they wanted to check for other stamps. I thought it prudent not to mention Israel and offered up a prayer of thanks that the entire trip had been arranged without documentation, so there was no trace.

He fired the names of a few individuals at me, all Saudi Arabian, and asked if I knew them. A few of them were familiar and I said so. I had nothing to hide on that score.

Was I suspected of being a spy for a foreign country?

I decided to ask a question of my own: 'Why am I here?'

My interrogator replied: 'I don't know. Don't ask this question because I cannot give you an answer. Just answer my questions because I am only doing my job.'

The same process continued for five days. By then, from watching TV, I was aware that the Colonel was back in the country and his silence was a blow to my hopes of a speedy release.

It was even more obvious that he was behind my arrest. Had it been some sort of terrible mix-up, or set up by the intelligence office, he would have got wind of it.

I can only assume that Gaddafi gave instructions for me to be well treated. I doubt many prisoners got the same perks, including food deliveries from the buffet of a five-star hotel. After it became apparent that I was going nowhere, my request for a better mattress and bed linen, courtesy of the Corinthia Hotel, was also granted.

Most of the time there was a policewoman with me in the villa. Occasionally I'd be on my own so I formed the impression that these women were there to protect, rather than guard, me. Dohaiba was my most frequent companion and, over time, she opened up and we became quite close. We watched television, following trashy Egyptian soap operas. In my normal life I would never have dreamed of wasting my time on such rubbish, but these programmes helped fill the day. I woke as late as possible, usually at about 11 a.m. For breakfast I ate bread and cheese and drank tea.

Dohaiba had no idea why I was there, so we just chatted about life in general. I enjoyed her company and apart from helping to pass the time she helped keep me sane. We shared the cleaning duties and I also became an avid reader, using this unexpected opportunity to study Islam.

After two weeks they brought my shisha pipe, which I carried on all my trips, and tobacco. It was good to have home comforts, but another sign that I was there for the long haul.

For one hour each day, under the eye of a security guard, I was permitted to walk in the communal garden and began tending its few plants. I also cleared away dead vegetation from around my own villa to try to keep the mosquitoes at bay.

However, for the rest of the time my only fresh air came from opening the inner wooden door and allowing the breeze to blow in through the metal bars of the outer gate. I craved sunshine and looked deathly pale. This was my life in 'Geneva'.

Contact with the 'guests' in the other villas was forbidden, but I soon discovered that one of my neighbours happened to be my old friend Nuri Al Mismari, head of the Libyan protocol office, who was accused of pilfering.

At first I also had a limited amount of clothes, which were regularly taken away by my driver to be laundered at The Corinthia. I was on good terms with the man, who'd worked with me for many years, and he was obviously distressed by my plight. He'd whispered to me that Reem was still in Tripoli, so during my third week in the villa I placed a letter to my sister in the pocket of a pair of trousers. Despite the risk of losing his job, or worse, he agreed to deliver the trousers directly to my sister and draw her attention to the note. He even had the presence of mind to steer Reem into the bathroom before having a conversation, in case the main room was bugged.

In my message I told my sister I was in danger and to urge the government, and the King of Jordan, to intervene on my behalf. Word came back next day that she was trying everything and that my brother, Ezalden, had flown to Libya to take up my case.

Although very grateful for his help, I was very worried that my family members would also end up under arrest. Reluctantly, next time my loyal driver made the laundry run, I instructed him to tell my brother and sister: 'Go home to Jordan and lobby on my behalf from there. You are at risk if you stay in Libya.'

I felt more alone than ever. I wondered how long my punishment, for whatever offence Gaddafi had deemed me to have committed, would last.

Chapter 21

Losing Faith

Life in the villa became a war of attrition as my captors tried to wear me down. Six excruciating weeks had passed since I'd flown back to Libya with Reem, my sister. I yearned for news of my family back in Jordan and wondered how Rasha and her new son, whom I could only assume had been delivered safely, were doing. The boy was to be called Firas, in honour of my late brother, so I already felt a close bond. I felt ill through worry and lack of sleep. Although my surroundings were comfortable I was still a prisoner, albeit one who was being fed five-star food.

With little to occupy my mind, other than reading and watching TV, I was going stir crazy.

Every morning I woke up praying: 'Today, maybe they will free me.' But with each sunset hope faded.

My birthday, in February, only added to my growing despondency. Bizarrely, my captors brought flowers and a cake to the villa, but I was in no mood to celebrate. The gesture was probably well meant, but it was almost as if they were taunting me.

It so happened that in March 2010 Libya was hosting an Arab League summit and I knew King Abdullah of Jordan was due to attend. Could his visit be the catalyst for my release?

It seemed that might be the case when, two days before the gathering, I was summoned to meet Abdallah Mansour. He was head of media and TV in Libya at the time and I counted him as a friend. It was dusk when I left the villa and was escorted past various buildings in the compound to a nondescript office block, where he was waiting. Mansour was the most senior individual I'd spoken to since being held, and I interpreted this as a positive sign.

As I entered the room, he rose from his seat at a round table and shook my hand. I felt underdressed in my tracksuit and trainers. He smiled smugly, as if nothing had happened and this was just an ordinary meeting. All the pent up fury over my arrest erupted.

I shouted at Mansour: 'Why are you holding me? How dare you? Do you think there are no laws? My country will make big trouble for you. Does Gaddafi even know that I am here?'

I lost control, cursing him as we stood just a metre apart, but the smile never left his face. Mansour's cool demeanour just made me even more agitated.

He waited for me to pause for breath then asked: 'Have you finished?'

The wind taken out of my sails, I replied: 'Yes'.

He motioned towards the table, adding: 'In that case sit, and we can talk. You know the president regards you like a daughter, so don't be angry with him. I don't know why you are here, but there is an order to hold you. Now, you know your king is arriving and President Gaddafi expects he will raise your case. He would like to release you, so you can fly home with the king.'

This was wonderful news, but Mansour went on: 'We want you to sign a statement confirming that you are a witness for some important cases and we placed you in a protection programme.'

We were straying into the realms of fantasy and worse was to follow. Mansour revealed that one of my fellow prisoners in the villas was Nouri Al-Mismari, the head of protocol and the man once abandoned by Gaddafi in the spa on our visit to Jordan. Now it was alleged that Mesmari had misappropriated government funds, and smuggled the cash out of the country to Jordan. If this was not enough, Mansour also wanted me to sign a statement against my close friend Salma Milad, the bodyguard. It was being alleged that she had plotted to kill Gaddafi.

I had no idea whether Mesmari was guilty but I knew for certain that Salma, who was as loyal as they came, would never conspire against the leader. She was utterly dedicated, and had no interest in personal gain.

Along with Naima she was my closest friend in Libya and if there was one person in Libya who was incorruptible it was Salma. She was always my direct route to Gaddafi and I suspected that was now being used against us both.

So I told Mansour: 'Number one, I am not the Central Bank of Jordan so I don't know where Mesmari keeps his money. Maybe you can ask the

King of Jordan when he arrives. Number two, I cannot be a false witness against one of my closest friends.'

Not for one moment did I contemplate signing. Plotting to kill Gaddafi was a capital offence, so I knew I could be signing my friend's death warrant. I couldn't live with that for the rest of my life.

Then Mansour pulled out a sheet of paper and jabbed at it. 'You transferred $2,000 to her three months ago,' he said, as if this was all the proof he needed.

I could explain exactly what that money was for. Salma did not come from a wealthy background and her mother had been ill so I'd gifted her the funds to pay for private treatment. In the past I'd also given her jewellery, I told Mansour, and that wasn't part of some plot either. It was preposterous and we both knew he was clutching at straws. If my position were not so precarious I would have laughed in his face.

Mansour looked embarrassed. I got the feeling he was reciting pre-prepared lines.

He sat back in his chair, spread his hands and said: 'OK. Gaddafi would like to compensate you for the time you have been held here, on condition you stay quiet and don't make trouble.'

This conversation was spiralling downwards. Now, if I hadn't misjudged the situation, I was being offered a cash bribe to keep my mouth shut.

'Keep quiet about what?' I demanded to know.

'You have many secrets about the president and now you are angry,' said Mansour. 'We would like you to leave on good terms, keep your office here and the relationship with Libya reverts back to normal. We will pay you a few million dollars to compensate you for the wasted time, the lost business and separation from your family.'

It was a typical, clumsy approach by the regime to buy its way out of a sticky spot. I wasn't having any of it.

'I don't need any money from Gaddafi to keep quiet, because I have nothing against him,' I said, not wishing Mansour to believe I posed any kind of threat to the Colonel.

Mansour changed tack again. 'Look,' he said. 'I don't think Gaddafi meant to have you placed under arrest. They misunderstood his orders. Now he is in a difficult situation.'

It was more nonsense. We both knew it.

'Gaddafi is like my father, I don't need money to stay quiet,' I repeated. 'I will not cause trouble.'

Mansour shuffled some papers. 'Why don't you just sign the witness statements and a declaration of confidentiality,' he said. 'Then you can return home with your king after the summit.'

We were going round in circles. I didn't sign. Our meeting was over.

Yet I was still confident that a deal would be reached between Libya and Jordan to release me. It was clear I'd become a nuisance to the Colonel and, in his own way, he was trying to solve the Daad problem.

Over the next three days I sat on the sofa in my villa watching blanket coverage of the Arab League summit, including images of King Abdullah of Jordan. To my dismay, his time in Libya did not herald a breakthrough in my case. Soon the king was gone, along with my hopes.

My food was still delivered daily from the Corinthia Hotel. I was still allowed into the garden for one hour per day. In other words, nothing changed.

I despaired as I thought of my ailing father, wondering if he was even still alive, and my 16-year-old daughter. How was she coping at school? Noor was used to my absences on business, with a full-time nanny and my sisters always around, but this was entirely different. Her ordeal, not knowing what had become of her mother, must be as awful as my own.

What about my business, with no one at the helm and bills and office staff to pay? Every quarter I wrote a report for each company I represented, and I worried how they would react to my silence.

There was also my case against the Saudi prince, over the millions of dollars in unpaid commission on the private jet sale, to fret about. I feared the British court would take a dim view of my absence and there was an important hearing approaching. All I could hope was that my lawyer in London, Richard Waller, was stalling for time and I would have my overdue day in court.

On top of all this, eating away at me was a sense of injustice. I had done nothing to merit imprisonment and no one had given me a proper explanation for the sudden downturn in my fortunes, so that I could at least try to rebut the allegations against me. Past experience told me that placing any faith in the Libyan legal system was futile.

I had no idea of the extent of any diplomatic efforts by my country's government to secure my release. These matters took time, I appreciated, but the longer I was locked up the more I was fearful that I would be forgotten. I felt let down that Jordan was not doing more. I had no way of knowing at the time if the king had raised my case, or demanded my release, but I was aware that protocol in the region dictated that such a request could only be made once without a second refusal causing loss of face. He was placed in a difficult position and I am grateful for his efforts. I now know that he did speak directly to Gaddafi and that I was always in his thoughts. So I attach no blame to the king, but I cannot forgive the diplomats and officials for their half-hearted attempts to resolve my case.

Mansour, my former friend, became my tormentor-in-chief. Every three weeks I'd be taken to his office and we'd go over the same old ground. Occasionally he'd ask a new question, usually covering subjects or individuals about which I had no knowledge. Never a direct allegation, just a fishing expedition. The longer this went on, the more confident I became that Gaddafi himself was orchestrating the interrogations.

Determined not to be bullied or tricked, I asked: 'Are you trying to design a crime for me, frame me? I will not answer any more of your questions.'

I felt sure that if I implicated myself in the slightest, on any matter, I would be dragged off to court. The outcome would be a foregone conclusion and I knew my position in Libya would only be made worse if I had a conviction hanging over me.

I learned that among my other neighbours were a Saudi Arabian man and his sister, who were sharing the nearest villa to my own. I caught glimpses of them and recognised him. I had opened doors for him in Libya, where he'd subsequently arranged many deals, and I wondered if his fate was somehow tangled up with mine. At one stage we'd been business partners, but we parted on bad terms after I discovered that he was exploiting my contacts and planning to set up on his own. I did not consider him to be an honest man and I'd made it clear to the Libyan government at the time, in writing, that our partnership was over. What exactly he'd been doing in the intervening two years I did not know.

On the other hand none of the barrage of questions from Mansour was about the Saudi, so maybe it was just a coincidence that we were both under glorified arrest.

Adding to my gloomy mood, my guard-come-companion Dohaiba was removed. I assume the Libyans feared we'd become too friendly.

And so my solitary existence stretched on, through the summer of 2010. Sometimes I would lose my temper, shouting at Mansour: 'Do you think there are no laws in the world and you can just hold me forever without charge? Why don't you take me to court if I've done something wrong?'

Not a soul from the Jordanian embassy had been to visit me and there had been no access to a lawyer. I'd encountered this treatment being meted out to Libya's own citizens, who seemed to have no legal rights, but never to an outsider. It was like reasoning with a brick wall. Mansour just grinned inanely.

In September, the second leg of that year's Arab League summit took place in Sirte. It was like a mirror image of the first meeting, with my hopes raised that I would be released only to be quickly dashed.

The Libyans were nervous that the spotlight would once more be on my case. The pressure on me to sign some sort of document, justifying my imprisonment, was ramped up. This time it got to the stage where I considered putting my name to some sort of vague agreement, but not amounting to any confession. I'd merely state that I was a witness to 'strategic issues' which had forced me to remain in Libya.

'Tomorrow we will send a hairdresser and some new clothes and you will be free,' Mansour assured me.

I had good reason to be sceptical about anything he uttered. The summit came and went.

I discovered that the King of Jordan, who'd been expected to attend, had cried off at the eleventh hour and sent his foreign minister in his place. The Libyans either did not think this merited my release, or had no intention of letting me go and this was all part of the campaign of mental torture. In the days after the summit I shed many more tears and my depression deepened. Triggers on TV, such as a familiar song, would set me off again. Family birthdays and other important events in the calendar, such as Ramadan, were also very tough.

There was, though, one improvement in my living conditions. From morning to dusk the barred outer gate of my villa was left open so I could wander around outside, still within the high walls of the compound.

I was reminded sternly that there must be no contact with anyone in the neighbouring villas. Should I forget, there were guards with guns in the watchtowers and security cameras trained on the area. Despite this, I tried to communicate with some of my fellow prisoners when we happened to be out walking at the same time. I was met with blank looks – they were clearly terrified to have anything to do with me.

It was good to be outdoors and get some sun on my bones, but as my captors gave with one hand, so they took away with the other.

Someone must have noticed that I'd become friendly with Adil, the man who brought my food every day. He clearly felt sorry for me and also gave me snippets of information. He'd spend half an hour at my villa in the morning as I ate, and I looked forward to our encounters. He was a kind man, who took no pleasure in my plight, and we struck up a good rapport over the nine months this routine continued.

Then, one morning in September, he was replaced without any warning by another man. In contrast to Adil, the newcomer was sullen and uncommunicative. I'm sure he was under instructions to have nothing to do with me.

When I asked what had become of my friend Adil, I was simply told he no longer worked in the compound. I later discovered that this was a lie and that he'd been assigned to other duties which kept him away from the villas.

The following month, I heard lots of screaming outside my villa and saw a group of women being escorted by General Abdul Hameed Al Saeh to a neighbouring building. I recognised them immediately as the wife and children of Nuri Al Mismari, the protocol chief.

'What's going on?' I shouted to the general as he left. Pausing briefly, he replied: 'Al Mismari has run away from Libya.'

That night I watched his defection reported on television. It emerged that Al Mismari had been released from villa arrest, but soon got wind that he was facing charges of embezzling state funds. He fled to Paris, where he was denouncing the Colonel. Members of his family were now paying the penalty for his disloyalty. They were later freed, unharmed.

All the time my health was deteriorating. I began suffering stomach pains, my blood pressure was low and I had constant headaches. My hand was also shaking uncontrollably and eventually a neurologist was called to the villa to examine me.

I hoped he would be sympathetic to a woman being held without charge like this, and might pass on messages or raise my case in the outside world. However, while he said he felt sorry for me, fear of angering the regime clearly outweighed that.

The neurologist told me only: 'Pray to God.'

I am sure it was heartfelt, but I didn't need this type of advice from him.

It was the doctor's opinion that I should be taken to hospital for tests, but this request was refused. I was given painkillers and they brought a machine to monitor my heart.

Yet I was reassured by the arrival of the neurologist and other medics. I concluded that although I'd become a thorn in his side, for reasons still unclear, Gaddafi did not want me to die in captivity.

Up until October 2010 I was dining on hotel food but then one day they arrived with military-style rations in a plastic bag. It was disgusting and I shouted: 'This is not fit for a dog. I'm not eating it.'

The reply came: 'What do you want? The people in the other villas have this food?'

I'm sure it was a punishment to break my spirit and put pressure on me to sign a false confession, which could result in me festering in a Libyan prison for years.

I complained about the poor food to General Al Saeh, who seemed surprised. He didn't say so, but I got the impression that this was a tactic, introduced behind his back, by the intelligence office.

I managed to persuade the general, who was not a brute, that my health would only decline further if my diet was restricted. Although I was no longer given food from the Corinthia Hotel, meals from local restaurants were brought to me in plastic boxes and one dish a day was always fish. It was a small victory.

The sullen man who brought my food was also replaced. To my disappointment it was not Adil who returned, but a guy of about 40 who had some nursing training and could also keep an eye on my health. I was grateful that he turned out to be friendly, because there wasn't much else to be thankful for.

After ten months in the compound I had lost all faith in Gaddafi. I had insomnia, a suspected stomach ulcer and was probably suffering from clinical depression. Every time the heavy metal gate to my villa was opened, grinding noisily on its hinges, I was a nervous wreck.

I tried to take comfort from still being in one of the villas, traditionally used to hold people temporarily, but also accepted that if the Colonel really wanted me freed it would have happened long ago. I was still bewildered that after so many years of dutiful service he'd obviously sanctioned this humiliation. I'd also lost faith in the government of Jordan to secure my release through diplomacy.

All that was preventing me from a total breakdown was my faith in God. Sitting alone for hours on end gave me plenty of time to reflect, but I never lost my belief. In fact it only became stronger – so many people had let me down that I placed all my trust in God and destiny. Surely my plight couldn't get any worse?

Then, one evening in December 2010, I flicked on the television.

Chapter 22

Bombs

It's now known as the Arab Spring, but tuning into Al Jazeera that chilly winter night I had no inkling of the momentous events that would unfold over the next few months. I was witnessing the beginning of the end for Gaddafi and would be caught up, helpless, in the firestorm.

For the record, on 17 December 2010 a Tunisian street seller called Mohamed Bouazizi was accused of working without a licence. His fruit and vegetables were confiscated, and in the dispute that followed he is said to have been slapped in the face by a policewoman. Bouazizi, who claimed to have been the victim of harassment and corruption, set himself alight in protest.

The immolation of Bouazizi did not at first attract much attention outside his home town, Sidi Bouzid, but over the next few days there were demonstrations outside the headquarters of the regional government. So the cogs were set in motion and it was during that period that I watched, with little more than idle curiosity, the first reports of the growing unrest in Tunisia. Television was my only link with the world outside the grim walls of the compound. Although I still didn't know my whereabouts in Tripoli, I had access to various foreign satellite channels in addition to Libyan state news. My other sources were two Saudi-owned channels, Al Arabiya, which covered the whole region, and MBC.

It didn't seem as though I was watching the start of a revolution but as the uprising gathered pace I became transfixed, trying to make sense of what was happening. The border was only 100 miles away, and was familiar from the days when I'd travelled overland to side-step the air embargoes. Tunisia was on my doorstep, but never did I dream for one moment that Libya would be affected. The region is volatile and localised trouble was not uncommon. Even when the Tunisian government was overthrown, there appeared to be no threat to the Colonel. I was sure he still had a firm grip on the country after more than forty years in power and maintained widespread popularity in most parts of Libya, despite my misgivings about his obsession with Africa. I'd warned that his ego would, eventually, kill him but I did not imagine the day of reckoning was not far away.

He had a strong army, bristling with military hardware which had been updated following the removal of sanctions. It came largely from Russia, but many countries including Britain and France helped arm Gaddafi – in exchange for his oil dollars, of course.

Libya struck me as a peaceful country, where a woman could walk the streets safely and I'd never detected much animosity towards the Colonel. His sons were scheming in the background, but there was no one seriously vying to replace him. Gaddafi was a survivor and I'm certain he also viewed the unfolding events in Tunisia with complacency.

In January and February, anti-government uprisings spread across the region to Egypt and Syria. Yet even when the revolution began in Egypt, resulting in the resignation of President Hosni Mubarak after thirty years in power, I still believed Gaddafi was untouchable.

In February, not long after Mubarak was removed, I was escorted to Abdallah Mansour's office. Expecting more of the same, I was sitting with a sense of resignation waiting for another grilling when he announced: 'Before you start bad-mouthing me, or screaming, I just want to tell you that your father is here and you are going to see him.'

For once I was speechless in Mansour's presence, but as my mind cleared I suspected it was just another of his tricks to unsettle me.

Mansour added: 'Your brother and one of your sisters are also here. President Gaddafi invited them. You will see them all tomorrow.'

Still convinced he was lying, I demanded to know: 'Why are they here? I don't want to see anyone unless you release me.'

Mansour continued: 'President Gaddafi has been giving much thought to finding a solution and now he thinks it can be arranged through your family. He called your father to Libya and the three of you will sit down together. Your father must promise that you will keep your mouth shut.'

Unsure how to react, I simply said: 'OK'. I was intrigued to see what Mansour had up his sleeve, but had zero expectation of sitting down the next day for this cosy chat he was promising.

I'd reached the point where I didn't allow myself any hope. In a perverse way it was easier to cope by taking that approach, so that my life was like a flat line. No ups, no downs; one day the same as the next and the day before.

Next morning it seemed like the charade was continuing. I was told to dress up and taken in a car, with a guard, to a police social club which was about thirty minutes away. I looked for familiar landmarks but I didn't recognise this part of the city, so I was still unable to pinpoint exactly where I was being held.

On arrival I was shown to an upstairs office. Sitting there were my father, in his wheelchair, my brother Ezalden, sister Reem and Yassin, my driver in Jordan, who was there to look after Baba. I also recognised a man called Mohessen, a Libyan, who worked for the government's legal department. He was sympathetic, sometimes making me coffee while I was being questioned.

For a moment I froze, overwhelmed by seeing my family for the first time in a year. My father burst into tears and I fell into his arms. He looked so frail that I was almost afraid to hug him. He was 80 years old and the trip from Amman to Tripoli had taken its toll. We clasped one another tight.

There was so much catching up to do, and I demanded to know all about my daughter. My brother handed me his mobile phone and I was able to speak to Noor for a few minutes. I could hardly believe I was hearing her voice. We were both crying. I tried to reassure her that I was fine, told her how much I missed her and to try to concentrate on her school work. I'm pleased to say Noor got excellent grades.

Then Ezalden told me he had two children – a son born just after I left Jordan and a baby girl, named Daad after her imprisoned aunt. All this just reinforced how long I'd been away.

I felt a whirlwind of emotions. While I was delighted to see them, part of me was angry that they had not done more to secure my release.

I screamed: 'Where is the ambassador of Jordan, why doesn't the king do something, why haven't you been to the media?' All the burning questions that had gnawed away at me for a year came pouring out. My father tried to cool me down, telling me they'd been scared of making matters worse. I discovered much later that my daughter had bombarded Gaddafi's office with faxes, demanding my release, but never got a response. My sisters, Linda and Rana, approached the offices of Jordanian intelligence, the prime minister and King Abdullah. More silence.

My brother told me, however, that they had been assured that as soon as Gaddafi returned from dealing with matters of state in Benghazi I would be on my way home to Jordan.

The meeting with my family seemed to last only a few minutes, although when I glanced at my watch we'd actually been together for an entire, precious hour. It was torture to be escorted back to the villa but, for once, I allowed myself a little optimism.

Two days later I had a second meeting with my family, in the same place. The date is etched in my memory, 1 February, my father's birthday. Again, I was told to prepare for my release which would happen in a day or two.

Still suspicious, I whispered in my brother's ear as we hugged goodbye: 'If this promise is broken, go home and make the biggest fuss you can. Contact everyone in the media.'

Day passed, then weeks. I should have known better than to trust my captors.

I resumed my television vigil and saw reports of the first trouble in Libya – in Benghazi, in the east of the country. Perhaps that was the reason for the Colonel's presence there?

Libyan state television played down the unrest, so inside my little bubble it was hard to make sense of what was happening.

A few days later, I heard the unmistakable sound of automatic gunfire in the distance. Now it seemed Tripoli was about to become a battleground and I had even more reason to worry. One of the guards told me the shots were fired by Gaddafi's troops, celebrating victory, but that was hard to believe.

I received a visit from General Al Saeh who informed me that my release had been delayed because of the trouble.

It was 15 February, the day after my second birthday in captivity. There were no flowers or cake this time. The Colonel and his henchmen had other things on their minds.

Al Saeh also revealed that my family had been instructed by the Jordanian ambassador in Tripoli to go home for their safety. Flights between Libya and Jordan were about to be suspended indefinitely.

However, I learned that my brother and sister had stayed to try to negotiate my release. I was touched by their loyalty, but Libya was clearly no longer a secure country. On a phone borrowed from one of my regular interrogators, it was with a heavy heart that I managed to speak to my brother and pleaded with him to go.

'I can look after myself,' I told Ezalden, not really believing what I was saying. 'The last thing I need is to be worrying if you and Reem are in danger. Leave with my sister as soon as possible.'

There was a pause then my brother said: 'OK, we will do as you say.' Little did I know at the time that both stayed in Libya to try to negotiate my release.

Over the next couple of weeks the gunfire intensified. Was it my imagination or was it coming closer?

I must confess that I had, a couple of months earlier, prayed for revenge on Gaddafi for what he'd done to me. Now, I prayed for him to remain safe because the alternative terrified me. Everyone knew I was his special advisor and that I'd been at his side for many years.

For the first time, I worried about my safety from this new threat, but the bottom line was that I was powerless to act. It wasn't as if I could just walk out of the door, hail a cab to the airport and go home to Jordan. No, whether I liked it or not, I believed that despite his apparent betrayal my fate was bound up with Gaddafi's.

By watching television I tried to piece together what was happening, and learned that NATO had issued the Colonel with a deadline to stop attacks on his own countrymen who were massing against him.

I'm sure that Gaddafi would not have been overthrown without the intervention of NATO. In his darkest hour his new allies in America, Britain and France went missing.

There is a saying: 'The Americans don't have friends, they have interests.' You can't rely on America – it will sell you out any time. It happened with Saddam Hussein, it happened with Mubarak and it happened with Gaddafi when he was no longer useful.

The justification for the NATO raids was to protect civilians, but the bombs killed Libyan civilians. It was all a front to oust Gaddafi. At the forefront of this campaign in the West was Nikolas Sarkozy, the president of France, who had rolled out the red carpet for Gaddafi at the Élysée Palace, signed arms deals with him and enjoyed Libyan hospitality.

On 19 March 2011, it was French aircraft that fired the first rockets at Gaddafi's armoured units and air-defence systems. I never thought they'd bomb Libya. I imagined a no-fly zone would be imposed, and the return of embargoes to try to force Gaddafi to the negotiating table.

But after more than forty years in power, the West had decided it was time for a regime change. Tony Blair, the former prime minister who'd praised Gaddafi as an ally in the war on terror, now wanted nothing to do with the Colonel.

I don't recall the precise date but one night, at 12.30, I heard the first bomb fall on Tripoli. The ground shook under my feet and people in the neighbouring villas began screaming. When dawn broke I could see thick black smoke, not far away.

And so a pattern emerged. During the day it was usually quiet, but every night the coalition aircraft dropped their explosive cargoes on Tripoli. On television they said the target was Gaddafi's compound, so using my knowledge of its location in the city I tried to work out where I was being held. From the plumes of smoke, I estimated that I was about a mile away. Too close for comfort. I could hear the sirens of fire engines and ambulances. People were dying around me. From March until September bombs rained down every night. Each evening I was locked in, behind the metal gate.

Not long after the bombing began, the Jordanian ambassador in Tripoli arrived to see me. I spent most of the time berating him for his inaction.

'What have you been doing for the last year?' I shouted.

He shrugged and tried to explain that he and his colleagues had been doing their best but the Libyan government ignored their requests. At one stage during our meeting he produced a wrapped piece of cake, which he offered as if he were making a house visit. This only set me off again and he left with my criticisms about his failings ringing in his ears. He promised to visit a week later, with good news, but I never saw the man again. I learned that the embassy had been evacuated and all the staff had returned to Jordan.

Then General Al Saeh visited and told me he would provide a female policewoman, each night, supposedly for my protection. He was not a stupid man – we both knew she could not catch a bomb. She wasn't very friendly, refusing to tell me her name, but at least we had one another for company.

The poor girl was terrified and her fear made her talkative. She let slip that I was being held in the notorious Abu Salim prison compound, where many opponents of the regime ended up. In 1996 it had been the site of a massacre which allegedly involved the deaths of more than 1,200 rioting prisoners.

I took reassurance from finally learning of my supposed location. I reckoned that the West would not target a prison which held opponents of Gaddafi, although I was not oblivious to the likelihood of a stray bomb or missile finding its way to Abu Salim. The margin for error in a war zone is small, but I relaxed a little.

At the back of my mind was always the question of how Jordan, on good terms with Gaddafi but also leaning towards the West, would react. I received the answer about a month after the bombing began.

One day the door to the villa was flung open and I was marched across the compound to a nondescript building. Inside I was bundled into a windowless room, measuring only a metre or so square. No washing facilities, no toilet.

'What's this about?' I asked.

'Your king is supporting NATO,' I was told. 'Now we will show him what we can do to you.'

It emerged that Jordan, while not participating directly in the attacks on Libya, was providing logistical support. Now there was no doubt among my captors that I was the enemy, and it was made obvious that their treatment of me would become harsher. My perilous situation had just taken another turn for the worse, and I could only imagine the Colonel's fury as an Arab country that he had courted assiduously lined up against him.

The door was slammed shut, leaving me in total darkness. All I could hear were screams from other rooms. It sounded like people were being beaten, and I wondered if this was also to be my fate.

I must have fainted in terror. When I awoke I was back in my villa, where I was soon visited by General Al Saeh.

'I had nothing to do with my king's decision, you must realise that,' I said. 'Why do you blame me for something that is beyond my control? Why do you punish me?'

He shrugged. 'I don't know. It was an order.'

I never discovered who gave it.

Soon after the bombing started, the prospect of my release was dangled again. Another document was produced by Abdallah Mansour – this time he wanted me to sign over my assets in Libya. I had about $3 million sitting in a Libyan bank account, earned through deals I'd completed, plus a villa and three cars. Matters were getting desperate so I agreed to put pen to paper, although I did not trust the man. I figured that effectively paying my own ransom was a gamble worth taking, but nothing came of it. Those assets were never recovered after the regime fell.

Life went on despite the carnage around me. I was still well fed and received supplies of tobacco for my shisha pipe. After my night in the tiny cell I tried to count my blessings and convince myself that events in Tripoli were not as bad as the TV news implied. The only change was the disappearance of the young woman who'd been sharing my villa.

I felt a strange sense of peace. If a missile hit directly there was nothing I could do, I told myself. So I tried to surrender myself to fate. I read the Quran, and prayed five times a day.

Lack of sleep, because of the night-time bombardment, was becoming an issue and I hardly recognised the gaunt woman in the mirror. Either a bomb fell, or I was waiting tensely for the next one. The following day's news programmes would show footage of the damage, and bodies being carried away from the ruins. I thought to myself: one day it will be me on TV, my body being carted away to the mortuary.

All the time I was trying to second-guess what might happen in Libya. I was shaken by the fall of Mubarak in Egypt, but I knew Gaddafi would not give up easily. I was certain he would not surrender, so more blood would be shed. Matters could only deteriorate, I concluded gloomily.

My continued imprisonment was pointless. There had been no direct accusation of wrongdoing, and no court case, but I figured that only Gaddafi could give the order for my release. Unfortunately, I was not high on his list of priorities.

The only chink of light was the unexpected return of my old friend Adil, who'd first brought my daily rations. I hadn't seen him for six months.

He would bring me extra food, and ask if there was anything I needed. Adil knew my background, and that I had a daughter waiting for me at home.

On one occasion my watch stopped and he took it away to replace the battery. It felt good to have him back, although he confided that the unrest in Libya was just as bad as some of the TV news reports suggested.

One day he told me: 'If the worst happens, I will do everything I can to help you.'

I appreciated the sentiment, although I doubted he could do much.

All summer the barrage continued. On 7 June, the leader's birthday, it was especially severe. I doubt that was a coincidence.

By the middle of August, the bombs were falling so heavily that I feared Libya must be in ruins. The explosions were deafening. Another month passed.

My routine was to sleep during the day when it was quieter.

The day I almost died I remember looking at my watch and it was only 5.30 on a balmy September evening. Outside it was still light.

Time dragged relentlessly and I wondered how I would fill the next hour and a half before Adil brought my food. That month I was fasting for the holy month of Ramadan, so I ate and drank only after sunset. I cursed myself for waking early, but it was hardly surprising my body clock was playing tricks.

When the bomb landed I was sitting on the bed, reading. There was a deafening blast and the building began to rock violently. I curled up like a baby in the womb, screaming over and over again: 'I'm dying, I'm dying'. But my shouting was futile, because no one could hear me.

The roof collapsed, showering me with chunks of concrete. One big piece struck my head a glancing blow, but I was so shocked, or more likely so terrified, that I felt no pain.

Although it could only have been a matter of seconds, the shaking seemed to last hours. Being caught in an earthquake must feel exactly like this. Clouds of dense, black, choking smoke and dust engulfed the room and I thought to myself: 'My body will never be found.'

And yet I was still alive. It was not just luck but a miracle that two huge slabs of fallen masonry formed a sort of protective tent above my bed.

I was scared to move in case my struggles brought the whole lot crashing down, crushing me to death, but after about ten minutes lying helpless in the dark I realised I had no other choice. Survival was in my hands alone.

Somehow I wriggled free from my tomb without disturbing the slabs and began to crawl, sharp debris on the floor tearing skin from the palms of my hands and knees.

I slowly felt my way through the murk and discovered that the main door frame was badly damaged, and I could feel faint breaths of air. But, my heart sank as I saw that the locked outer gate with its impenetrable iron bars was still intact.

In any case, it dawned on me that even if I could escape where could I go? Out on the streets, I would be in even more danger.

'Think Daad, think,' I repeated to myself, as my reserves of courage ebbed away.

As I stood gazing through the bars, pondering what to do next, the smoke gradually cleared. I could see the outline of a man walking purposefully towards me. He was carrying an automatic rifle.

The words of my father, from all those years ago, were ringing in my ears: 'Daad, I am begging you, don't go to Libya. It is not safe. If anything happens we cannot help you there.'

I wondered, is this where my story ends?

Then, to my amazement, I realised that the figure striding through the black smoke was my friend Adil. He'd kept his promise to help me!

Shouting to me to stand back, he levelled his gun at the padlock on the gate and fired once. The gate swung open and I was able to stagger out of the ruins of the villa. My first thought was for my neighbours, the Saudi businessman and his sister, and I urged Adil to help. He fired again to free them from their building, which was badly damaged but still standing. Other parts of the complex had clearly not been so fortunate.

As we moved through the rubble Adil warned me: 'Close your eyes. I will guide you.'

He did not want me to see the terrible aftermath of the bombing, but I knew we were still in peril and wanted all my senses.

I was confronted by a vision of hell. Nearby was a huge crater. I could see bodies and severed limbs. Much as I've tried to forget, that image is forever in my memory. No one should ever have to see something like that. Even now I don't want to dwell on those scenes.

I could see that the main building, where General Al Saeh had his office and I'd often been interrogated, was destroyed. By chance the general had survived, because he was away from his desk.

Now he noticed us and demanded to know: 'What are you doing?'

Adil explained what had happened and Al Saeh instructed him: 'Take them all to Abu Salim prison.'

This didn't make sense to me and I said to the general: 'But we are already at Abu Salim.'

He gave me a look, as if to suggest I had gone mad, and replied: 'No, this is the Office against Terrorism.'

I'd been fed false information. All the time I was thinking I was in the relative safety of the prison I had actually been held at a complex which was a prime target for NATO.

'Your country is being turned upside down and you still worry about me,' I shouted at the hapless general. 'Why don't you just let us take our chances?'

Al Saeh replied: 'The last call we had from the president was to put you in a safe place.'

Maybe I should have been flattered. Even as his regime was crumbling the Colonel still had me in mind.

We all bundled into a four-wheel drive vehicle and about ten minutes later I saw a sign: Abu Salim Prison.

Along with the two Saudis, I was escorted to a villa, larger but not dissimilar in style to my home of the last twenty-one months, which was normally reserved for prison officials.

I didn't relish moving into the villa which I feared could be the next target for a NATO smart bomb. How ironic it would be to escape so narrowly, only to die in the very next raid.

'Put me in the prison,' I urged the officer who was in charge of Abu Salim. He wasn't budging but at least he agreed that the three of us could remain together.

The interior of the villa was a mess, infested with rats and strewn with rubbish. We were shown to a room which looked like it hadn't been occupied for months. There was no bed, only a sofa, and water was dripping from the air-conditioning unit. We were given a few dates and milk.

Bombs were still falling on the city and I could hear the screams of hundreds of inmates from the nearby cells. Every time there was an explosion the wails would intensify, and I prayed that my original hope that NATO would spare Abu Salim prison would prove correct.

The only saving grace was that we were not locked in. Through the window I could see the commanding officer, wearing a pair of shorts and calmly smoking a shisha pipe as the bombs rained down. It looked for all the world as if he were on holiday.

That night none of us slept.

Next morning I sought out the commander. The door to his office was smashed and the telephone line cut. It emerged that he'd fled during the night. In another room I found some dates, bread and milk, which I shared with the Saudis and two Libyan nurses who were being held in the same building on suspicion of helping the revolution.

After a while some soldiers, loyal to Gaddafi, arrived and directed me back to the villa. Once again, I found myself locked in and for three days I cowered in the stinking room.

There was no television, so the three of us had no way of knowing what was happening in Tripoli and the rest of Libya.

Regular explosions still punctuated the night, but I got the impression that they were from land attacks, not the usual NATO aerial bombardment. I could hear rockets landing near the prison perimeter walls, but the walls were thick and did not fall.

Was Gaddafi still in power? In all the chaos would my enemies within the regime have me executed? If the Colonel was overthrown or fled to his traditional power base in Sirte, what would happen to me if I fell into the hands of rebels? To all these questions I had no answer.

All this was happening during Ramadan and so the holiest night of the Muslim calendar arrived, Laylat Al Qadr. Falling on the twenty-seventh day of Ramadan, it marks the date that the Quran was revealed to the prophet Muhammad. On this night it is believed that God is most likely to listen to your prayers.

The following morning there was an urgent knock on our door.

Chapter 23

Losing Hope

It was with a sense of trepidation that I walked to the locked wooden door and called: 'Who's there?'

Starved of news over the past three days, I had no idea who was in control of the city. For all I knew my executioner could be standing a few feet away.

'Open the door,' said the male voice but I did not have a key, even if I wanted to obey.

'Move away,' he commanded and I did as I was told. There was a crash, a splintering of wood and the flimsy barrier was gone in a few brutal kicks. I was confronted by a man, in his late sixties, who was wearing white robes.

'Who are you? Why are you here?' he barked. 'Your accent is not Libyan.'

I explained, as quickly as I could, that the three of us were prisoners of the regime. I prayed that I was not signing our own death warrants, but thankfully my response seemed to satisfy him.

'Come I will get you out of here,' he said, beckoning for me to follow.

I hesitated, reluctant to place my trust in this stranger, although I knew I had little choice.

'Who are you?' I asked.

He replied: 'This is not the time for questions. Come, follow me, quickly.'

I pleaded with him to take the two Saudis and the Libyan nurses. Another door was hastily smashed open and, with the nurses also now free, we all ran to the main prison gate. There was no sign of any guards. Outside I could see ruined buildings and rubble-strewn streets.

Our rescuer told the two Libyan women: 'You know the city? Then find your way home.' He gestured for the Saudis and me to follow him.

I tried to get my bearings and take in my surroundings. Although we were in a war zone, cafes were still doing business. Outside, old men smoking shisha pipes were sitting on the pavements. The streets were still busy with cars, picking their way through all the fallen debris. It was surreal. I could hear gunfire, not far away, but on the surface at least daily life was continuing as normal.

We walked for about a mile until we arrived at a small house, in a poor district of the city. The man opened the door and welcomed us inside.

'This is my home,' he said.

Now he introduced himself, along with his wife and sister, telling me he was called Ali Abdulhadi. Some children were playing in another room, oblivious to the arrival of three foreigners. In the relative safety of the house Ali visibly relaxed and began opening up.

'I don't know what took me to Abu Salim prison,' he said. 'This morning I woke and just began walking. Normally, no one can enter the prison and we are scared to even go near. But today the gate was open and I was curious. I rescued some other prisoners, who were being held in a van, and they told me they'd seen people trapped in the villas. That is when I found you.'

Ali, who explained that he was a taxi driver, offered us food and as we ate I reflected on how fate had again intervened. Why else would this guardian angel have come to my rescue?

Ali offered me his mobile telephone and I tried to call my father's landline. I heard Baba answer but the line immediately went dead so I called my sister Linda, whose number was the only other I carried in my head. When Linda heard my voice she began crying, my daughter was with her, I was able to speak with her and she sounded collapsed and wrecked down but we were able to speak for a minute or two before I reluctantly handed back the phone, which was low in credit. I was grateful that at least they knew I was alive and unharmed, yet I knew I was still far from safe as Libya imploded around us.

We discussed what to do next. Ali said: 'It's not secure here, because I've heard Gaddafi's son Saif is hiding in this area. The fighting is coming closer. We need to move you.'

He proposed taking the three of us by taxi to a rural area in the Ain Zara district where his brother, Mohammad, lived on a farm. Once there we'd have more time to figure out a plan to get us out of Libya, or simply hide. Getting away from the city seemed like the most sensible option, as all the fighting appeared to be confined to the centre and suburbs. The

30-mile journey south was uneventful and eventually we were greeted by a man, with a babe in arms, who introduced himself as Ali's younger brother. Yet again I was struck by the kindness being shown by strangers. Here was a family man who was willing to welcome three strangers into his home and share his food, not to mention the risk he was taking by offering us sanctuary. He never even questioned how long we would stay. I will never forget the extraordinary generosity of these people.

I had my first shower for days, immediately feeling refreshed, and we ate pizza cooked over the fire. It emerged that Ali's story about his own home being unsafe was only half true. He was also worried that he had little food, and we would go hungry. He knew supplies of fresh vegetables were plentiful on his brother's farm.

A generator was turned on so mobiles could be charged and I was again able to speak to my sister, using the brother's phone. I got hold of the telephone number for the Jordanian foreign ministry and made a call.

'I need to get out of Libya,' I said. 'There is blood everywhere and people are being killed.'

An official took the brother's number and promised that I would be contacted the following day. Sure enough, the phone rang and it was the Jordanian ambassador to Libya, calling from his office in Benghazi.

He said: 'If you can reach here I can get you to Cairo, then to Jordan.'

I was momentarily stunned. Benghazi is in the east of Libya, about 600 miles from Tripoli. Did he seriously expect me to make my own way there, without any documents or money? Even in peacetime it wasn't an easy overland journey. Now, I was certain it would be fraught with danger and my good luck must run out some time.

Perhaps I should have bitten my tongue, but I was in no mood for diplomacy and exploded in anger.

'Are you the ambassador to China or Libya?' I raged down the phone. 'Do you know how far that is? Do you know there is a war? If I can get to Benghazi by myself I don't need your help in the first place.' I hung up on him, furious.

Once more I was overwhelmed by despair. In my hour of need my country was effectively abandoning me. What did one dead citizen mean to Jordan?

I called the foreign ministry of Jordan and gave an official hell. I uttered every bad word you can imagine. It made me feel better, but did not improve my dire situation.

For four nights I stayed with this hospitable family, drinking water from a well and eating fresh vegetables. At any other time it would have been idyllic, but I felt guilty that I was eating their food and using their telephone. The two Saudis were in the same boat, after discovering their embassy was unwilling to intervene. All we could do was wait.

At one stage my daughter called. She'd spoken to her father in Saudi Arabia and he'd been making calls on my behalf. If I could somehow get to Djerba, in Tunisia, they could arrange for me to be rescued. To my surprise, Prince Al-Waleed, from whom I'd arranged the purchase of Gaddafi's private jet, was offering to fly me home despite our unresolved dispute over the commission. I appreciated the gesture but although the Tunisian border was much closer than Benghazi, less than 100 miles away, reaching there would no doubt be equally perilous. Without help I had no chance.

Then, on the fourth day at the farm, the phone rang. The caller introduced himself as Hany, a Libyan who worked in my office in Tripoli.

'We've been searching for you,' he said. 'We've been to every prison in Tripoli. I called your family and they gave me this number. I will help get you out of Libya.'

I was taken aback, asking: 'Why are you willing to do this? Why will you take this huge risk for me?'

Hany replied: 'Don't you remember me?'

I racked my brains but my office in Libya had many employees over the years and I could not recall him.

'I came to you four years ago when my mother was ill,' he said. 'She needed a kidney operation and you gave me money. Now I am repaying the debt. I am part of the revolution now.'

I didn't know it at the time but he'd also promised my father and brother, when they visited me while I was being held, that he would do everything to help me.

Giving gifts of money to Libyans on my payroll was not uncommon. I was well rewarded by the Colonel and I always tried to share a little of my wealth. That wasn't entirely motiveless – I learned early in my business career that you can buy loyalty. I was about to reap the dividend.

I gave Hany my location, wondering what he had in mind. The answer came about an hour later when a military-style truck, with an open back, thundered into view. It was crammed full of men brandishing guns.

My host panicked at first, only relaxing when I walked outside and greeted Hany. He had a long beard but, finally, I remembered him. He clasped me and kissed the top of my head.

'Say your goodbyes,' he said. 'Tonight you will stay with me and tomorrow we will take you to Tunisia.'

I had known the farm owner and his wife for a matter of days but we parted like lifelong friends. We hugged and kissed and cried. As I said my final farewell, I felt a few notes being pressed into my hand.

'It's a few Tunisian dinars,' said the man. 'It's all I have but it might help.'

Then I climbed into the cab of the truck, leaving behind the two Saudis who had decided to stay and wait for a rescue organised by their own country. Much later I discovered, to my relief, that they got safely out of Libya.

That evening I stayed with Hany's parents, in a small villa in central Tripoli. He revealed that his plan was to take me to the border town of Dehiba, in Tunisia. It was about 200 miles away, twice as far as the nearest crossing, but he was confident the route was controlled by rebels. It should be plain sailing. I called my family to ask them to try to make arrangements so I could cross the border without a passport. At least the Jordanian foreign ministry, which I now regarded with contempt, should be able to organise this for me!

We set out at dawn in a convoy of about forty vehicles, driving through ravaged parts of Libya. I was in the rear seat of a pick-up truck, driven by Hany. The third occupant was an armed revolutionary.

It broke my heart to see the country like this. There were plumes of smoke and buildings pockmarked with blast holes. People were crying in the street and wearing black for mourning. It felt like being on the set of a war film, although there was no sound of gunfire or explosions. Tripoli, it seemed, had fallen to the rebels.

Then, after about an hour, we stopped. It was announced that we were changing direction, to take the most direct route to Tunisia. Now we were aiming for the coastal border town of Ra's Ajdir, which was only an hour away. However, it would mean running a gauntlet of soldiers loyal to Gaddafi. The explanation for this more risky strategy was that the rebels wanted to clear the shortest route to Tunisia, and reckoned they had sufficient firepower in our convoy to achieve this.

I was handed a military helmet and bulletproof vest. Hany told me to lie on the floor of the pick-up cab.

'There will be a fight,' he said, calmly.

Yet again I was giving myself up to fate, but I knew this was my only opportunity to escape Libya. I tried to take solace from the youthful confidence of the rebels, but the pessimist within me nagged away that bravado does not stop a flying bullet.

However, as the minutes ticked by in the cramped footwell I dared to hope that we might reach the border unimpeded. The revolutionaries were spoiling for action, but all I had in mind was crossing into Tunisia as quickly as possible and getting home to Jordan.

Then I heard the unmistakable sound of automatic weapons. Within a few seconds we were in the middle of a fire fight. I cannot begin to describe the ear-shattering noise and my terror, although I couldn't see a thing as I curled up on the floor trying to make myself even smaller. Up front the two men were shouting. While one drove like the wind the other returned fire from the passenger window. The NATO bombs, dropped from unseen aircraft on Tripoli while I was a prisoner, felt somehow remote but this was a real war. There was no way of telling how close our attackers were, but there was no doubt that, yet again, my life was in the balance. And again, I had to rely on others for my survival.

This went on for about fifteen minutes, but it seemed like fifteen hours. Bullets hit the windscreen of our car as we raced along the desert road. There was nowhere to take cover.

At some stage Hany took the decision to divide our convoy. While about two-thirds stayed to fight Gaddafi's troops, our smaller group of about twenty men broke away and kept speeding towards the border. Earlier, I'd questioned how these revolutionaries would cope when the chips were down. Now I had my answer. They are the bravest men I've met. I know that some of those who stayed behind to fight that day were killed.

As we approached the border, I knew there would be one more hurdle. I had no passport or identification, so I called the Jordanian embassy in Tunis. I should have known better than to expect assistance – no one seemed willing to lift a finger to help. Even now, many years later, I still feel bitter about the manner in which I was abandoned by my country in my hour of need. On the other hand, I also learned that you often find great kindness and self-sacrifice where you least expect it.

Having delivered me safely to the border, Hany had one last surprise. While I pondered how I would cross from Libya into Tunisia at the dusty town of Ra's Ajdir, it became apparent that this was not his first time here. Tunisian policemen and border guards were shaking Hany's hand and saluting him. I'm sure that in the febrile atmosphere of the Arab Spring the fact that he and his men were heavily armed also helped, but somehow my path was smoothed from Libya to Tunisia. I'd crossed that border many times, but never had I breathed such a huge sigh of relief.

Belatedly, an official from the Jordanian embassy arrived to deal with this troublesome woman, and I was taken to a hotel. On this occasion, Prince Al-Waleed was as good as his word and four hours later a private jet landed at the airport at Djerba, about twenty minutes away. I was going home in style, the only passenger on the six-seater aircraft.

I slept for most of the 2,000-mile flight, utterly exhausted. It was my first proper sleep for nine months.

At 7 a.m., I touched down at a military airport in Jordan. It was twenty-one months, from January 2010 to September 2011, since I'd last set foot in my homeland.

I could see sisters, cousins, uncles and friends lined up on the airport terrace to greet me. They were being held back by security guards, but as I walked down the steps my daughter was allowed to run to the plane. I felt my heart bursting. We hugged and cried, then walked across the tarmac to where my family was gathered. I barely managed to kiss my father's hand, as tears rolled down his cheeks, before I was at the bottom of a scrum of people – sisters, cousins, uncles.

Mixed in with joy was a feeling of numbness. This was the moment I'd dreamed about, but now it was happening I couldn't take it all in. My memories of my arrival are little more than a blur. It felt unreal. Looking back, I was probably still in shock from the fire fight in the desert. Overwhelmed, my mind shut down.

I do know that my first act was to kiss the floor, and I've been told that the aircraft crew were also in tears as they watched my reunion with Noor.

From the airport, we drove straight to my father's house. The place was full of relatives, friends and media. Baba had arranged for a big tent to be put in the garden and for the next three days my homecoming was celebrated in traditional style. Guns were fired in the air. A lamb was sacrificed and roasted over an open fire. It's the Arab way of thanking God.

There was music and dancing although, truth be told, all I really wanted was a long bath and more sleep.

In the Hollywood version of my life this is where the final credits would roll. However, in the real world I still had some unfinished business.

Chapter 24

The Arrogant Prince

After the initial euphoria of my homecoming came a reality check. Two weeks after escaping from Libya I returned to my desk in Amman. Unsurprisingly, my business had suffered badly due to my enforced absence. Contracts had been cancelled and my non-appearances at the various military hardware shows around the world had not gone unnoticed. Only a handful of close contacts knew the real reason; most thought I had been deliberately ignoring their messages for the best part of two years, and understandably did their business elsewhere. To my dismay I also discovered that my sister Reem, who'd done her best to keep a grip on my finances, had authorised payments which were far in excess of the actual amounts owed. Some unscrupulous people had taken advantage of her lack of business acumen and simply inflated their bills. In a few cases, she'd even been persuaded to fake my signature.

In addition to the financial cost of my imprisonment in Libya, was the heavy toll on my health. Soon after I came home I noticed that one of my hands was shaking, so I went for a health check. I was referred to a neurologist and an MRI scan revealed a tumour in my brain. It was a devastating diagnosis, as I tried to rebuild my life and business, but I resolved not to feel self-pity. I told myself that I was lucky to be alive, and tried to be grateful for every day with my family. Frequent flashbacks of the bodies I'd seen in Tripoli were a reminder of my good fortune.

The good news was that the tumour, growing on the surface of my brain, was benign, but the specialist told me I would probably require surgery. He decided the best course was to monitor the tumour, to see how fast it was growing.

Perhaps I should also have seen a counsellor or psychiatrist after witnessing those horrible scenes in Tripoli, and my several brushes with death. I'm sure now that I was suffering from post-traumatic stress but, as usual, my coping strategy was to throw myself head first into work. I didn't set foot out of Jordan for a year.

The unfinished business I have mentioned was my legal battle with Prince Al-Waleed of Saudi Arabia, over the unpaid commission for Gaddafi's private jet. I wasn't about to let the $10 million I was owed slip through my fingers.

I remain extremely grateful that the prince sent his private jet to Djerba to bring me home, and I expected this gesture would be the trigger for some sort of settlement to be thrashed out. In my fragile state I would have been happy to agree a compromise, settling for half the money owed, but the telephone call from his lawyers never came. So I set about resurrecting the court case which, like everything else, had been placed on hold while I was detained in Libya.

I began thinking that maybe the gesture he made by flying me home was nothing more than a cynical ploy. My gratitude for his intervention, which I expressed publicly in interviews with newspapers at the time, didn't extend to writing off $10 million!

Throughout 2012, there was a flurry of legal letters as I sought to prove to the High Court in London, which was hearing the case, that the two-year delay was out of my control. Lawyers for the prince claimed I'd fabricated the whole episode in Libya, and the case should be dismissed, but I was able to convince the judge to proceed. I was shocked that Prince Al-Waleed would fight dirty in this way, but it was just a taste of what was to come. His tactic was to drag the matter out, knowing I had financial problems. I'm sure he thought he could wear me down, but I am made of sterner stuff.

I was forced to sell some assets, including land I owned in Jordan, to pay my legal fees, but his attitude made me even more determined to seek justice. I knew I was in the right and my lawyers told me I had a robust case. I felt like a caged lioness, ready to come out fighting with claws bared.

I had to battle hard to get the hearing in London, where I had negotiated the key part of the deal. It was one of the few places in the world where I was confident of getting a fair hearing against the wealthy prince.

At the start of proceedings, in 2008, Prince Al-Waleed tried to have the case heard in Libya. My lawyers argued successfully that the deal for the jet was sealed at the Ayoush restaurant in Mayfair, so London was the proper place. This was crucial and a big hurdle cleared.

Then, when he lost that argument, he tried unsuccessfully to have his evidence heard via video link from Dubai. In fact, the billionaire prince tried to thwart me at every step of the way. I learned that during my captivity his lawyers offered a miserly $500,000 to settle – one-twentieth of what I was owed.

Prince Al-Waleed is arrogant, and I'd witnessed his treatment of women. I'm convinced that had I been a man he would have handled the whole matter very differently. For him it was not about the money, because he made a healthy profit on the sale of the Airbus to Gaddafi, but belittling me and putting a woman in her place. He was driven by his huge ego.

The date was set for 24 June 2013, at the High Court in London. However, as the day loomed, my doctors in Jordan became concerned about the tumour in my head. It was becoming apparent that I would need surgery sooner rather than later, or risk becoming paralysed as the growth pushed on my brain. I did my homework and decided on Neil Kitchen, a consultant neurosurgeon at the National Hospital for Neurology and Neurosurgery in London. We discussed my pending date at the High Court and agreed that I would go under the knife after I'd given evidence, but before the judgment.

The surgeon cautioned: 'Even now you should try to avoid stress. When you study for your court case, take your time.'

Mr Kitchen assured me that although it was a delicate operation, the chances of success were good. Nonetheless there was a 5 per cent possibility that I would be left blind or unable to walk. I'm not a betting woman, but I figured the odds were stacked in my favour. Anyway, there wasn't an option to do nothing and at least the impending surgery helped take my mind off the daunting prospect of giving evidence at the High Court.

The case lasted eight days and I attended every one, unlike my adversary who breezed in only for two days for questioning. I wasn't there to make history, but I was told this was a landmark case because it was the first time a member of the Saudi royal family had been cross-examined in an English court.

The whole saga of the sale, including our meeting on the prince's yacht in the south of France, the aftermath when the jet was spirited away to

Saudi Arabia and his visit to Libya to apologise to Gaddafi, was outlined. In court documents, his fortune was described as over $20 billion.

My position was that I was responsible for achieving the sale of the prince's surplus Airbus A340 to the Colonel, for $120 million, and was therefore entitled to the $10 million commission we had agreed. The prince, described on the court sheet as His Royal Highness Prince Al-Waleed bin Talal bin Abdul Aziz Al-Saud, denied we had any such deal. His lawyers claimed that I played only a minor role in the long-drawn-out sale, playing down all my efforts to get the deal over the line and salvage it when everything went awry. The prince's lawyers claimed I'd 'stabbed him in the back' by colluding with the Libyans, but this was nonsense. I'd never made any secret of my good relations with Gaddafi and, indeed, Prince Al-Waleed would never have approached me otherwise. The prince also denied ever having apologised to the Colonel for effectively trying to snatch the jet back. More nonsense. The judge was shown a short video of the start of the tented meeting between Gaddafi and a sheepish-looking prince, in which I am seen being warmly welcomed by the Colonel.

Speaking in court was nerve-wracking but I emerged feeling pleased that I'd done my best. The opposition barrister was quite aggressive in his questioning, but I knew I was telling the truth, which always helps in this type of pressure situation. I made sure I knew my own case inside out, and my lawyer schooled me on how to behave in court.

My satisfaction only intensified when I watched Prince Al-Waleed squirm under cross-examination by our barrister, Clive Freedman, QC. I think the prince underestimated me and that worked in my favour, because in my view he came to court under-prepared. I thought he presented his evidence carelessly. When I spoke I made sure always to address the judge as 'my lord,' as I'd been told, but I noticed that the prince did not always show the same respect. He thought that because he'd rubbed shoulders with Prime Minister David Cameron and the British royal family, and owned The Savoy Hotel, in London, he was somehow above the law.

In court, the prince was forced to admit that I'd 'opened the door' to Gaddafi, but gave me scant credit. I was shocked by some of the words that spewed out of his mouth after he swore on the Quran to tell the truth. At one stage the prince said: 'I don't lie at all under oath – and even not under oath.' It was all I could do to keep my composure, and not snort derisively. I wished Gaddafi was there because it would have appealed to his sense of humour to see this pompous man put through the wringer.

Prince Al-Waleed looked thoroughly uncomfortable in the witness box, probably not helped by me sitting in eyeshot just a few feet away.

I was also pleased by the performance of Said Elturk, an aviation specialist, who was my expert witness. He told the court that the commission I claimed I was due on the aircraft, amounting to about 8 per cent of the sale price, was reasonable given the huge price tag.

Throughout all eight days I watched the judge like a hawk for any hint of the way in which he was leaning. Everything boiled down to which of us was considered to be the most credible witness. However, the body language of the Honourable Mr Justice Peter Smith, who had a reputation for being unpredictable, gave nothing away.

After the evidence is presented in such complex cases it's normal for judgment to be delayed, or reserved, to give the judge time for careful consideration. We were told to prepare to wait a month. The hearing finished on 5 July and my operation was scheduled for 27 July. The timing wasn't ideal because I'd still be recuperating when judgment was made, but it couldn't be helped. I never considered trying to reschedule the procedure or the court case, which had dragged on long enough for one reason or another.

Predicting the outcome of a court case is a risky game, because it can turn on a single fact or legal document, but I felt reasonably confident.

Then, three days after all the evidence had been given, there was an unexpected development. The prince's legal team asked for a meeting in London and I agreed to sit down with his advisors. The Savoy Hotel, which Prince Al-Waleed owned, was initially suggested but I insisted on neutral territory. We eventually opted for the plush surroundings of the Four Seasons Hotel, in Park Lane.

On the other side of the table was the prince's senior legal advisor Mark Mazo, a suave hotshot from the Washington DC office of the international legal firm Hogan Lovells. The cavalry had been sent in to try to rescue Prince Al-Waleed! Accompanying him was the prince's top personal assistant, a young Saudi Arabian woman called Nahla Al-Anbar. Alongside me was my lawyer Richard Waller from TLT Solicitors.

After a few formalities, Mazo laid out his cards: 'The prince knows that you are due to go in to hospital soon and so you don't have this hanging over you would like to offer a settlement.'

It was almost laughable that they were trying to pretend they were doing me a favour. Clearly, following his disastrous performance in court, the prince had been told the writing was on the wall. At this late stage, when it seemed that I had the upper hand, I wasn't in the mood for compromise or to be patronised.

However, I listened as an offer was made. The figure of $6.7 million was bandied about, but it came with strings attached. As part of the deal, the prince was insisting on a no-publicity clause, and was not willing to offer an apology to me.

By nature lawyers are cautious and Richard Waller quite correctly asked me to carefully consider the offer. It was a tidy sum, the judge was known to be unpredictable and if I won there could be an appeal by the prince.

However, I felt indignant that he was trying to sweep his disgraceful behaviour under the carpet. The prince thought he could simply buy me off and walk away as if nothing had happened. Also, I wasn't willing to budge on the matter of an apology. For me the case was not only about money, but integrity and principles. After about an hour of talking, the offer was rejected and we wished them a curt goodbye.

It appeared, however, that the prince was not for giving up. After his lawyer and the PA were sent away, tails between legs, I was telephoned by him personally several times. On one occasion Noor happened to pick up the phone at my flat and he even beseeched her to persuade me to accept his offer. The more desperate he became, the more determined I was to hold my ground. All I could do was wait for the judgment, place my faith in the English justice system and hope I hadn't made the mistake of my life.

There was to be one more sting in the tail. A few days before I was due to go into hospital I received a call from Richard Waller, telling me there had been an urgent development and to make my way immediately to our barrister's chambers near the High Court.

It was late in the afternoon as I dashed through London by taxi, from my flat near Oxford Street. I wasn't sure what to expect as I was ushered into a large meeting room.

It emerged that the judge, knowing I was about to have serious surgery, did not want me to go into the operating theatre burdened by the additional worry of the unresolved case. So he'd pulled out all the stops and reached his decision early. Whether I won, or lost, I was very grateful for this.

I was handed a weighty document and began reading, trembling with anticipation, but I barely understood a word! It was written in English legal language but might as well have been in Mandarin. I looked at my poker-faced barrister, Mr Freedman, for help.

'Congratulations,' he said, breaking into a broad smile from across the desk. '$10 million, plus interest and legal costs. It's all you could wish for.' He shook my hand. With add-ons, the total was more than $13 million.

My first reaction was: 'Are you joking?' The barrister shook his head.

'This goes no further, for now,' he said, explaining the English legal custom of giving sight of the judgment to both sides a week before it is made public in court. This allows for both sides to seek clarification, or corrections.

Mr Freedman continued: 'If you discuss this with anyone, even your close family, and word somehow leaks out then you risk the judgment being cancelled. Nothing leaves this room. Can you contain your excitement for a week?'

You know, for that sort of money, it was easy to keep my mouth shut for a few days! Inside I was celebrating, but my main emotion was satisfaction that I had been vindicated. If I'd been awarded a million I would have been just as happy and I never for a second dreamed that I would receive the maximum amount.

Everyone thought I was crazy to sue a rich guy like Prince Al-Waleed. They said he was too powerful and that I should not make an enemy of him.

He made me angry. He thought that because I am a woman he could disregard me. He thought he was untouchable.

Throughout my adult life I have fought to prove that Arab women are not weak, that we are not slaves. By going to court I wanted to prove a point that women have brains, should be respected and treated equally. I think he got the message.

The 132-page judgment could not have been more damning. I didn't follow much of the legal-speak but, in plain English, Prince Al-Waleed got his backside well and truly kicked. Maybe he regrets now that he didn't pick up the phone immediately after I escaped from Libya, when I was in the mood to settle for half the money I was due. In his ruling, the judge praised my unique ability to gain access to the Colonel, and concluded that the private jet sale could not have happened without my involvement. He wrote: 'It is, in my view, impossible to exaggerate her importance in the deal.'

The judge concluded that he found Prince Al-Waleed's evidence 'completely unsatisfactory', adding: 'At the end of the day I simply found the prince's evidence confusing and too unreliable and Mrs Sharab's was more credible on any dispute of fact between them ... it is not necessary for me to determine that he was telling lies in the witness box. He came close to admitting it.'

Reading on, other parts of the prince's evidence were dismissed as 'hopeless' and concocted in court to suit his argument as he went along. I could almost imagine his fury at also being described by the judge as 'frankly pathetic'.

On the other hand, my schooling on court etiquette and ensuring I knew my case thoroughly had clearly paid off, as the judge described me as 'an impressive witness'. He completely rejected the prince's assertion that I'd somehow 'stabbed him in the back'.

It was a thorough vindication. My lawyers told me they could not remember having seen a more comprehensive trashing of an individual's character and reputation.

All this I had to keep under wraps as I settled into my hospital bed in room 13 of the National Hospital for Neurology and Neurosurgery three days later, on 27 July, a Saturday. The number 13 is considered unlucky in many cultures, including Britain, but I felt like I'd just won the lottery. I had surgery the same day and my daughter Noor, sister Linda and a friend called Mona all flew in from Jordan to be at my side.

I was expected to recuperate there for at least a week. Although the four-hour operation went as well as could be expected, afterwards I was still weak and my head was swathed in bandages.

The judgment, about which I had not breathed a word, was due to be read in court on 31 July when the whole world would also find out. We agreed that my daughter Noor would afterwards provide a short statement for the gathered media on the court steps, and explain that I was in hospital.

However, at the last minute I changed my mind. I'd fought so long and hard for this day, more than nine years in all since the prince broke his word, so I had no intention of missing out. My absence could be interpreted as weakness and, for me, the case was also about showing that a woman could stand up to a rich and powerful man like Prince Al-Waleed. Another reason to be there was to demonstrate my respect for the English legal system, which has always treated me fairly.

Against doctors' orders, I gingerly got dressed and made my way to the High Court, on the Strand, by taxi. The judge was surprised to see me and even more taken aback when I removed my hat, as is the custom in court, to reveal my heavily bandaged head. Later, I posed for newspaper photographers and the television cameras on the steps of the famous court building. I wondered if Prince Al-Waleed was watching back in Saudi Arabia. I hope so.

There was still one more hurdle, an attempted appeal by the prince. His last throw of the dice was to bring in one of England's leading lawyers, Lord Pannick QC, to try to have the judgment overturned. The previous year he had been ranked in the Top 10 of an influential list of the nation's best barristers.

To my relief, the appeal never got off the ground. Further embarrassment was heaped on the prince when a fresh judge branded his case 'hopeless'. He's an intelligent man but it took a long time for the message to sink in. Much to his dismay, I'm sure, Prince Al-Waleed was left with no choice but to pay up the whole sum.

After the court case and the successful operation I was overwhelmed by tiredness. I realised I had been running on adrenaline and euphoria. It wasn't just physical tiredness, but a tiredness with life itself. I wanted to take stock, think about the direction in which my life was going and spend more time with Noor.

First step was to have a long holiday and I opted for Bodrum, on the south-west coast of Turkey. My daughter accompanied me and when the time came for her to return to university I turned off all my various mobile telephones, except one I used solely for speaking to Noor. It felt quite liberating to know that the world was still revolving without me!

I shaved off my hair and bathed the scars on my head in salt water. I checked into the Rixos Hotel for four months, but fell so much in love with this charming resort on the Aegean Sea that I decided to invest some of my court winnings in a holiday villa. I spent some more having the place, which was formerly two semi-detached houses, renovated and decorated to my taste. I still retreat here every summer, for three months, to relax and find peace of mind. Being there is my therapy. I named my new holiday home Villa Noor.

There's an amusing postscript to the court case. One summer I happened to bump into the prince at the marina in Bodrum. Before he could react, I grasped his hand and shook it warmly.

'Hi, how are you Prince Al-Waleed?' I smiled, then couldn't help adding: 'Welcome to Bodrum.'

His mouth just gaped open in disbelief, before he stalked away without uttering a word. It was a sweet moment.

Chapter 25

Reflections

I was resting at my home in Amman a few weeks after escaping from Libya when Noor came running into the room.

'Mama, they've caught Gaddafi,' screamed my daughter. 'Come and see. It's all over the TV.'

Gathering my thoughts I leapt out of bed and dashed downstairs to the living room. It was 20 October 2011 and Al Jazeera was broadcasting a shaky video showing the last moments of the Colonel's life. His final mistake was to think he would be safe in his home city of Sirte, but he was cornered like a rat. Looking dishevelled and bewildered, Gaddafi was dragged from a storm pipe where he'd sought shelter from a pursuing mob. It was like an animal feeding frenzy as he was beaten and tortured by his own countrymen. They were kicking him and pulling at his hair. I couldn't bear to watch any more. Muslims should not behave like this. It was inhuman.

No matter what he'd done to me, I did not want it to end like this. I wanted to see Gaddafi put on trial, in a civilised way, given the chance to defend himself in a proper court and be punished if convicted. I also wanted to hear from his own lips why he'd imprisoned me.

In my last sight of the Colonel, before I told Noor to turn off the television, he was covered in blood. That clip, leading up to his death, is still widely available on the Internet but even now I don't have the stomach or the desire to watch it in full. Not just because it's Gaddafi, the man I knew for more than twenty years, but because it is a human being. His final words are said to have been: 'What did I do to you?'

There are conflicting reports of exactly how he died, either caught in crossfire or executed by a bullet to the head. His son Mutassim was killed at the same time, and after the bodies were put on gruesome display both were buried at a secret location in the desert.

In the aftermath I was very disappointed by the reaction of Hillary Clinton. Asked about Gaddafi's death she made a joke, apparently trying to take credit for his downfall.

'We came, we saw, he died,' she laughed. It was not the behaviour of a stateswoman, with aspirations for high office, to make fun of him and she fell in my estimation at that moment. In her defence, I can only think that she was caught off guard by the TV crew and reacted without having being properly briefed. It was the sort of stupid bravado you'd expect from Trump. I thought she was better than that and recalled our dinner in New York, when she seemed so keen to work with the regime in Libya.

The response of Nicolas Sarkozy in France was even more hypocritical. He described Gaddafi's death as a milestone in the Libyan people's battle 'to free themselves from the dictatorial and violent regime that was imposed on them for more than forty years'. The same Gaddafi that he'd embraced many times, and whose hospitality he and his former wife Cecilia happily accepted. Even now, years later, the allegations that Gaddafi bankrolled Sarkozy's election campaign could still come back to haunt him.

In fact, Vladimir Putin was among the few politicians who did not appear to relish Gaddafi's downfall. He was critical of the US's role, asking: 'All the world saw him being killed, bloodied. Is that democracy?'

I remain a great admirer of Putin, now president of Russia, but I regret he did not become involved in the rebuilding of Libya after the revolution. Had he been given a prominent role, I believe he could have united the country and the place would not be the mess it is today.

Over the years, I have spent countless hours trying to make sense of what happened to me in Libya. I did nothing wrong, so why did the Colonel turn against me?

The only conclusion I can reach is that someone, or quite likely more than one person, got inside Gaddafi's head. The main suspects are his son Saif, Abdullah Senussi from the intelligence office, and Mabrouka Sherif, who became increasingly influential. None of them wanted me around the leader and each was equally ruthless.

I will never be sure of what was going through his mind, but with the passage of time my feelings have gradually mellowed. Once I felt only anger but now, while I still can't forgive him for having me placed under house arrest and the painful separation from my daughter, when I think of Gaddafi a whole range of emotions are stirred.

It might surprise you to learn that gratitude is among them but, looking back, when the NATO raids started it would have been all too easy for

220 The Colonel and I

me to have disappeared. The Libyans could have simply blamed my death on a stray bomb, expressed a few trite condolences and that would have been the end of me.

It's my opinion that although I'd become a headache for Gaddafi, who did not know what to do with me, he wanted me alive. I firmly believe that even as his grip on power was loosening he was still protecting me. However, I cannot forget that by authorising my arrest he also unwittingly almost signed my death sentence.

I never hated Gaddafi, even in my darkest hours in the villa, but I did not cry when he died. Neither did I celebrate, or have the same thirst for revenge as his countrymen in Sirte. I was disgusted that they threw his body into a supermarket cold room, where it was laid out on a grubby mattress, and turned the bloodied corpse into some sort of tourist attraction. I can't help thinking of the death of Saddam Hussein, who was hanged five years earlier. At least he was allowed some dignity at the end. The manner of Gaddafi's death was horrible, but deep down I think it is always what he feared most and why he tried to keep such an iron grip on the many factions in Libya.

Just as I have mixed emotions over the Colonel's death, I am also torn when I consider his legacy. For most of his rule he was focused on doing his best for ordinary Libyans. In many ways he was a progressive leader and he did not flaunt his wealth by building palaces or having collections of sports cars. He wanted girls to have the same education as boys and illiteracy was almost non-existent. The healthcare system in Libya was excellent by standards in the region.

Gaddafi was more intelligent than the snapshots of his rambling speeches show. He spoke good English and passable Italian but always insisted on a translator being present because he was a proud man and didn't see why he should be the one to compromise.

However, as I've explained, the Gaddafi I respected became sidetracked by all the King of Kings nonsense and his obsession with creating a pan-African state.

From about 2005 onwards, Gaddafi was consumed by his ego, and no one really dared to steer him back on track. The lifting of sanctions, after a solution was found to the Lockerbie problem, should have been a defining moment for the Colonel and Libya but he squandered it. Even towards the end I am sure he could have sneaked out of Libya, somehow, but his ego did not allow it.

I doubt anything I write will alter most of the Western world's opinion of Gaddafi; for some people he will always be the monster. I didn't see everything, so I can't be his judge, but I did not deliberately close my eyes just because I was working for him. Gaddafi was no angel but neither was he the devil. I've tried to show, from all I witnessed, that he was a more rounded individual than some of the cartoonish depictions would have everyone believe. It's for others to decide, because he was a man of contradictions.

I will never feel comfortable about witnessing the procession of young women who were brought for Gaddafi's sexual pleasure. His embracing of terrorist organisations such as the Irish Republican Army, at least in the early part of his rule, cannot be ignored.

Yet, in other areas his treatment of women was exemplary. The Colonel promoted women to senior positions, in government and the military. You only have to look at my own experience; I prospered in Libya in a way that would have been impossible for a woman in the rest of the Middle East. The Colonel did not look down on me, or treat me differently, because of my gender. How do you possibly reconcile those two extremes: Gaddafi the abuser and Gaddafi the feminist?

Throughout my life I've tried to overcome sexual prejudice, from the day I first set foot in the Jordan Investment Bank to the time I took a Saudi prince to court. I had to develop a hard exterior. I would love to be able to say that I raised the bar for Arab women but, although I am proud of what I have achieved as a single mother and a businesswoman, I fear not much has changed over the past twenty-five years. I have never been one of those Arab women who sits at home and lets the husband pay all the bills. I want to be a role model for bright young Arab women but, sadly, I don't see too many following me. In the Arab world many men still consider the woman's place is in the bedroom or the kitchen, and her primary role is to bear and rear children. They feel threatened by powerful and successful women, so they place barriers in our way at every step. My former husband, for example, is an educated man but he could never accept a reversal of the old order. Too many women with good brains end up in minor administrative and secretarial jobs, and get passed over for promotions.

However I hope I've showed that with faith, determination and a stubborn streak it's possible to overcome the odds. Likewise, I hope that I've showed Arab women that combining motherhood and a career is not only for their Western counterparts.

I wonder that the future holds for my own daughter? Noor did not have an easy upbringing. Following my divorce, when she was two-and-a-half years-old, I played the dual roles of mother and father. She endured my frequent absences on business, then the agony of her mother being arrested in Libya and worrying if I'd ever return home. She has always been very understanding and, despite it all, we have a wonderful relationship.

Now in her mid-twenties, she graduated from UCL in central London with a first degree in Economics and Business with East European Studies and a Master's degree in Management. At that age they keep changing their minds, but whatever path Noor eventually takes I will support her.

However, I don't want her to go through the same experiences and have the same struggles to be taken seriously. Noor's personality is softer, gentler, than mine and business is still primarily a very cut-throat man's world.

Libya, and Gaddafi, shaped my character in other ways. When I first went to the country I was always in a hurry but I learned patience. I used to get frustrated when I'd go to the Colonel's office for a meeting, or to sign a document, and be kept waiting. I recall once throwing a sheaf of papers in the face of some hapless official but I eventually realised that this was just the Libyan way. For Gaddafi, time meant nothing. I'm much calmer now and that's entirely down to him.

For me life goes on, with the usual mix of highs and lows.

In February 2015 I lost my beloved father. He never fully recovered from the road accident, along with losing my mother and brother. I sometimes wonder whether the stress caused by my captivity also took time off his life.

I was with Baba when he died in my arms, at my home in London, after suffering a heart attack. He'd been suffering pain in his toes and needed a minor operation to open a vein in his leg. All seemed to have gone well and he was recuperating at my flat. He was in good spirits and we stayed up late one night to see in my birthday. My brother, Ezalden, and Noor were also there and we all ate cake.

Next morning my daughter came running to say that her grandfather had collapsed. At that stage we had two private nurses staying with us to look after Baba while he recovered from surgery, and they tried frantically to revive him. Then paramedics arrived and also did their best, but Baba could not be saved. One of the medics just looked at me, as I sat with my father's head resting in my lap, and said: 'Sorry, we lost him.'

Can you believe it, he died on my birthday? I remember the flowers, which had just been delivered for the occasion, were placed around his body. Since that day I've never really been able to enjoy my birthday, because the memories are just too painful. I also give thanks for his 82 years, and console myself that Baba was not a young man when he died.

I'm also grateful that I remain healthy. In the beginning I used to lose sleep about the brain tumour returning, and who would look after my daughter, but with the passage of time the nagging fear recedes. For the first four years after the operation I had an annual scan, but that's now been reduced to every two years. Whatever happens, I'm a fighter.

I continue to work as a mediator and advisor for Western companies with interests in the Gulf, such as the Italian military company Leonardo, but I have no links with Libya. For my own safety I will never be able to return there, which breaks my heart because it is a country I learned to love like my own.

For different reasons I will never forget some of the people I met. Some remain lifelong friends, but it's harder to stay in touch with others who chose to stay in the fractured country that is now post-Gaddafi Libya. I fear for them.

Naima, who first took me under her wing when I arrived in Libya, is still like a sister to me. We speak often, by telephone. I won't say where she lives but it's somewhere in Europe, with her Libyan husband and son, after they fled Libya during the revolution. They live a quiet life.

Salma, my other close bodyguard friend, also managed to escape and lives in North Africa with her mother and brother. The bond between us will never be broken.

Adil, who saved my life when the compound where I was being held was bombed by NATO, is still in Libya and works for the government. His mobile phone number changes often, so I rely on him contacting me. He is in good health and has promised to visit me in Jordan one day.

I also owe a huge debt to Ali, the taxi driver who found me at Abu Salim prison and gave me shelter. A few years ago I was able to repay a small part by arranging for his father to have urgent medical treatment. His family still lives on the same farm where I briefly hid out before my perilous dash through the desert to Tunisia. Ali still drives a taxi in Tripoli where, despite the turmoil, livings have to be made and families supported.

Hany, who worked in my office in Libya and risked his life to drive me to the Tunisian border, has visited me in Jordan many times. He's like one of the family and we speak regularly. He was part of the revolution but I think it is best not to seek his views on how it has turned out. He has a wife and children now, so we talk about them instead. It's safe ground.

And what of my tormentors?

Moussa Koussa, whose last post in Libya was Minister of Foreign Affairs, abandoned Gaddafi the moment the regime began to crumble. After his defection, he fled to the UK where he was questioned about Lockerbie. Koussa is as slippery as an ice cube, always serving his own interests, so it was no surprise to me that he was welcomed by the West in return for information. He's now living in Qatar. Koussa called me after I escaped from Libya in 2011 to offer his congratulations, assuring me that he'd tried to secure my release. Do I believe him? It doesn't matter now. He blamed the Jordanian government for not putting enough pressure on Libya, which does have a ring of truth.

I have no feelings now, either way, for Koussa but Abdullah Senussi is another matter. I've had no contact with him and I hope it stays that way. Last I heard he was in prison in Libya, where he has been sentenced to death, but God will be his judge for what he did to the Libyan people. Mabrouka Sherif, the so-called brothel madam, is said to be living in Algeria where I understand she has a very nice lifestyle with plenty of money. Where did all this wealth come from? You can draw your own conclusions.

After the revolution, Gaddafi's son Saif was caught trying to flee across the Sahara desert to Niger. He was held in prison, in Zintan, in the north-west of Libya, but it has been claimed he's been released. They say Saif still has political ambitions but that seems unlikely, given that he is still on the International Criminal Court's wanted list for crimes against humanity.

I don't fear retribution from any of them. They all have bigger problems in their lives than me to worry about and, in any case, their influence and reach is gone.

I'm starting to think of winding down, maybe in the next two or three years, and I've opened a beauty company. Soon I will be 60 and I feel weary. For much of the time I've been both mother and father to my daughter. I would like my former husband to step up.

I am still single following my divorce and with no one at my side it is often tough, although I am financially secure. It has been suggested that I enter politics, but dealing with the likes of Sarkozy doesn't appeal to me. In any case, I don't like being told what to do and having to toe a party line!

It's almost ten years since Gaddafi died. For all his faults, I believe Libya is worse off without him. I know I will be condemned for saying this, but he was a big personality who brought stability. His death created a huge void. Libya today is a much more dangerous and divided country. Roads from the borders became unsafe for Westerners who used to be welcomed with open arms, passenger ferries stopped running, foreign airlines cancelled flights to Libya, most embassies shut and foreign workers fled. In 2010, the year before the Colonel's death, there were fifty-three murders in Libya; in the year after he died there were more than 500. In 2016, Barack Obama said the worst mistake of his presidency was not preparing better for the aftermath of Gaddafi's overthrow. I wonder what Hillary Clinton thinks now.

Old conflicts have erupted again, between west and east Libya, between cities and between tribes. I also wonder if anyone will ever unite Libya again? As I write, the country has two rival governments and is in a state of civil war. One faction is led by Khalifa Haftar, who was part of the coup against King Idris that brought Gaddafi to power in 1959.

The Colonel is rarely far from my thoughts. On my office wall in Amman there is a gallery of photographs. In one I am with Hillary Clinton; in another with George Bush. Pride of place goes to an image of the Colonel, standing next to me and with his hand protectively on my daughter's shoulder.

Many people ask: 'How can you display a picture of this man who imprisoned and nearly killed you?'

My answer is simple. He was part of my life. I have no regrets. Read my book and judge him for yourself.

Timeline

7 June 1942: Muammar Gaddafi born in Sirte, Libya;

14 February 1961: Daad Sharab born, in Jeddah, Saudi Arabia;

September 1969: Gaddafi seizes power in bloodless coup, overthrowing King Idris;

April 1986: Libya blamed for death of two US servicemen in bomb attack on Berlin nightclub;

April 1986: US launches air strikes against Libya. Gaddafi's adopted daughter, Hana, is claimed to have been killed;

March 1988: Daad attends Women's Union conference in Tripoli and Benghazi, meeting Gaddafi for the first time;

December 1988: Pan Am Flight 103 blown up over Lockerbie resulting in the deaths of 259 passengers and 11 Lockerbie residents;

September 1989: French flight UTA 772 brought down by a bomb over the Sahara Desert;

August 1990: Saddam Hussein invades Kuwait, triggering the first Gulf War;

November 1991: Warrants issued for the arrest of Abdelbaset al-Megrahi and Al-Amin Khalifa Fhimah, who are accused of planting the Lockerbie bomb;

March 1992: UN imposes sanctions on Libya over Lockerbie;

May 1992: Daad meets President George Bush in Texas;

25 May 1994: Daad's daughter Noor is born;

April 1999: Sanctions against Libya suspended after two Lockerbie suspects are handed over for trial;

October 2000: Gaddafi makes official visit to Jordan;

January 2001: Abdelbaset al-Megrahi convicted of the Lockerbie bombing. His co-defendant is found not guilty;

August 2001: Deal between Gaddafi and Prince Al-Waleed for private jet is brokered by Daad Sharab;

May 2002: Libya accepts blame for Lockerbie;

March 2003: Start of second Gulf War;

April 2003: Libya agrees to pay compensation to families of all 270 Lockerbie victims;

July 2003: Daad meets Abdelbaset al-Megrahi for first time at Barlinnie jail, in Glasgow;

December 2007: Gaddafi makes state visit to France;

July 2008: Daad flies to Tel Aviv for meeting with Shimon Peres;

August 2008: Gaddafi proclaimed 'King of Kings' by a group of African rulers;

January 2010: Daad placed under house arrest in Tripoli;

December and January 2011: Waves of anti-government protests across the Middle East herald the start of the Arab Spring;

March 2011: NATO begins bombing raids against Libya, ostensibly to protect civilians;

September 2011: Daad Sharab survives air raid and escapes through desert to Tunisia;

20 October 2011: Gaddafi captured and killed near Sirte;

June 2013: Daad successfully sues Prince Al-Waleed at the High Court, in London.

Acknowledgements

This book is a gift for the souls of my father Mohammad, mother Amal and brother Firas. Baba, I hope I made you proud.

It is also dedicated to my beautiful daughter. Noor, when all seemed lost, thoughts of you gave me the courage to keep fighting to survive. To women everywhere work hard, chase your dreams and never feel inferior to a man.

My heartfelt thanks to my great friend Osama Imseeh, who convinced me to open my diaries and publish this book. He also encouraged me to stand up to Prince Al-Waleed bin Talal. When others doubted, telling me it was impossible to succeed against such a powerful man, Osama was always at my shoulder urging me on. Gratitude also to Said Elturk, for his impressive expert testimony in my court case against Prince Al-Waleed.

For factual information about Libya's history I am indebted to Lindsey Hilsum for her excellent book *Sand Storm*. Likewise, *Libya: The Rise and Fall of Quaddafi*, by Alison Pargeter. I have also drawn on contemporaneous accounts from a wide range of news outlets including the BBC, Al-Jazeera and the *Dallas Post* newspaper.

Finally, I remind everyone that my primary purpose in writing this book is to share my experiences, good and bad. I am not Gaddafi's judge. I leave that to the reader.

Daad Sharab, Amman, 2021